# CAHSEE
## CALIFORNIA HIGH SCHOOL EXIT EXAM

# ENGLISH-LANGUAGE ARTS

# Available Online

## TAKE THE ONLINE DIAGNOSTIC QUIZ AND WRITING TASK

Go to kaptest.com/cahsee.

The address is case sensitive, so enter it carefully. Choose English-Language Arts. To register, you will need to have your book in front of you because you will be prompted for a word found in the text. Type that word when prompted by the computer.

Registering your program online is important because it gives you access to the diagnostic quiz and essay practice, as well as any late-breaking information on the CAHSEE. Once you have registered, it's simple to access your Online Companion whenever you want.

## FOR ANY TEST CHANGES OR LATE-BREAKING DEVELOPMENTS

kaptest.com/publishing

The material in this book is up to date at the time of publication. However, the test makers may have instituted changes in the test after this book was published. Be sure to carefully read the materials you receive when you register for the test. If there are any important late-breaking developments—or any changes or corrections to the Kaplan test-preparation materials in this book—we will post that information online at kaptest.com/publishing.

## RELATED TITLES FOR HIGH SCHOOL STUDENTS

SAT Comprehensive Program 2008

SAT Premier Program 2008

SAT Strategies for Super Busy Students, 2007

ACT Strategies for Super Busy Students, 2007

ACT Comprehensive Program 2008

ACT Premier Program 2008

AP Series 2008

# CAHSEE

## CALIFORNIA HIGH SCHOOL EXIT EXAM

# ENGLISH-LANGUAGE ARTS

## 2008 Edition

### by the staff of Kaplan

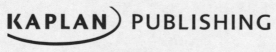

KAPLAN PUBLISHING

New York

Vice President and Publisher: Maureen McMahon
Editorial Director: Jennifer Farthing
Acquisitions Editor: Allyson Rogers Bozeth
Development Editor: Janell Lantana
Production Editor: Karina Cueto
Interior Book Designer: Ivelisse Robles Marrero and Sokie Lee
Typesetter: Joe Budenholzer
Cover Designer: Carly Schnur

Published by Kaplan Publishing, a division of Kaplan, Inc.
1 Liberty Plaza, 24th Floor
New York, NY 10006

Excerpt from "The Masque of the Red Death" by Edgar Allan Poe. *The Works of Edgar Allan Poe—Volume 2*. Project Gutenberg. 1997. www.gutenberg.org/etext/1062.
Excerpt from "The Tell-Tale Heart" by Edgar Allan Poe. *The Works of Edgar Allan Poe — Volume 2*. Project Gutenberg. 2000. www.gutenberg.org/etext/2148.
"Mending Wall" by Robert Frost. *North of Boston*. Project Gutenberg. 2002. www.gutenberg.org/catalog/world/readfile?fk_files=3903.
"The Tiger" by William Blake. *Songs of Innocence, Songs of Experience*. 1999. www.gutenberg.org/catalog/world/readfile?fk_files=39605.
Excerpt from "The Premature Burial" by Edgar Allan Poe. *The Works of Edgar Allan Poe — Volume 2*. Project Gutenberg. 2000. www.gutenberg.org/catalog/world/results.
"If" by Rudyard Kipling. *Rewards and Fairies* . Project Gutenberg. 1996. www.gutenberg.org/catalog/world/readfile?fk_files=36516.
"Bill and Joe" by Oliver Wendell Holmes. *Poetical Words of Oliver Wendell Holmes*. Project Gutenberg. 2004. http://www.gutenberg.org/etext/7400
"Out of the Morning" by Emily Dickinson. *Poems by Emily Dickinson, Series Two*. Project Gutenberg. 2001. www.gutenberg.org/catalog/world/readfile?fk_files=1209

Printed in the United States of America

January 2008

10 9 8 7 6 5 4 3 2 1

978-1-4277-9600-4

# Table of Contents

## Chapter 3: Literary Response and Analysis

# SECTION 2: WRITING

## Chapter 4: Writing Conventions

## Chapter 5: Writing Strategies

# How to Use This Book

If you're a high school sophomore, junior, or senior, or an adult learner, you are approaching the California High School Exit Examination (CAHSEE), the exam that all California students must pass to get their high school diplomas.

For many students, facing a high-stakes test like the CAHSEE can be intimidating. But you already have a head start: You've bought this book, putting yourself on the best path to mastering the topics on the exam —and succeeding on test day.

This part will provide you with information about how the CAHSEE English-Language Arts Exam is structured, and how you can best study for it. The rest of the chapters in this book will examine in detail the skills that the test measures, providing you with a solid foundation for success.

# Introduction

## What You Will Be Tested On

The English-Language Arts exam is one of two exams that make up the CAHSEE, a test that all high school seniors in California must pass in order to graduate. The other half of the test is the CAHSEE Mathematics exam. The CAHSEE English-Language Arts exam includes a Reading section and a Writing section. Reading questions are all multiple choice and will test your understanding of vocabulary words and your ability to read and understand informational (nonfiction) and literary (fiction) texts. Half of the passages on the Reading portion of the exam will be informational, and the other half will be literary.

The Writing part of the exam includes multiple-choice questions that test your knowledge of English language conventions (grammar and usage, capitalization and punctuation, and paragraph structure), as well as your ability to use writing strategies to find errors and improve the flow of text. You will also be asked to write an essay; the prompt may require that your response take the form of a business letter, a response to something you've read, a factual or persuasive essay, or an autobiographical piece. The writing task accounts for about 20 percent of your total score, so it's important to be prepared with strategies that will help you write a high-scoring essay.

*Word Analysis, Fluency, and Systemic Vocabulary Development (7 questions)*

*Reading Comprehension (Focus on Informational Materials) (18 questions)*

*Literary Response and Analysis (20 questions)*

*Writing (27 questions)*

*Writing Applications (Essay Item)*

You may find that your exam includes more than 72 multiple-choice questions. Many administrations of the CAHSEE English-Language Arts exam have 79 questions, 7 of which are experimental test questions that are not scored. However, you have no way to distinguish these experimental items from the questions that will be scored, so it's important to approach each question with your full attention.

The good news is that, unlike many tests, the CAHSEE English-Language Arts exam has no set time limit. Students are generally expected to finish within one full school day, which means you have a good deal of time to really evaluate, work through, and answer each question without watching the clock.

## How Do I Prepare for the CAHSEE English-Language Arts Exam?

The fact that you've opened this book means you've taken a major step toward being ready for the CAHSEE English-Language Arts exam. You can use the book to determine where your strengths and weaknesses lie and then use the techniques and resources provided to help build your knowledge in the areas in which you need improvement.

If you're like most people, taking time out of your day-to-day responsibilities and commitments in order to study can be daunting and difficult. You'd probably prefer to spend your time doing more exciting activities. We also know that not everyone studies in the same way, nor does everyone need to prep in the same way for each section. Some of this material will feel like a review, and you'll ace the questions. For other topics, you may have to give the content some more consideration. To maximize your study time and minimize the hours needed, we've made a few suggestions for how to study with this book. We realize that you're a person in need of options—the option of when to study, where to study, and, most of all—*how to study*. That's why the CAH-SEE English-Language Arts program contained here is *your* program—flexible and customizable. What's unique about it is that *you* control the variety and amount of study that best suits your needs.

First, we know you want practice. We've included that. But to make sure that you don't get bored with a big book of lessons, quizzes, and tests, we've made this program interactive, so we encourage you to start off by going online to take our short diagnostic quiz—just to see what you know and what you need to work on. That said, you don't have to go by a predetermined order set by us. Jump around all you want—to a specific chapter in the book, or straight to a full-length practice test!

Here's the step-by-step plan.

## STEP 1: REGISTER YOUR PROGRAM ONLINE

Go to kaptest.com/cahsee.

The address is case sensitive, so enter it carefully. Choose English-Language Arts. To register, you will need to have your book in front of you because you will be prompted for a word found in the text. Type that word when prompted by the computer.

Registering your program is important because it gives you access to the diagnostic quiz and essay practice, as well as any late-breaking information on the CAHSEE. Once you have registered, it's simple to access your Online Companion whenever you want.

## STEP 2: TAKE THE ONLINE DIAGNOSTIC QUIZ

Taking the short diagnostic quiz is the first thing we recommend you do. It will help you figure out your strengths and weaknesses. With that information, you can customize and focus your study time.

**GOING ONLINE**

If you don't have access to a computer at home, don't worry! You can access this at the library, a school, or a friend's house. If getting online is impossible, it's still okay—the diagnostic quiz is good to take, but it doesn't mean you can't skip it and dive right into the lessons and practice in the book.

### STEP 3: TRY AN ONLINE WRITING TASK

Your Online Companion includes an essay prompt similar to what you will see on the CAHSEE.

- Choose a prompt, and allow yourself 30 minutes to write your essay.
- When you are finished, compare it to the model essay provided and check it against the scoring rubric found on page 266.

How did you do? There are additional essay prompts in Chapter 8 to try over the course of your study, so you will be able to gauge your improvement.

### STEP 4: IDENTIFY YOUR WEAKNESSES

Check your answers to the diagnostic quiz, noting how many questions you answered correctly and how many you answered incorrectly. Look for patterns. Did you ace the Word Analysis questions? Did the tough usage questions trip you up?

Don't limit your initial review to the questions you got wrong. Read all of the explanations—even those you got right—to reinforce key concepts and sharpen your skills. As time permits, go back to the question types that you aced so you can keep that material fresh.

### STEP 5: CUSTOMIZE YOUR STUDY PLAN

The best study plan will adapt to your individual needs and should start with a review of content weaknesses and include practice on weaker topics to boost skills and understanding. However, only you can determine the course of study that's right for you. We suggest the following:

- If you were able to do the online practice, target your study in the order of what you need to work on the most—are you stronger in writing than reading? Start with reading. If you aced the reading parts but struggle with writing, start there. Use the detailed table of contents to point yourself in the right direction. Devote time to reinforcing content strengths within the chapters through lessons and practice quizzes.

- If you weren't able to go online, start going through the book in order of the areas you know are sometimes a struggle for you. Once you've gotten through the chapters you've targeted for skill building, try the first full-length practice test—your first milestone. How did you do?

- Think about the topics that you need to focus on, and go back to the chapters, if needed. Plan to read the remaining lessons in the book and take the quizzes at the end of each chapter. As time permits, return to the question types that you found easy so you can keep that material sharp.

- When you've finished the chapters, take the second full-length practice test.

## STEP 6: REVIEW, REINFORCE, AND BUILD SKILLS

Again, you know what you need to study, so feel confident that the content you need to practice to pass the CAHSEE is right here. Go ahead and skip to the first practice test and find out what you know. Or, start on the first page, and dive into the material in sequential order, leaving no sentence unread, if that's how you need to prepare. Whatever your study needs are, form a study plan, and make a commitment to follow it. Block time out of your day to study, and give yourself rewards for sticking to your schedule. Don't push yourself too hard, but do try to keep a good long-term perspective on your goals and the work you need to do.

Take a look at the Table of Contents for the topics covered in each chapter. Try to make a realistic plan for how much time you'll need to spend preparing for the exam. Perhaps you've always been good at taking tests—if that's the case, you have a head start. For most people, though, taking standardized tests can be a real challenge, so make sure you give yourself enough time to fully cover and understand the information and techniques in this book.

## How Do I Find the Time to Study?

You probably have a busy life and many commitments outside of school, particularly if you are an adult or a graduating senior. It can be difficult to free up several hours out of your day to devote to studying. Instead, think about setting aside just a small amount of time each day—you may not have time to study for three hours, but you can surely find an extra 20–30 minutes in your day.

- Create a timeline. Making a timeline of your study plan will give you a concrete way to see the progress you're making as test day approaches. It's good practice, too: On the Reading portion of the test, you can make timelines to clarify the progression of events in a passage. On the Writing portion, you might make a timeline to help plan the way your essay will unfold.

- Make outlines and mind maps. As you read and evaluate the material in this book, create your own outlines and notes that review the important concepts you want to remember. Add new information to the facts and ideas you already know, and see whether you can find a short, memorable way to make note of those concepts. The process of articulating and writing down your thoughts will help you to remember them later.

- Get help from your friends and family. Studying alone can get tiresome—you should know that studying with another person can be just as productive. Ask a friend or family member to help you review notes, vocabulary, or flashcards. If you are in high school, you're in an especially good position, because many of your classmates will also be preparing for the CAHSEE exams.

- Make flashcards. Flashcards are one of the simplest and most effective study tools you can use, and they are indispensable in helping you learn new vocabulary, memorize key terms and concepts, and review material you already know.

- Find creative times to study. If you have a free moment, you have time to be preparing for the CAHSEE English-Language Arts exam. Waiting for a ride? Review the flashcards you've made to test your knowledge of punctuation. Commercial break during your favorite television show? Ask a family member to give you a quick vocabulary quiz.

- Have fun! Finishing high school opens up a world of possibilities for you—in your career and your further education. If you can think of the CAHSEE as a stepping stone on the way to your ultimate goals, rather than just a requirement for school, you might find that you get excited about studying for the test, passing it, and moving on to the next stage in your life. This is an opportunity to learn essential basic skills, hone your study habits, and make a commitment to do your best for the future.

## Kaplan's 4-Step Method for Multiple-Choice Questions

**Step 1:** Read the question carefully.

**Step 2:** Rephrase the question.

**Step 3:** Read all the answer choices.

**Step 4:** Look for matching or mirroring language or concepts.

### Step 1: Read the Question Carefully

One of the most common reasons that test takers miss an item is that they misunderstood or misinterpreted the question, and answered a question that wasn't being asked. You probably feel that you're too careful to make this mistake—but are you positive? In a tense situation like a high-stakes exam, it's easy to let stress push you into working faster. However, working faster doesn't equate to working harder or getting a better score. What's essential is not to rush through the test, but to be well prepared and approach each item carefully and thoughtfully.

Many difficult questions rely on a fit between the language used in the question and that used in the correct answer choice. This means that your awareness of language will be key in understanding the clues that are contained in each question. Many test takers find it helpful to circle or underline important words and phrases as they read. Key words and phrases make each question unique, differentiating it from other questions and leading to a unique correct answer. These words and phrases might point to a particular relationship (e.g., *Which BEST describes . . .* or *Which is MOST likely to agree with . . .*), or they might qualify or limit the range of correct answers (e.g., *on the day before the family moves . . .* or *At the end of the story . . .*).

As you work through the exercises in the book, practice this method of marking up your book. That way will be second nature to you on test day.

When a passage is followed by a set of questions, try skimming over the questions before you read the passage itself. Questions might direct you to a specific phrase or word (e.g., *this sentence from the selection*) or ask for a more general response to the passage (e.g., *What is the author's purpose in writing this story?*). If you have an idea of what to look for in the passage, you'll be more focused and directed as you read, and be able to use your time effectively.

### Step 2: Rephrase the Question

A question that begins with *which of the following . . .* can be challenging to rephrase. If the question is *Which of the following is the MOST accurate description of the story's plot?*, you could rephrase it so that you think to yourself, *One of these (answers) is the best summary of the events that happen in the story.* This helps you approach the answer choices with a clear knowledge of exactly what you're looking for. After you've rephrased the question, see if you can predict what a correct answer might say, without looking at the answer choices. This will help you recognize the correct answer from choices that may be plausible, but are incorrect.

### Step 3: Read All of the Answer Choices

You might be tempted, especially if you've already predicted an answer, to select the first choice that looks good, then move on to the next question. However, there are frequently two very similar choices in a set, only one of which is the correct answer. If you never read past choice D, you won't see choice

E, which could be the correct choice. Instead of settling on the first choice you like, mark off the ones you don't like as you read through. Crossing off answers that are incorrect means you never have to think about them again; each time you cross off an incorrect answer, you narrow the field of possible correct answers from which to choose.

### Step 4: Look for Matching or Mirroring Language or Concepts

You may have eliminated two choices, but find yourself unable to choose between the remaining two possible correct answers. To solve this dilemma, you'll need to return to the question. Look at the words or phrases you marked the first time you read it, and reread, marking any additional words or phrases you might have missed. Now reread the remaining answer choices, looking for language that lines up with the language used in the question.

## Kaplan's 4-Step Method for Writing Task Questions

### STEP 1: READ EACH QUESTION CAREFULLY

Just as with multiple-choice questions, it's essential that you understand exactly what the question is asking. Pay attention to the words that are used in the question. Prompts for constructed-response questions frequently include an important idea or reference that you can expand upon in your essay. Focusing on the choice of words in the question will also help you get a sense of what type of response is being sought.

### Step 2: Make a Note of How Many Parts the Question Includes

The CAHSEE English-Language Arts writing task often includes more than one part. In order to write a successful response, you must address all parts of the question fully. For example, a question that asks about *emotional, mental, and physical health* is really asking for three different pieces of information. Count carefully and then write the number of parts next to the question so that you can refer back to it as you begin crafting your response.

### STEP 3: BRAINSTORM

Many students feel anxious or stressed out during exams like the CAHSEE, and they go right from reading the question to writing a response, trying to make the most of their time. The trouble with this approach is that you might be halfway through your response and realize the angle you're taking isn't detailed enough to answer the question—or that you have three more points to make and only one paragraph in which to make them. Putting all of your thoughts down before you begin will make your writing go more smoothly when you're ready to start your essay.

After you read the writing task, take a minute or two to think about the question. How can you relate it to your own experiences, or to movies you've seen, books you've read, or stories you've heard from other people? Write down your thoughts as they come to mind, using just a word or two to describe each idea. At this point, write down anything you think of, not evaluating whether it will be useful as you write your essay.

### STEP 4: ORGANIZE

Now that you've brainstormed, you have all of your thoughts in one place, and you're ready to organize them. The ability to convey your thoughts in writing is crucial in high school and college, in the workplace, and in the rest of your life. The teachers who score your essay want to see that you can use written language to express your thoughts sensibly. Take some time to think about how you will move from one idea to the next, introduce and end your response, and support each of your ideas.

It may seem silly, but you should also be sure that your handwriting is legible—there's no point writing a stellar essay if no one else can decipher what you've written.

## CAHSEE ENGLISH-LANGUAGE ARTS EXAM EXPLAINED

The questions on the English-Language Arts exam will test your understanding of six strands—groups of standards that are included in California's K–12 curriculum. The questions on the CAHSEE, however, will cover material that is taught through only the tenth grade.

**Word Analysis (7 questions)**

Can you identify the meanings of words, understand how they are derived, and distinguish between multiple meanings?

**Reading Comprehension (18 questions)**

How well can you compare and contrast materials and understand the structure of what you've read? Can you determine whether a piece of writing is well organized and presents a logical argument? Are you able to perform your own critique of the information in the passage?

**Literary Response and Analysis (20 questions)**

When you read a literary work, are you able to understand how the author develops the characters, their traits, and the plot? Do you understand how literary devices are used? Can you compare various works of literature and see how they differ and/or how they reflect on their author(s)?

**Writing Strategies (12 questions)**

How well can you develop a thesis, revise a piece of writing, and use evidence to support your argument? Do you understand how to use outside sources in your work?

**Writing Conventions (15 questions)**

Can you demonstrate an understanding of the conventions of written English (usage, grammar, punctuation, and syntax)?

**Writing Applications (1 essay)**

Are you able to compose an effective and well-rounded expository or persuasive essay, business letter, response to literature, or biographical narrative?

## RESOURCES

The lesson chapters that follow will provide you with more detailed information about, and strategies for, preparing for these types of questions. Here are some online resources that offer more information or background in a particular area.

www.cde.ca.gov/ta/tg/hs/documents/eng05studygde.pd

> Preparing for the California High School Exit Examination: An English-Language Arts Study Guide. Published by the California Department of Education, this guide provides guidelines on the content strands covered on the test, as well as sample questions for each strand.

www.geocities.com/soho/Atrium/1437

> The Five Paragraph Essay Wizard. Comprehensive, detailed information on formulating, writing, and editing an essay and avoiding common writing pitfalls.

owl.english.purdue.edu/handouts/grammar

> Grammar, Punctuation, and Spelling from Purdue University. Printable handouts, many with practice exercises, explain specific problems such as pronoun use, punctuation, and adjective versus adverb use.

www.how-to-study.com

> Includes "A Strategy for Reading Textbooks" and "A Strategy for Reading Novels" that provide information on story elements, active reading, and retaining the information you read.

## SCORING THE CAHSEE ENGLISH-LANGUAGE ARTS EXAM

The English-Language Arts component of the CAHSEE has 90 possible points—one point for each multiple-choice answer, and 18 possible points for the writing task. (The writing task receives a score between 1 and 4; this number of points is then multiplied by 4.5 to determine your essay's raw score.) Your score report will convert this raw score to a scaled score between 275 and 450. In order to pass this portion of the CAHSEE, you must receive a scaled score of at least 350, or roughly 56 of the 90 possible points.

## CAHSEE ENGLISH-LANGUAGE ARTS TEST DATES

The CAHSEE English-Language Arts exam will be administered on these dates for 2008–2010.

February 5, 2008

March 11, 2008

May 6, 2008

July 29, 2008

October 7, 2008

November 4, 2008

December 6, 2008*

February 3, 2009

March 17, 2009

May 12, 2009

July 28, 2009

October 6, 2009

November 3, 2009

December 5, 2009*

February 2, 2010

March 16, 2010

May 11, 2010

*Saturday administration

Students who plan to graduate in June 2008 should take the CAHSEE prior to the May administration so that their scores are received before graduation.

**NOTE ON RETESTING:**

High school seniors and adult students may take the part(s) of the CAHSEE that they have not passed up to three times during the school year, and may take the test on two successive test dates.

Juniors may take the part(s) of the CAHSEE that they have not passed up to two times during the school year. However, juniors may not take the CAHSEE on two successive test dates (e.g., February and March).

Sophomores are required to take the CAHSEE, and may take the test only once during the school year.

# Section 1
# Reading

# Word Analysis

The Word Analysis strand of the Reading portion of the California High School Exit Exam (CAHSEE) will focus on your ability to analyze and understand vocabulary. You will need to apply your knowledge of word origins to unfamiliar words that you will encounter in the CAHSEE reading passages and determine how to use the new words correctly.

This chapter will help you understand and master literal, figurative, denotative, and connotative meanings of words. You will learn how to draw on your knowledge of literature, context, and synonyms to understand a word's origin and meaning. You will also become skilled at breaking words into parts (such as roots, suffixes, and prefixes) to find the meanings of unfamiliar words. Finally, this chapter will offer you the best strategies to approach the Word Analysis questions on the CAHSEE.

## FIGURATIVE VOCABULARY

Have you ever heard someone describe clouds as fluffy pillows or kittens as balls of fluff? These are examples of figurative language, or language that goes beyond the basic dictionary meaning of a word. Authors often use figurative language as a tool to create colorful and vivid pictures in the reader's mind.

In order to understand many poems, stories, and other pieces of literature, you need to be able to identify figurative language and understand its meaning. When authors use figurative language, they expect you to interpret it based on the context and theme of the passage. The CAHSEE will test your ability to understand the difference between literal and figurative language.

Here are some common types of figurative language and their examples.

| Figurative Language | Definition | Example | Meaning |
|---|---|---|---|
| *Personification* | To give an animal, object, or idea characteristics that are considered human | The branches groaned under the weight of the snow. | The author has given the tree the human ability to groan. |
| *Metaphor* | A word or phrase that compares two different things, but does not use the words *like* or *as* | The toddler was a tornado, ripping and tearing through the house. | The author compares the toddler to a tornado. |
| *Simile* | A phrase that compares two things using the words *like* or *as* | The discarded umbrella lay crumpled like a dead bat. | The author compares an umbrella to a bat, using the word like. |
| *Symbol* | An object that stands for something with greater meaning, often an abstract concept | She gave her heart to him and he cast it aside. | Heart is a symbol of devoted love. |

## Personification

On the CAHSEE, some questions will address personification. Writers, especially poets, use personification to give an animal, plant, object, or idea some essentially human characteristics and traits. The qualities given to nonhuman things may include personalities, feelings, actions, expressions, and speech.

Look at the following examples to distinguish the difference between a personification statement and a literal statement.

**Literal:** *Julia arranged the flowers in the basket so that the colorful petals were the first thing visitors saw when they came in the door.*

**Personification:** *Julia arranged the flowers in the basket so that their bright smiling faces greeted visitors at the door.*

Does a flower have a face? Can a flower smile? Can a flower greet visitors? The answer is no, but in literature, personification is a literary device to make the text more engaging to the reader.

Let's examine the following personification question.

**In this line from a poem, the word *whispered* suggests that the wind is—**

> The wind whispered its secrets to me . . .

**A**   a movement of air.
**B**   a small gust.
**C**   a person.
**D**   a scent.

This line is an example of personification. Choices A and B are incorrect because although they are literally correct, the poet wants the reader to think of the wind as more than just air or a gust. The poet has given the wind the human ability to whisper like a person. People can whisper secrets, so the correct answer is **C**.

## Metaphors

Metaphors are very important to understanding certain reading passages because they help create a picture in the reader's mind. Using metaphors is often more interesting than using straightforward, literal language, which is why writers often use them. Look at the difference between these two statements, one of which is literal and one of which is metaphorical.

**Literal:** *Angela's bike was fast, and we rode very quickly down the hill.*

**Metaphorical:** *Angela's bike was a hawk, and we flew down the hill.*

Can you see the difference between the two sentences? In the first sentence, you can imagine the bike, but the image is not very exciting. In the second sentence, the reader can see a bike with wings attached, speeding downhill. One mental picture is clearly more exciting than the other. Take a look at the following example.

**What is the meaning of the phrase *class clown* in the following sentence?**

> Mike was the class clown, always telling a joke or a silly story in science homeroom.

**A**   Mike was a toy doll.
**B**   Mike was a circus performer.
**C**   Mike was a funny person.
**D**   Mike was the school mascot.

You know that *class clown* is probably not literal. Mike is not actually a toy doll or a circus performer. Mike is a student. Perhaps Mike could be the school mascot, but from the context of the sentence, it seems more likely that Mike is simply a funny person who makes everyone laugh. So you could reasonably guess that this is a metaphor, and you can determine that the meaning is not literal, but figurative. The correct answer is **C**.

## Similes

A phrase that compares two different things using the words *like* or *as* is called a **simile**. In writing and conversation, people often use similes to make a point or add emphasis. Some examples of similes would be the phrases *He's as sharp as a tack,* or *The dog's tail was like an exclamation point when it saw the rabbit.*

You might see an example like the following example on the CAHSEE. Here, the author uses literal and figurative language to help the reader picture the force of the ocean. You will need to select the phrase that is a simile to answer the question correctly.

**Which sentence is an example of a simile?**

A   The waves were rough and frightening.
B   The waves turned into a frothing, mad fury.
C   The waves became angry and threatening.
D   The waves were like grabbing, violent hands.

In choice A, the meaning of the sentence is fairly literal. It describes the condition of the waves and the effect they had on the narrator. In choice B, the waves are identified as a fury (metaphor), which has the quality of being angry (personification). You know that waves have no feelings, angry or otherwise, but this helps you see that this statement is both a metaphor and an example of personification. The words *like* and *as* are not used in the second statement, so you know this is not a simile. Choice C is an example of personification and is similar to the second statement. Waves cannot have emotions or make threats, but reading this helps you imagine the destructive force of the waves. In the final choice, the waves are compared to grabbing, violent hands. This phrase is an example of a simile because it compares two unlike things using the word *like*, so choice **D** would be the correct answer.

Look at the following example and determine what type of figurative language is used.

> The large mob swarmed the state capitol like angry bees.

**What kind of figure of speech does the writer use to help us visualize the mob?**

**A**   metaphor

**B**   simile

**C**   idiom

**D**   symbol

The correct answer is **B**. The mob is compared to bees using the word *like*, so this is an example of a simile. You know that when bees are upset or angry, they sometimes attack. The simile *like angry bees* helps you make a connection between the mob and the bees—they are both angry and taking action. This sentence could have been stated literally but using a simile creates a stronger visual image and meaning for the reader.

## Symbolism

In fiction, a character or object often stands for, or symbolizes, something with greater meaning. Think about people's names. These often symbolize something personal. For example, the name Felicity means "happiness" and the name David means "beloved."

Sometimes writers use symbolism to make their writing more meaningful and colorful. In the novel *The Grapes of Wrath*, one of the main characters, Rose of Sharon, is a symbol of hope and redemption. In one of the final scenes from the book, she saves the life of a starving man. This act turns her from an ordinary person into a saintlike figure.

Writers often use characters as symbols in their text, but sometimes they use objects as symbols. In Ireland, potatoes were once considered the basis of life. People depended on their potato crops to provide most of their daily food. To the Irish, potatoes symbolized life, so when the potato famine of 1845 occurred, it devastated Irish culture. The potatoes did not grow, and as a result, many people died and many people left Ireland for America. Authors have seized this image of the potato as a symbol to represent and reflect many ideas and concepts about Irish culture.

Let's try to identify an example of symbolism.

I always look forward to summer when pineapples are fresh and ripe. After I take a bite of pineapple, I always remember the first time I tried pineapple with my parents while on vacation as a young child.

**In the passage, what do pineapples symbolize to the narrator?**

**A**   warm weather

**B**   the grocery produce section

**C**   a childhood memory

**D**   backyard barbecues

While *pineapple* could symbolize any of these choices, from the context of the information, you know that pineapple symbolizes a childhood memory for the narrator. The correct answer is **C**, a childhood memory.

## CONNOTATIONS

All words have the meaning that you can find in the dictionary, which is called their denotative meaning. But how do you describe the happy or scared feeling that some people get when they hear certain words? A word's emotional meaning is called the **connotation**.

Connotations can be either positive or negative. Some words, such as *medicine* or *vaccine*, have positive connotations for some people and negative connotations for other people. But many words have universal connotations. For example, the words *tiresome* and *nasty* usually have negative connotations, but the words *celebration* and *victory* usually have positive connotations.

Take a look at the illustrations of people exercising below. Do you think the illustrations are good examples of the positive and negative connotations of exercise?

Authors often rely on the connotations of words to create a mood and tone. For example, a poem that has a lot of words with positive connotations usually has an upbeat tone and a happy mood, while a poem with a lot of words that have negative connotations has a somber tone and a sad mood.

In addition to applying connotations to the mood and tone of a piece—concepts covered later in this book—you can use the connotations of words to determine their meanings. For example, if you come across an unfamiliar word, you can often determine the connotation of the word and use that to determine its meaning. Let's look at a CAHSEE example.

**What does the word *longevity* mean in the following sentence?**

> If you exercise and eat properly, you will
> probably have longevity and good health.

A  malnutrition
B  disease
C  sadness
D  long life

You may not know what the word *longevity* means, but you can determine its connotation from the context of the sentence. Eating properly and exercising generally lead to a positive result, good health. It is likely that longevity also has a positive meaning. The only positive connotation in the answer choices is long life, so choice **D** is correct.

## WORD ANALYSIS SKILLS

On the CAHSEE, you will most likely be asked if a word has a similar meaning to another word. Sometimes answer choices will be words that are similar in meaning. When two answers are similar in meaning, you can often eliminate both answers as incorrect choices. Knowing words that are similar in meaning can help you tackle many of the questions that you will see on the CAHSEE.

### Synonyms

A **synonym** is a word that is similar in meaning to another word. *Fast* is a synonym for *quick*. *Garrulous* (whether you know it or not) is a synonym for *talkative*. Some of the CAHSEE Word Analysis questions involve selecting a synonym. Look at the following example.

**In the passage, *genuine* suggests something that is—**

**A** authentic.

**B** valuable.

**C** ancient.

**D** damaged.

 **Questions with the phrase *suggests* are synonym questions. Look for a word in the answer choices that means the same thing as the word in the question.**

Sometimes you'll know the word in the question, and sometimes you won't. Sometimes you'll know all the words in the answer choices, and sometimes, you won't. For those times when you're stumped, here is Kaplan's 3-Step Method for Synonym Questions. Then, we'll give you some great tactics to use when you don't know all the words in the question.

## KAPLAN'S 3-STEP METHOD FOR SYNONYM QUESTIONS
**Step 1:** Define the stem word.
**Step 2:** Find the answer choice that best fits your definition.
**Step 3:** If no choice fits, think of other definitions for the stem word and go through the choices again.

Let's take another look at the *genuine* example, using Kaplan's 3-Step Method.

### Step 1: Define the Stem Word
What does *genuine* mean? Something genuine is something *real*, such as a real Ming vase, rather than a forgery. Your definition might be something like this: Something genuine can be proven to be what it claims to be. It is *authentic*, not fake.

### Step 2: Find the Answer Choice That Best Fits Your Definition
Go through the answer choices one by one to see which choice fits best. Your options are *authentic*, *valuable*, *ancient*, and *damaged*. Something genuine could be worth money or not worth anything at all, it could be old or new, or it could be in good shape or bad. The only word that really means the same thing as genuine is choice **A**, *authentic*.

### Step 3: If No Choice Fits, Think of Other Definitions for the Stem Word and Go through the Choices Again
In this instance, only one choice fits all the conditions of being genuine as based on the context of the sentence. That word is *authentic*. Choice **A** is the correct answer.

Now, take a look at the following example.

***Grave* most nearly suggests—**

**A**   regrettable.

**B**   unpleasant.

**C**   serious.

**D**   careful.

Maybe you defined *grave* as a burial location. You looked at the choices, and didn't see any words like *tomb* or *coffin*. What do you do? Move to Step 3, and go back to the stem word, thinking about other definitions. Have you ever heard of a *grave* situation? *Grave* can also mean serious or *solemn*, so you can see that choice **C**, *serious*, now fits perfectly. If none of the answer choices seems to work with your definition, there may be a secondary definition you haven't considered.

## WHAT TO DO IF YOU DON'T KNOW THE WORD

**Technique 1:** Look for familiar roots, prefixes, and suffixes.

**Technique 2:** Use your knowledge of foreign languages.

**Technique 3:** Remember the word in context.

**Technique 4:** Use word charge.

**Technique 5:** Work backward to eliminate answers.

Let's examine each technique more closely.

### Technique 1: Look for Familiar Roots, Prefixes, and Suffixes

Having a good grasp of how words are put together will help you tremendously on synonym questions, particularly when you don't know a vocabulary word. If you can break a word into pieces that you understand, you'll be able to answer questions that you might have thought too difficult to tackle.

Look at the following words, and circle any prefixes, suffixes, or roots that you know.

*benevolence*          *verify*

*conspire*             *inscribe*

*insomnia*

*Bene* is related to good; *somn* has to do with sleep; *scrib* has to do with writing; *con* is related to together; and *ver* has to do with truth. So, if you were looking for a synonym for *benevolence*, you'd definitely want to choose a positive, or "good," word.

Refer to the end of this chapter for lists of roots, prefixes, and suffixes.

### Technique 2: Use Your Knowledge of Foreign Languages

Do you know or study a foreign language? If so, it can help you decode many vocabulary words on the CAHSEE, particularly if it's one of the Romance languages (French, Spanish, Italian, or Portuguese).

Look at the following example words. Do you recognize any foreign language words in them?

*facilitate*

*dormant*

*explicate*

*Facile* means *easy* in Italian; *dormir* means *to sleep* in Spanish; and *expliquer* means *to explain* in French. A synonym for each of these words would have something to do with these general meanings.

### Technique 3: Remember the Word in Context

Sometimes a word may look strange on the page by itself, but if you think about it, you realize you've probably heard it before in other phrases. If you can put the word into context, even if that context is cliché, you're on your way to deciphering its meaning.

**In the following sentence, what does *field* mean?**

> Her field of study was architecture.

A    garden

B    area

C    space

D    object

A *field* is an open space.  However, using the context of study can help you avoid going down a wrong path to begin with.  Because field is used in the phrase *field of study*, we are not talking about a real open space with grass, but rather a *general area* or *subject*.  Given that definition, move on to Step 2, so choice **B** fits best.

Here's another example.

**In the passage, *laurels* most nearly means—**

A    branches.

B    accomplishments.

C    lavender.

D    cushion.

Have you heard the phrase *Don't rest on your laurels*? What do you think it might mean?

The phrase *Don't rest on your laurels* originated in ancient Greece, where heroes were given wreaths of laurel branches to signify their accomplishments. Telling someone to not rest on his *laurels* is the same thing as telling him to not get too smug, living off the success of one accomplishment, rather than striving for improvement.  *Don't rest on your laurels* doesn't mean rest on your *branches*; it means don't rest on your *accomplishments*.  In this case, the answer is dependent on the context of how the word is used in the passage. Choice **B** is the correct answer.

### Technique 4: Use Word Charge

Even if you know nothing about the word, have never seen it before, don't recognize any prefixes or roots, and can't think of any word in any language that it sounds like, you can still take an educated guess by using word charge.

Word charge refers to the sense that a word gives you as to whether it's a positive word or a negative word. Often, words that sound harsh have negative meanings, while smooth-sounding words tend to have positive meanings. If *cantankerous* sounds negative to you, you would be right: It means "difficult to handle."

You can also use prefixes and roots to help determine a word's charge. *Anti-, mal-, de-, dis-, un-, in-, im-, a-,* and *mis-* often indicate a negative, while *pro-, bene-,* and *magn-* are often positives.

Not all words sound positive or negative; some sound neutral. But, if you can define the charge, you can probably eliminate some answer choices on that basis alone. Word charge is a great technique to use when answering antonym questions, too.

### Technique 5: Work Backward to Eliminate Answers

What if you just can't think of a definition for the underlined word? Try working backward. What is working backward? It may sound hard, but it's actually just a nifty way of approaching questions when you can't answer them directly. Basically, you skip past the question and head straight for the answer choices.

Working backward means plugging in your answer choices and asking yourself if they could possibly mean the same as the underlined word. This technique is especially useful for words-in-context questions. Let's examine how this works.

**In this line from the poem, the expression *dry wit* most nearly means wit that is—**

A     sarcastic.

B     moldy.

C     unusual.

D     pathetic.

Given the context, we know that *dry* here can't mean the opposite of *wet*. The context already clues us in to the fact that dry has something to do with *wit*, or being clever. Let's say you just don't know what *dry wit* could be. Go to the answer choices and ask yourself if each one could apply to the context and, therefore, mean the same as the word *dry*.

**Choice A:** Could you have *sarcastic* wit? Yes, someone could be sarcastically witty.

**Choice B:** Could you have *moldy* wit? *Moldy* wit? That doesn't make sense. Eliminate this answer choice.

**Choice C:** Could you have *unusual* wit? Perhaps, but it doesn't sound as good as choice A.

**Choice D:** Could you have *pathetic* wit? No, that doesn't make sense. *Pathetic* means *pitiable*. Pitiable cleverness doesn't make sense. Eliminate this answer choice.

Choice **A** is the best answer. You've got it!

## TEMPTING WRONG ANSWERS

The test makers choose their wrong answer choices very carefully. Sometimes that means throwing in answer traps that will tempt you, but that are incorrect. Be a savvy test taker; don't fall for these distractions!

What kinds of wrong answers are we talking about here? In synonym questions, there are two types of answer traps to watch out for: answers that are almost right and answers that sound like the stem word. Let's illustrate both types to make them concrete.

**The author uses the word *delegate* to mean—**

A delight.

B assign.

C decide.

D manage.

> I tend to favor citrus fruit over other types of fruit.

**In the passage, *favor* suggests a feeling of—**

A service.

B preference.

C respect.

D improvement.

In the first example, choices A and C might be tempting, because they all start with the prefix *de-*, just like the stem word, *delegate*. It's important that you examine all the answer choices, because otherwise, you might select choice A and never get to the correct answer, **B**.

In the second example, you might look at the word *favor* and think, oh, that's something positive. It's something you do for someone else. It sounds a lot like choice A, *service*. Maybe you select A and move on. If you do that, you would be falling for a trap! The correct answer is **B**, *preference*, because *favoring* someone or something is to like it better than something else—in other words, to *prefer* it. If you don't read through all of the choices, you might be tricked into choosing a wrong answer.

At this point, you have a great set of tools for answering many Word Analysis questions. You know how to approach them and you know some traps to avoid. But what happens if these strategies don't work for you? Should you just give up and move on? No way! Here are some more strategies and tools to help you figure out the meaning of a tough vocabulary word by learning some basic roots, prefixes, and suffixes.

## WORD PARTS

When you come across a word that you do not know in a CAHSEE passage, you can often approach the word like a math problem. Many words are made up of two or more building blocks called roots, prefixes, or suffixes.

A **root** is the part of a word that provides the general meaning of the word. A **prefix** is a group of letters added to the front of a word to change the meaning. A **suffix** is a group of letters added to the end of a word to change the meaning.

For example, the word *aquarium* can be divided into the root *aqua-*, meaning "water," and the suffix *-arium*, meaning "a place for or relating to." So the word *aquarium* means "a place for or relating to water."

How familiar are you with the meanings of different word parts? Examine the following words and identify the word parts to determine their meaning. The answers can be found in the following box.

| Word | Root | Prefix | Suffix | Meaning |
|---|---|---|---|---|
| microbiology | | | | |
| preview | | | | |
| dermatology | | | | |
| monochromatic | | | | |

| Word | Root | Prefix | Suffix | Meaning |
|------|------|--------|--------|---------|
| microbiology | *bio* | *micro-* | *-ology* | the study of small life |
| preview | *view* | *pre-* | | to view before or in advance |
| dermatology | *derm* | | *-ology* | the study of skin |
| monochromatic | *chrom* | *mono-* | *-ic* | having to do with one color |

If it was difficult for you slice up these words to find meaning, you may want to spend some time reviewing word parts. The following charts list common roots, prefixes, and suffixes.

## Roots

| Root | Meaning | Example |
|------|---------|---------|
| *ami, amic* | love | amiable |
| *brev* | short | brevity |
| *culp* | guilt | culpable, culprit |
| *dys* | abnormal | dysfunctional |
| *her, hes* | stick | adhesive |
| *loc* | place | location |
| *mor, mort* | death | immortal |
| *ped, pod* | foot | pedal |
| *sec, sect* | cut | dissect |
| *tens* | stretch | tension |

## Prefixes

| Prefix | Meaning | Example |
|---|---|---|
| *anti-* | against | antisocial |
| *dia-* | through | diameter |
| *hyper-* | excessive | hyperbole |
| *mal-* | bad | malign |
| *syn-, sym-, syl-, sys-* | with, together | sympathetic |

## Suffixes

| Suffix | Definition | Example |
|---|---|---|
| *-ia, -y* | act, state | hysteria, lucidity |
| *-ism* | the belief in | activism |
| *-ness* | having or possessing | fairness |
| *-or, -er* | one who takes part in | tutor, painter |
| *-sis* | state, condition of | stasis |

Let's try using word parts to determine the answer to the following question.

**What is the meaning of the word *rehash* in the following sentence?**

> Politicians often rehash political points in their campaign speeches.

A    take away

B    state again

C    reduce

D    deduct

You know that the prefix *re-* can mean "to repeat" or "do again." You may not know what *hash* means, but from the context of the sentence, you might guess that it means "state" or "speak." Choice **B** is also the only answer that is an action repeated or done again. The meaning of the word *rehash* is to "state again."

## USING A DICTIONARY

How many times do you see an unfamiliar word while reading? If you're like most people, you would simply skip the word you did not understand. However, as you prepare for the CAHSEE, use a dictionary as often as you can to learn the meanings of new words. This book can offer you strategies to decode unfamiliar words, but the dictionary can help you remember those vocabulary words. This step will save you time on the test for other questions that might be more difficult.

Here are some quick tips for using a dictionary.

Look at the top of the dictionary page to see the first and the last words on the page. They are called *guide words*. Compare the first three letters of your unfamiliar word to the guide words. If your word falls alphabetically between the guide words, the definition will appear on that page.

For example, would the word *drowsy* appear on a page with the guide words *distance/disorder* or *drool/drudge*?

*Drowsy* comes alphabetically between *drool* and *drudge*, so you would look at the second of the two pages.

Read the definitions of the word *drowsy*. The dictionary offers more than one definition for each word. You need to find the definition that best fits the context of the sentence.

For example, you are reading a story about a cross-country driver who has been on the road for nine hours. She pulls over for the night because she is drowsy. Which of the following definitions would you use?

**Drowsy, adj. A. sleepy or half-asleep; B. peacefully quiet or inactive**

The correct answer is definition A, *sleepy* or *half-asleep*. This describes the driver as being sleepy. Definition B would describe someone's personality or the attitude of a town.

Now that you know the unfamiliar word's meaning, you might want to write the definition in your own words. This step can help you remember what you just learned. You can also use the new word in a sentence. You are more likely to use the word in your daily speech or writing.

No matter what the question type, having a strong vocabulary is a large part of doing well on the CAHSEE, and we'll discuss how to build your vocabulary. Obviously, the more words you know, the better. But our goal is to rack up points on the test, not to memorize every word in the dictionary. The strategies covered here will help you get closer to the correct answer choice, even if you don't always know the exact meaning of the word in question.

## USING FLASHCARDS TO STUDY

Dictionaries, memorization, and logic strategies are good ways to approach the CAHSEE. One of the best ways to prepare for the CAHSEE is to memorize words that you have trouble with before the test. Likewise, knowing word parts will help you figure out the meanings of unfamiliar words quickly.

One way to memorize words is to make flashcards. Flashcards will help you not only memorize the vocabulary, but also review the concepts covered in chapters throughout this study guide.

To make flashcards, buy a package of 3 × 5 or 4 × 6 index cards. Write the term on one side of an index card and the definition on the other side of the card. As you make your way through the rest of this study guide, you may even want to write examples of each vocabulary term below the definitions.

## SUMMARY

You learned a lot in this chapter. Let's review the most important points.

- Figurative language goes beyond the dictionary meaning of a word.
  - **Personification** gives an animal, object, or idea human characteristics.
  - A **metaphor** uses a word or phrase to compare two different things, without using the words *like* or *as*.
  - A **simile** is a phrase that compares two or more things using the words *like* or *as*.
  - **Symbolism** is a character or object that stands for something with great meaning, often an abstract concept.
- A **connotation** is the emotional meaning of a word.
  - Words have negative and positive connotations, which can help you determine the meaning of an unfamiliar word.
- A **synonym** is a word that means the same thing as another word.
- There will be words in the passages that are difficult or challenging.
  - Look for familiar roots, prefixes, or suffixes.
  - Use your knowledge of foreign languages.
  - Remember the word in context.
  - Use word charge.
  - Work backward to eliminate answers.
- Many unfamiliar words can be divided into word parts.
  - A **root** is the main part of a word that provides the meaning.
  - A **prefix** is a group of letters added to the beginning of a word to change the meaning.
  - A **suffix** is a group of letters added to the end of a word to change the meaning.
- To prepare for difficult vocabulary words in a passage, use a dictionary to find the meanings of unfamiliar words.
  - Look at the guide words on the top of the dictionary page.
  - Find the word and the definition that best fits.
  - Write down the word and its meaning.
- Flashcards are a tool that can be used to study vocabulary words and word parts.

# Chapter 1
# Word Analysis Quiz

Read the following passage and answer questions 1 through 4.

# Narrative Painting

1 Gustave Courbet painted his realist masterpiece, *The Wheat Sifters*, in Ornans in 1853 to 1854. The picture depicts an agricultural subject, two rural women and a small child sifting wheat in a bolting room flooded with golden light. The main figure is a powerful woman, dressed in orange and yellow, kneeling on a white cloth. She is seen lifting a large round sieve or colander-like object over her head. Kernels of wheat fall onto the cloth before her. A younger woman in pale blue and gray at the sifter's left picks at bits of chaff or fiber from a dish in her lap. A curious boy in blue is shown peering into the black recesses of a tartare, a mechanical device for cleaning grain. A kitten naps among tall sacks of wheat.

2 Art historian Michael Fried sees Courbet's painting not only as an illustration of labor and work, but also as a picture of painting itself. The women's work is a thematic proxy for the painter's effort, with the group of sifters and child representing the artist. The creamy expanse of the large, rough white cloth and the sticky red kernels of wheat should be compared to canvas and pigment, with the latticed shadow cast on the brilliant wall opposite the main sifter representing the frame of a painting. The round sieve is a painter's palette and the sacks of grain are tubes of paint, which were fairly recent inventions in Courbet's time.

3 Industrialization threatened to change the ways of farm life, as well as the painter's craft. The menacing presence of the dark tartare at the heart of Courbet's picture suggests as much. Fried shows that these images place Courbet in the position of predicting the problems of modern art, in which the abstract parts of art, no longer interested in telling a story, would become the most important concern of painting.

1. Read this excerpt from the first paragraph of the passage.

> . . . a bolting room flooded with golden light.

What is the meaning of the word *flooded* in the passage?

A    overwhelmed

B    irrigated

C    illuminated

D    dampened

2. Read this part of the passage.

> The women's work is a thematic proxy for the painter's effort, with the group of sifters and child representing the artist.

What is the meaning of the word *proxy* in the passage?

A    attorney

B    substitute

C    manager

D    definition

3. What figure of speech is the following statement?

> The round sieve is a painter's palette and the sacks of grain are tubes of paint, which were fairly recent inventions in Courbet's time.

A    a simile statement

B    a metaphorical statement

C    a personification statement

D    a literal statement

4. What is one of the concepts that the tartare symbolizes in the passage?

A    a painter's canvas

B    tubes of paint

C    modern art

D    industrialization

Read the following passage and answer questions 5 through 8.

# Philosophy in the 20th Century

Influential philosopher Ludwig Wittgenstein was an important 20th-century philosopher. He was born in Austria in 1889. The English language version of his early treatise, *Tractatus Logico-Philosophicus*, was published in 1922. It contained a preface, or foreward, by the logical positivist Bertrand Russell, who was Wittgenstein's mentor and colleague. The book's crystalline structure was easy to understand, and it was immediately recognized as a brilliant masterpiece.

*Tractatus* is perhaps the single most important work of philosophy written in the 20th century, and the only work published during Wittgenstein's lifetime. In this terse, compact book, the philosopher presents a set of concise, elegant paragraphs known as *Propositions*, in which the machinery of language attempts to describe an elusive, undefined sense of reality.

The structure of the *Propositions*, and the nature of inferences and conclusions that they show, are the first topics Wittgenstein addressed. This section is followed by the theory of knowledge, the principles of physics and ethics, and, finally, the mystical. In the last *Proposition*, Wittgenstein famously summarizes his argument by stating, "What we cannot speak about we must pass over in silence." The relationship of the mystical to the Greek *mystos*, and to the concept of silence, may be considered in this contradictory case as a criticism and praise of language itself.

In the book *Philosophical Investigations*, the topics are written in a circular style and make a subtle negation of the direct, linear style set forth in the *Tractatus*. Taken together, these two works demonstrate the impossibility of making language simpler. They show how language's limitations define and restrict the boundaries of human action.

**5. Read this part of the passage.**

> Its crystalline structure was easy to understand, and it was immediately recognized as a brilliant masterpiece.

**What is the meaning of the word *crystalline* in the passage?**

A    clear

B    sparkling

C    mineral

D    hard

**6. Read this part of the passage.**

> In this terse, compact book, the philosopher presents a set of concise, elegant paragraphs . . .

**What is the meaning of the word *terse* in this sentence?**

A    curt

B    brief

C    unfriendly

D    rambling

**7. Read this part of the passage.**

> . . . the machinery of language attempts to describe an elusive, undefined sense of reality . . .

**What is the meaning of the word *elusive* in this passage?**

A    exclusive

B    specific

C    inexplicable

D    distinct

**8. Read this part of the passage.**

> . . . the topics are written in a circular style and make a subtle negation of the direct, linear style set forth in the *Tractatus*.

**What is the meaning of the word *circular* in this passage?**

A    curved

B    round

C    indirect

D    straight

Read the passage and answer questions 9 through 12.

# An American Symbol of the Individual

Popeye the Sailor is the main character of a comic strip originally created in 1919. Popeye, himself, did not appear in the comic strip until 1929. The strips were quite beloved, and Popeye was later featured in a series of animated short films. Fleischer Studios produced the best of these during the 1930s. A number of unique characters show up in these films. Popeye is a feisty "salty dog" who has a distinct and expressive voice. His primary way of speaking is a garbled, singsong muttering, often addressed only to himself. His bulging forearms bear tattoos of anchors and he clenches a corncob pipe in his mouth. Although Popeye is short, very quarrelsome, and odd looking, many fans consider him a predecessor to the muscular superheroes who appeared in the 1950s American comic books.

Popeye cartoons are usually very simple. Popeye's arch-nemesis, a bearded, burly brute named Bluto, mocks the little sailor while wooing Popeye's sweetheart, Olive Oyl. In a show of strength, Bluto abuses Popeye, who finally declares, "That's all's me can stand, and me can't stands no more!" At this point, Popeye downs a can of spinach, which gives him an instant boost of energy, and he quickly defeats his foe. Olive Oyl is

defended, and Popeye's status is assured. The character's unapologetic code of honor is represented by his personal motto, "I yam what I yam, and that's all that I yam." This repeated bit of nonsense is at the center of Popeye's personal character and principles. In this light, Popeye is best understood as an expression of American individualism.

**9. Which sentence from the passage is an example of figurative language?**

A   Popeye the Sailor is the main character of a comic strip originally created in 1919.

B   The strips were quite beloved, and Popeye was later featured in a series of animated short films.

C   A number of unique characters show up in these films.

D   Popeye is a feisty "salty dog" who has a distinct and expressive voice.

**10. Read this part from the passage.**

> His bulging forearms bear tattoos of anchors . . .

**What is the meaning of the word *bear* in the passage?**

A support
B display
C tolerate
D carry

**11. Read this statement from the passage.**

> . . . Popeye downs a can of spinach, which gives him an instant boost of energy . . .

**What is the meaning of the word *downs* in the passage?**

A consumes
B defeats
C shoots
D gags

**12. Read this part from the passage.**

> This repeated bit of nonsense is perhaps at the core of Popeye's personal character and principles.

**What does the word *character* mean in the passage?**

A figure
B role
C ethic
D cipher

**13. What does the word *quizzical* mean in the following sentence?**

> In the game of chess, a very bad move is technically referred to as a blunder, and is recorded in match notation with the quizzical sign ??.

A expressing concern
B mildly teasing
C gently mocking
D expressing disbelief

14. What does the word *aesthetic* mean in the following sentence?

> Japanese culture has a particular aesthetic and understanding of the world that extends not only from its art and architecture, but also to its carefully prepared cuisine, streamlined industrial design, and even its polite conversation.

A    practice of anesthesiology

B    preference for no decoration

C    philosophy of the afterlife

D    interest in a pleasing appearance

15. What is the meaning of the word *anchor* in the following sentence?

> For many years, the two impressive neo-Gothic structures of limestone and granite, which anchor the span on either side of the East River, were the tallest towers in the world.

A    a large column

B    a device that is cast into water

C    to provide steady support

D    to hold loosely in place

16. What is the meaning of the word *break* in the following sentence?

> Jackie Robinson was the first African American player to break the race barrier in Major League Baseball.

A    separate into parts

B    turn over

C    burst through

D    ruin

17. Read the following sentence. What does the word *binding* mean?

> Although linseed oil remains the most widely used oil for binding pigments, thinning paint, and varnishing finished paintings, poppyseed oil is sometimes used in its stead.

A    tying up

B    blending into a paste

C    restraining movement

D    creating an agreement

**18. What is the meaning of the word *slim* in the following sentence?**

By the time of Walt Whitman's death, *Leaves of Grass* had grown from a slim 12 poems to a lush 400, and the book was on its way to becoming, as Ralph Waldo Emerson had presciently called it, "the most extraordinary piece of wit and wisdom America has contributed."

A    graceful
B    frail
C    skinny
D    small

**19. What is the meaning of the word *harsh* in the following sentence?**

The unequal measures were ultimately deemed too harsh, and were humanely revised when the board met the next week.

A    glaring
B    discordant
C    punitive
D    inhospitable

**20. What does the word *scrapped* mean in the following sentence?**

The limited Morgenthau Plan was totally scrapped in favor of far more comprehensive policies advocated by General George C. Marshall, who was named U.S. Secretary of State after the end of the war.

A    abandoned
B    revised
C    converted
D    rethought

# Answers and Explanations

**1. C**

The incorrect answer choices for this question are all true definitions of the word *flooded*, but they are not correct in the context provided. Choice A is incorrect because a person can be *flooded* or *overwhelmed* with emotion, but a room cannot be considered *overwhelmed* by light. Choices B and D are incorrect because the words *irrigated* and *dampened* imply a soaking by water, and not illumination by the sun or by candles.

**2. B**

The key word *representing* provides a clue that *proxy* means "substitute." Choice B is correct. While sometimes a *manager* or an *attorney* can be a stand-in, or *proxy*, the use of *manager* or *attorney* does not fit into this context, so choices A and C are incorrect. Choice D is incorrect because *proxy* does not mean "definition"; it means a "delegate, representative, or substitute."

**3. B**

If you read the statement carefully, you can see that the correct answer is B, a *metaphorical statement*. The sentence compares two unlike objects, a sieve and sacks of grain to two other unlike objects, a painter's palette and tubes of paint. This is an example of a metaphor. You can eliminate choice A because the sentence does not use *like* or *as* to draw a comparison between the objects. You can eliminate choice C because the objects are not given human qualities or characteristics; they firmly remain inanimate objects. You can eliminate choice D because the statement is not literal; a sieve is not a painter's palette nor are sacks of grain actually tubes of paint, but you can understand the metaphor that Courbet is trying to draw between the objects.

### 4. D

In the passage, the writer points out that industrialization threatened rural life as well as the painter's craft. Courbet chooses to represent this threat as a dark machine called a tartare, so the correct answer is choice D, *industrialization.* You can eliminate answer choice A because the tartare does not represent a painter's canvas. You know that the white cloth represented a painter's canvas. You know that choice B is incorrect because the sacks of grain represent the tubes of paint. While answer choice C may look tempting, if you read the passage carefully, you will know that Courbet is more concerned with the problems of industrialization than with modern art. While his work anticipates some of the future problems with art, even Courbet is not skilled enough to see directly into the future.

### 5. A

In the passage, *crystalline* means "easy to understand." Something that is easy to understand is lucid, or *clear*, so the correct answer is choice A. The words *sparkling*, *mineral*, and *hard* are more compatible with the description of semiprecious stone such as quartz, which has a crystal-like structure.

### 6. B

The key words *compact* and *concise* imply that Wittgenstein's paragraphs are *brief* and to the point. The correct answer is choice B. While *terse* can mean "curt" or "unfriendly," the terms usually apply to social interactions, not formal writing. In this case, choices A and C are synonyms. By using the process of elimination, you can determine that neither answer is correct because the test cannot have two correct answers. You can determine that choice D is incorrect because *rambling* is an antonym of *compact* and *concise*.

## 7. C

Take a look at the words in the sentence and see if you can find a synonym of *elusive.* The word *undefined* is a synonym of *elusive.* You know that the suffix *un-* means "not" and the base word *define* means "to state the nature of something exactly." Something that is *not defined exactly* cannot be *specific* or *distinct.* Therefore, you can eliminate choices B and D because they are antonyms of *elusive.* You know that *exclusive* means "something that not everyone is able to have or take part in." While *exclusive* may be a synonym of *elusive* in some cases, in this case they are not synonyms. *Inexplicable* means "something that cannot be defined." This is the best synonym of *elusive* based on the context of the sentence. The correct answer is choice C.

## 8. C

You must use antonyms to determine the meaning of *circular.* The key words *direct* and *linear* are antonyms of *circular.* *Negation* is also a key word. *Negation* means "not" and implies that the topics are neither *direct* nor *linear,* so choice C is correct. *Round* and *curved* may describe aspects of physical, concrete objects such as paintings, furniture, or buildings, but they are not often used to describe abstract things such as ideas or topics, so you know that choices A and B are incorrect. You also know that choice D is incorrect because something that is *circular* is not *straight.*

## 9. D

If you read the passage carefully, you can tell that the last answer is an example of figurative speech, so the correct answer is choice D. In this sentence, a *salty dog* is a metaphor for *sailor.* Even if you didn't know that, you are aware that Popeye is not really a dog, and it should not be taken literally. You know that comparing two unlike things is a metaphor, so this sentence is an example of figurative language. In choice A, the sentence describes who Popeye is, but it does not have any figurative expressions. It is simply a straightforward statement, so you know that choice A is incorrect. Choice B is incorrect because, like choice A, the sentence is descriptive, but it is not figurative in any sense. Choice C, while descriptive, is also a literal statement, so it cannot be an example of figurative language.

## 10. B

The key word *tattoos* implies the forearms *bear* images of anchors, or are inscribed with imagery, so the correct answer is choice B. A series of columns that *support* a structure above them are said to bear its weight, but tattoos do not need support, so choice A is incorrect. If a husband can hardly *tolerate* his mother-in-law's screeching voice, he can be said to scarcely *bear,* or *tolerate* her presence, but you cannot say *bear* means *tolerate* in the passage, so choice C is incorrect. Choice D is incorrect because people don't *carry* tattoos, they *display* them.

## 11. A

The key word *spinach* implies that a can of the vegetable is *consumed,* or *eaten,* so that implies choice A is correct. Choices B and C are incorrect because a fighter pilot may shoot or *defeat* his enemy, but Popeye is not trying to *defeat* anyone, he is *consuming.* While you may *gag* if you had to down a can of spinach in a gulp, Popeye likes spinach and he does not *gag,* so choice D is incorrect.

## 12. C

The key word *principles* implies a discussion of moral standards and *ethics,* so choice C is correct. Choices A and B are incorrect because the sentence is not discussing Popeye's physical *figure* or the *role* that he plays; the sentence is discussing Popeye's beliefs. Choice D is incorrect because a *cipher* may be a person who plays a mysterious role, or has an inscrutable visage, but Popeye is not a cipher; if anything, Popeye is not mysterious in any way.

## 13. D

There are key words in the sentence that imply the meaning of the word *quizzical.* The notation *??* suggests an expression of *disbelief* or *puzzlement* at the very bad move known as a *blunder.* The question marks themselves also indicate *questioning, surprise,* or *stunned amazement,* so choice D is correct. Choice A is incorrect because a bad chess move may result in the end of game and may call for more than an expression of *concern.* Choices B and C are incorrect because in chess, a very bad move is serious, not something to be *mildly teased* about or *gently mocked*; such a move is more likely to cause *disbelief.*

**14. D**

To understand the correct answer, read the entire sentence and look for context clues that help determine the meaning of the phrase. You know that Japanese *aesthetics* extend to many different areas of Japanese life. Key words such as *carefully prepared*, *streamlined*, and *polite* suggest a preference for a *pleasing appearance*. So you might infer that *aesthetics* might be an *interest in a pleasing appearance*. However, if you're not sure, you can eliminate the other answers by determining if the context of the sentence supports them or doesn't. Choice A is incorrect because *anesthesiology* is the practice of using drugs to prepare patients for surgery. Choice B is incorrect because you know from the sentence that the Japanese are interested in *presentation* and *appearance*, so an answer that suggests *no decoration* is incorrect. Choice C is incorrect because the sentence is not discussing the concept of an *afterlife*, but instead the concept of *appearance*. If you had been in doubt about choice D, crossing out all the incorrect answers would have helped you arrive at, and confirm, the correct answer, choice D.

**15. C**

In order to understand the correct answer, read the entire sentence and look for context clues that can help determine the meaning of the word. Parsing the phrase *structures of limestone and granite, which anchor the span* show that the correct choice is a verb, and not a noun. The structures anchor, or *support*, the bridge. Choice C is correct. If the word *anchor* is a noun, it may indeed be a large column that provides support. It may also be a device thrown from a boat to prevent it from moving, but in the sentence, *anchor* is not a noun, so choices A and B are incorrect. Anchor means to provide steady, firm support, so choice D is incorrect.

**16. C**

To understand the correct answer, read the entire sentence and look for context clues that can help determine the meaning of the word. Robinson was the first African American player to *break* into the big leagues, and this implies that he *burst* through a barrier. Choice C is the correct one. A waiter may break a crusty loaf of bread into small pieces, or *separate* it into parts, before placing it on the diner's table, but that meaning does not fit the context of the sentence, so choice A is incorrect. A farmer will *turn over*, or *break*, the soil in his fields before planting his crops, but again, this does not fit the context of the sentence, so choice B is incorrect. Choice D is incorrect because a child may *break* a vase and *ruin* it, but this does not fit the context of the sentence.

### 17. B

Read the entire sentence and look for context clues that can help determine the meaning of the word. As the sentence mentions the thinning of oil paint and the application of varnish, the context implies oil is a liquid that is essential in *binding* or *blending* pigment into a paste, making it ready for use. Choice B is correct. *Tying up*, or *restraining movement* means binding, or preventing movement, but that is not what is happening here, so choices A and C are incorrect. Choice D is incorrect because a legal *agreement* between two parties may be described as a *binding contract* to which both parties are held, but this answer does not fit the context of the sentence.

### 18. D

Read the entire sentence and look for context clues that can help determine the meaning of the word. Whitman's *slim* book originally contained a *small* number of poems, 12, but eventually grew to 400. Choice D is the correct one. Choice A is incorrect because while the poems may be *graceful*, there is nothing in the sentence to suggest whether the poems are graceful or not. This is not a better answer than *small*. Choice B is incorrect because a *frail* poem doesn't make much sense in this context. People may be *frail*, but writing is not referred to as frail. A *skinny* child may be said to be *slim*, but *skinny* is not a word used to describe poetry, so choice C is incorrect.

### 19. C

*Unequal* measures that were revised to reach a more humane outcome may originally have been thought to be too *punitive*. Choice C is correct. Choice A is incorrect because *glaring* refers to the visual sense, and in this case, you can't see the unequal measures, you can only think about them. Choice B is incorrect because a *discordant* note is a note that clashes or does not fit with the rest of the music. This has nothing to do with the sentence or its context.

Choice D is incorrect because something that is *inhospitable* is something that you cannot live in, and the context of the sentence does not support this conclusion.

**20. A**

In order to understand the correct answer, read the entire sentence and look for context clues that can help determine the meaning of the word. The fact that the limited Morgenthau Plan was *totally scrapped* in favor of other policies suggests that choice A is the correct answer. The plan was *abandoned*, and a more *comprehensive*, or "total," plan was drafted in its place. Choices B and C are both synonyms, which can immediately eliminate them as answers. A *revised* plan would have retained some of the components of the original plan, and a *converted* plan would have adopted its premises for a different use, so these answers are incorrect. Choice D is incorrect because a *rethought* plan would have retained the spirit of the original plan, if not some of its policies; here, nothing of the original plan was kept.

# Chapter 2

# Reading Comprehension

## DEVELOPING READING COMPREHENSION

The CAHSEE will have 18 questions to test your ability to comprehend what you read. There are two types of reading passages on the CAHSEE: informational materials and literary texts. Informational materials are nonfiction documents such as encyclopedia entries. You read these nonfiction passages for a specific purpose, such as learning how to assemble a new bike or finding information about tree frogs. Literary texts are plays, poems, and stories that offer a theme or a message for readers to take away.

This chapter will offer general reading comprehension strategies that you can apply to all types of passages. Skills such as reading comprehension strategies, workplace communication, finding the main idea, and summarizing are invaluable tools for any reading passage. This chapter will also focus specifically on how to read, comprehend, and apply these tools to the types of nonfiction passages that might appear on the test.

## HOW READING ON TESTS DIFFERS FROM EVERYDAY READING

You don't usually read to gather points, do you? Remember, as you approach the CAHSEE reading passages, the points come from the questions, not the passages. If you spend your time focusing on all the subtle nuances or details of a given passage, you may not have time to answer the questions (and earn points). Yes, you may know all the details of the history of space flight, but this won't help you on the test.

Therefore, as you work through this chapter, there are two things you need to do:

1. Be aware of your reading habits. Notice how you approach each passage and whether you are getting bogged down in the details.
2. Make the questions your priority.

How do you do that? Use our systematic approach to focus on the questions and the points.

## Kaplan's 4-Step Method for Reading Comprehension Questions

**Step 1:** Read the passage.
**Step 2:** Decode the questions.
**Step 3:** Research the details.
**Step 4:** Predict the answer, and check the answer choices.

Let's see put this plan into action.

## Step 1: Read the Passage

The first thing you're going to do is read through the passage, but don't memorize it or take it apart. Instead, look for the main idea and paragraph topics (note the general idea and where it seems to be going).

For example, if you saw the following passage on the CAHSEE, these are some things you might want to note.

Benjamin Franklin is well known as a founding father, an inventor, and a philosopher. He is remembered for the clever yet humorous writings of *Poor Richard's Almanac*, which offered advice, such as, "Early to bed, early to rise, makes a man healthy, wealthy, and wise." The scientist Franklin discovered electricity through his experiments with lightning. He was also the first American diplomat. From 1776 to 1778, Benjamin Franklin led a three-man envoy to France in an effort to win French support for American independence.

 **Franklin was remembered for many things; he was also a diplomat.**

In Paris, Franklin charmed French aristocrats and intellectuals. They welcomed him as the embodiment of the New World Enlightenment thinking. His likeness was etched on medallions, rings, watches, and snuffboxes. Fashionable upper-class ladies wore their hair in a style imitating Franklin's fur cap. Franklin used his popularity and diplomatic talent to convince France to recognize American independence and sign the Treaty of Alliance with the 13 states. The treaty was negotiated brilliantly, and Franklin managed to include an article stating that no payment would need to be made to secure the alliance.

 **Franklin was popular and successful in France.**

After the American Revolution, Franklin became the first American Minister to be received by a foreign government. He was 73 years old at the time. In 1785, Thomas Jefferson followed Franklin as ambassador to France. When the French Foreign Minister asked Jefferson, "It is you who replaced Dr. Franklin?" Jefferson replied, "No one can replace him, Sir; I am only his successor."

Notice that we've kept our comments very broad on this initial reading of the passage. The goal is to recognize the major themes and perhaps a few details. There's no reason to focus too closely on any particular thing because we don't know exactly what the questions will ask.

## Step 2: Decode the Questions

A few questions will follow each passage. The first thing you'll need to do with each question is figure out exactly what it is asking before you can answer it.

Here's an example of a question that might follow the Benjamin Franklin passage.

**According to the passage, what was the goal of Franklin's first mission to France?**

A     to charm the French people

B     to win support for the American Revolution

C     to get help drafting the Constitution

D     to be received by a foreign government

 **In other words, why did Franklin go to France?**

This is a detail question. However, we did not originally note details when we first read the passage. We were waiting to see which ones were asked about in the questions. Now that we know, we can move on to Step 3.

## Step 3: Research the Details

Now that you know the detail that is being questioned—why Franklin went to France—you can go back and find it. You should have noted when you read the passage that the first paragraph is about Franklin's role as a diplomat. Scan this paragraph for details about where he went and why.

Even if you have some memory of the detail, avoid answering based solely on your recollection. Check the passage to make sure your memory is right. This technique will also keep you from trying to memorize details, which is a waste of time on the test.

## Step 4: Predict the Answer, and Check the Answer Choices

When you find the detail in the passage, think about its purpose. Why does the author mention Franklin's effort to win French support for American independence? What does that mean? It could mean he wanted financial support or to form an alliance against the British. Now that you have an idea of the correct answer, look for an answer choice that matches your idea.

**According to the passage, what was the goal of Franklin's first mission to France?**

A   to charm the French people
B   to win support for the American Revolution
C   to get help drafting the Constitution
D   to be received by a foreign government

Choice **B** is the only one that fits the idea you've already come up with.

## THE QUESTIONS

Knowing what types of questions to expect will help you read the passage constructively. There are three question types that you could be asked.

## Main Idea Questions

A main idea question asks you to summarize the topic of the entire passage. You may see a main idea question in a variety of forms. Some examples of these forms are as follows:

- What is this passage mostly about?
- Which of the following is a good title for this passage?
- The information in this passage could help you answer which of these questions?

If you decode the questions, you'll realize that they are asking the same thing.

**KAPLAN TIP**

A key strategy for main idea questions is to look for an answer choice that summarizes the entire passage, not just a detail or a paragraph.

## Detail Questions

A detail question asks you to research information that is directly stated in the passage. For example:

**Which of the following is a result of photosynthesis?**

A   Plants transform light energy into chemical energy.

B   Roots transport water to all the plant's cells.

C   Tree rings are formed.

D   Leaves are shed in the autumn.

**What is the first stage of child development?**

A   Children start rolling over.

B   Children learn how to laugh.

C   Children learn how to walk.

D   Children recognize a parent's voice.

**Which Roman Emperor conquered the Celts?**

A   Caesar

B   Claudius

C   Augustus

D   Octavius

All you have to do is locate the information in the passage. A key strategy is to research the details by relating the facts from the question to a specific paragraph and then rereading that paragraph to find the detail you're looking for.

## Inference Questions

The answers to inference questions will not be stated in the passage, but will be hinted at strongly. It is your job to figure out what those hints mean when put together. Here are some examples of inference questions. You may not know the exact answer to the question, but by using clues (like the art shown below), you can make inferences about which answers are the best choices.

**This passage is most likely found in—**

A   a fictionalized version of an astronomical discovery.

B   a scientific magazine on chemistry.

C   an archaeological report.

D   a manual on museum preservation.

**The author of this passage is probably—**

A   a bilingual teacher.

B   an archaeologist.

C   a historian.

D   a political scientist.

**The next thing that will most likely happen is—**

A   the site will be excavated.

B   the site will be left alone.

C   the site will be turned into a historical monument.

D   the site will be bulldozed.

Inference questions usually ask you to predict what might happen next or what would be a logical next paragraph. Likewise, questions that ask you about the author's purpose, or the author's attitude toward the topic, are inference questions.

For instance, if a passage goes on about the wonders of exploring archaeological excavations, the author is, most likely, an archaeologist. If, on the other hand, the passage discusses the negative impact of archaeological digs, the author is probably not an archaeologist.

We will discuss what skills are involved in answering inference questions more in this chapter.

## READING COMPREHENSION STRATEGIES

Have you ever reached the bottom of a page you were reading and had no idea what you just read? Staying focused as you read the passages is the most fundamental building block of reading comprehension, but it can also be the most challenging. There will be passages that are difficult for you to read or that are just not interesting, so it will be difficult to stay focused. This section will offer tools to help you focus on what you are reading and get the most out of each passage.

### Reading for the Test

As you learned earlier, reading for the CAHSEE is not exactly like the reading you do in school or at home. In general, you usually read to learn or read for pleasure. It's a pretty safe bet that you're not reading the passages on the test for the fun of it. You are reading them to answer questions and earn points. Anything that doesn't help you get a point is a waste of time. The questions will ask you about the main idea, a few details, and a few inferences. Keep in mind that you need to get enough out of the passage to help you deal with the questions. Here are some strategies to do just that.

#### LOOK FOR THE MAIN IDEA

The way a passage is organized can help you understand it. Most passages state the main idea in the first paragraph. The first sentence of a paragraph usually provides the main idea of the paragraph. The last paragraph will usually summarize the passage. Remember that you can research the details as you need them, as long as you have an idea of where to look.

## PAY ATTENTION TO STRUCTURE

**Transitions** are words or phrases such as *however*, *therefore*, and *in addition to* that signal a change in the passage. As you read, spot these words or phrases, which usually appear at the beginning of a paragraph, and look for the change of topic that follows.

Most passages follow a particular order or sequence. Some passages follow a chronological, or time, sequence while others follow a logical sequence. As you read, try to identify the sequence of ideas in the passage and use this sequence to make predictions.

Noticing the sequence of the passage as you read will also help you answer questions that ask you what happens *before*, *next*, *after*, *first*, or *last*.

## MARK IT UP

You can write in the test booklet, so use this to your advantage. You do not need to take a lot of notes, but do not leave the passage and surrounding space blank. Use it to keep track of the main idea of the whole passage and of the various paragraphs. Your notes will help you find the information you need to answer the questions later.

## USE THE PARAGRAPH TOPICS

The first two sentences of each paragraph should tell you what it's about. The rest of the paragraph is likely to be detail. Just as you should pay more attention to the beginning of the passage, you should also pay more attention to the beginning of each paragraph.

## BREAK IT DOWN

Sometimes you'll come across difficult language or technical jargon in the passages, especially in the science passages. Don't get bogged down by language that you find confusing. The underlying topic is usually pretty straightforward. It can be very helpful to put confusing language into your own words. Remember, you don't have to understand every word to summarize or paraphrase. All you need is a general understanding.

### HOW TO SKIM PASSAGES

Most questions on the CAHSEE require you to go back to the passage in order to find the answer to the question. You do not have time to reread the passage for every question related to that passage. One of the ways to quickly find information in a text is to skim the passage for the information. **Skimming** a passage means to scan the passage quickly without reading every word, in order to find the information you are looking for.

## SUMMARIZING

For the purposes of the CAHSEE, **summarizing** means capturing in a single phrase what the entire passage is about. We've already shown you the types of main idea questions you could see; these questions ask about the passage as a whole. Incorrect answers will include choices that deal with only one paragraph or some other smaller component of the passage. You will need to look for the answer that deals with the entire passage. If you've thought about the main idea ahead of time, you're more likely to go directly to the correct answer choice.

The Homestead Act was one of the most important bills passed in the history of the United States. Signed into law in 1862 by Abraham Lincoln, this act made vast amounts of public land available to private citizens. Under the Homestead Act, 270 million acres, or 10 percent of the area of the United States, was claimed and settled. For a small filing fee of $18, five years of residency, and a lot of backbreaking labor, anyone dedicated to land ownership could win an impressive 160-acre parcel of land.

The qualifying requirements were seemingly scant. A homesteader simply had to be the head of a household and at least 21 years old. Each homesteader had to build a home, make improvements to the land, and farm it for five years. After this time, the settler would be eligible to "prove up," or prove all the conditions had been met. If successful, he or she would be able to keep the land. Hopeful people from all walks of life came to the West lured by the promise of "free" land.

**This passage is mainly about—**

**A**  how to apply to be a homesteader.

**B**  proving requirements for homesteaders.

**C**  the Homestead Act's effect on land ownership.

**D**  all the acts that Abraham Lincoln signed.

This question basically asks which choice best summarizes what the entire passage is about. Only one answer choice sums up the contents of both paragraphs. Choices A and B are both details. Choice D is too broad; all the acts that Lincoln signed are not discussed in the passage. Choice **C** summarizes the whole passage, which discusses the importance of the Homestead Act making public land available for people to own. Although there are a few details explaining how the land was given out, the main idea of the passage is that the Homestead Act made it possible for people to own land.

## RESEARCHING

Whereas summarizing is important in helping you answer main idea questions, researching is important in helping you answer detail questions. Generally, if you jot down paragraph topics in the blank space around the text, you should have a good map to help you locate the details. Once you know where to look, just scan the paragraph for key phrases found in the question.

From fall through winter, extratropical storms dominate the weather across much of the United States and other parts of the globe. These extratropical storms originate outside the tropics and generally move west to east across the oceans and continents. In areas of the storm that are ahead of a warm front, warm air flows over colder air that is closer to the ground. Thus, one layer of air that is above 32 degrees Fahrenheit is caught between a layer of colder air near the ground and a layer of colder air higher up.

**Your notes might read: extratropical storms, layers of cold and warm air**

Whether we experience snow, sleet, or freezing rain is determined by the temperatures of the layers of air where precipitation begins. Precipitation that begins as snow in the higher level of colder air will become rain if it meets a layer of air that's above 32 degrees Fahrenheit. However, if the layer of cold air near the ground is relatively thick, the falling rain will freeze into ice pellets, which are generally called sleet. On the other hand, if the layer of cold air near the ground is relatively thin, the falling rain will not become ice unless it hits something. This is freezing rain. In places where there is no layer of warm air, precipitation falls all the way to the ground as snow. Often, rain, freezing rain, and snow will fall together as a storm moves by, leaving an icy coating on exposed surfaces.

 **Your notes might read: rain, sleet, or snow determined by temperature of layers**

Look again at the passage and paragraph topics you just read. The topics are very general. If you came across the following questions, could you find the answers in the passage quickly?

**Which of the following is TRUE of extratropical storms?**

A They dominate winter weather.

B They originate in the tropics.

C They move from east to west.

D They cause tornados.

**According to the passage, what causes precipitation to fall as snow?**

A Precipitation meets a layer of ice as it hits the ground.

B Precipitation begins high in the atmosphere.

C Precipitation does not meet any layer of warm air as it hits the ground.

D Precipitation moves from west to east as it travels the globe.

# MAKING AN INFERENCE

**Making an inference** means coming to a conclusion that is not directly stated, based on the information given. In other words, making an inference means reading between the lines. What did the author almost say, but not state outright? Inferences will not stray too far from the language of the text. Incorrect answer choices on inference questions often fall beyond the subject matter of the passage. Here's an example.

As the saying goes, Rome wasn't built in a day. Writing a top-notch essay takes time, planning, and careful revision. But to revise your writing, you must first have something down on paper. Many students feel that this is the most difficult part of the composition process. Brainstorming is often a helpful way to overcome writer's block. Sit quietly somewhere with a piece of blank paper and your chosen topic. Note all the things that occur to you on that topic. For example, if you were writing an essay about horses, you might jot down fast, beautiful, Arabian Stallion, workhorses, or anything else that jars your imagination. Once you have some ideas down on paper, you can begin to organize them.

**According to the passage, the FIRST step in the writing process is—**

A   carefully revising.
B   purchasing necessary supplies.
C   daydreaming about the topic.
D   jotting down ideas.

This short passage discusses the writing process. The question asks about the first step in the process. Yet, there is no sentence in the passage that states directly: "The first step of the writing passage is. . ." However, in the first paragraph, the author mentions that before you can revise, you must have something down on paper. Getting something down must be the first step.

Choice **D** is the only choice that is close to your predicted answer. You can't revise until you have written something *to* revise (choice A). Purchasing supplies, choice B, is not getting something down on paper; neither is daydreaming (choice C).

## A WORD ABOUT TYPES OF PASSAGES

There are many different types of passages on the CAHSEE. You will see poetry, short stories, plays, and nonfiction texts. Each of these categories is called a **genre**. When you read a passage, it is important to identify the genre right away because you will use different tools to understand each genre. While the tools discussed in the rest of the chapter will offer general strategies for all passages, it will specifically focus on the tools that you need to apply to nonfiction passages. Chapter 3 will focus on skills specific to literary passages.

**Nonfiction** is a broad category that includes biographies, textbooks, encyclopedias, newspaper and magazine articles, historical and scientific books, essays, and persuasive arguments.

When you see a nonfiction passage on the CAHSEE, you will be asked to gather and identify information from the text, identify the purpose of the passage, or evaluate its credibility. This chapter will help you identify the passage as nonfiction, use the tools of the passage to gather information, and evaluate the credibility of the text.

### The Purpose of Nonfiction

The purpose of nonfiction is to convey information to the reader. For example, the newspaper attempts to convey the news, a biology textbook communicates information about bodies and animals, and a biography tells the reader about the life and times of a specific person.

When you finish reading a nonfiction passage, you should be able to identify the purpose, or what the point of the passage is.

For instance, let's look at the following example. Read the short excerpt and use it to answer the question that follows.

# Ski Area Safety Brochure

Cadillac Mountain is a gorgeous terrain that offers ski slopes for every level of skier. To get the most out of your stay here, please observe the following rules.

- Keep your distance from other skiers.
- Stay on the slopes that fit your level of skiing.
- Always ski with a partner or a friend.
- Keep all equipment and body parts in the lifts.

**The main purpose of this brochure is—**

A    to explain how to get to the mountain.
B    to explain how to use a ski lift.
C    to present safety guidelines for visitors to Cadillac Mountain.
D    to present services offered by Cadillac Mountain.

Because the point of nonfiction texts is to give information, the **purpose**, or the main point, of a nonfiction passage is often directly stated in the passage. In this case, the purpose of the passage is stated in the title, as well as in the final sentence before the bullets. The correct answer is choice **C**. The purpose of the brochure is to present safety guidelines for Cadillac Mountain.

## Characteristics of Nonfiction

Nonfiction passages have a different feel and appearance than fiction or poetry. Here are some examples of their characteristics:

- Nonfiction passages generally have a lot of information to present, so the passages are dense.
- There are often more unfamiliar words that relate to the topic of the passage, but most words are defined in the text.
- There are often a lot of titles and subheadings in a nonfiction passage.

- Nonfiction texts are often accompanied with graphics, maps, pictures, and diagrams to help illustrate the main ideas of the text.
- Many nonfiction passages, such as instruction manuals, follow a specific sequence or order.

Many of these characteristics *can* be intimidating on the page, but they are actually useful tools meant to help a reader understand the information presented. For example, unfamiliar words, while intimidating at first, are probably unique to the topic and defined right in the text.

Let's look at some examples of how the characteristics of nonfiction texts can help you understand the passage.

**What does the word *Mesozoic* mean in this sentence?**

> The Mesozoic era, or the prehistoric time about 250 to 65 million years ago, was dominated by dinosaurs.

A    a type of dinosaur
B    a prehistoric era
C    the name of a scientist who discovered a fossil
D    present day

It is possible you may have never seen the word *Mesozoic* before, but you need to know what it means in order to understand the passage. That's why the author of the article provides the definition right after the word. The correct answer is choice **B**.

The subheadings in the text advertise the main idea of the section and help you make predictions about what you will find in that section.

**Read the passage and answer the question that follows.**

# How to Become a Vegan

### What Is a Vegan?

A vegan is a type of vegetarian who does not eat any animal products. Most vegetarians eat dairy products like cheese, eggs, and milk. But vegans do not eat or consume any products that come from animals, ruling out all dairy products, including chocolate!

### Vegan Diet

Vegans eat a lot of soy protein. Although they don't eat traditional cheese, they do eat cheese made out of soy. Vegans also substitute nuts and beans to make up for the protein they miss by not eating meat and dairy products.

**What is the main idea of the second paragraph?**

A   why people might decide to be vegans

B   things that vegans eat

C   how vegans are different than vegetarians

D   how to make a vegan breakfast

The subhead of the second paragraph advertises the main idea of the paragraph. The subheadings help you determine the main idea before you even read the paragraph. The correct answer is choice **B**.

Graphics, maps, tables, and diagrams may look complicated, but they are included in many nonfiction passages in order to increase your understanding of the topic. They are meant to be used *with* the text and are most likely explained there.

Let's look at an example of a reading passage with a table.

# Healthy Food Choices

The school cafeteria offers a large variety of food. Some of the food has high nutritional content, while other food offers only fat and calories. In order to maintain a healthy diet and weight, people need to understand what they are eating and how to read a label.

Nutritional food offers fewer calories and more vitamins and minerals. Ideal nutritional foods are packed with natural ingredients such as fruit, grains, and proteins. Food that is good for your health contains more protein, folic acid, potassium, fiber, and vitamins than preservatives, salt, and sugar.

Food that is not as nutritional often has a long list of ingredients that are not natural, such as color, high fructose corn syrup, and trans fats. The labels of unhealthy snacks might also list salt and sugar as two of the main ingredients. Unhealthy food is also high in calories and low in nutritional things such as folic acid, fiber, and protein.

Food packaging is required by law to list the calories, fat content, protein, vitamins, and ingredients on the label. Ingredients on a food label are listed from highest to lowest. For example, if salt is the first ingredient on the list, it means that it is the most prominent ingredient in the item. The label also offers a serving guide. The serving guide tells you how many servings are in each package. It is important to multiply the number of servings in the package by each of the food measurements. For example, if there are 110 calories in the snack but three servings per package, you are actually eating 330 calories if you eat the entire package.

| Healthy Ingredients | Unhealthy Ingredients |
| --- | --- |
| protein | corn syrup |
| potassium | fructose |
| vitamin C | polysaturated fat |
| folic acid | sodium |
| fiber | artificial flavor |
| whole grain | artificial color |

**The table at the end of the passage illustrates information that can primarily be found in which paragraphs?**

A    paragraphs 1 and 2

B    paragraphs 2 and 3

C    paragraphs 3 and 4

D    paragraphs 1 and 4

The table at the end of the passage serves as a visual aid to help a reader remember which ingredients are signs of healthy food and which are signs of unhealthy food. Ingredients of healthy food are discussed in paragraph 2 and ingredients of unhealthy food are discussed in paragraph 3, so the correct answer is choice **B**.

# TYPES OF NONFICTION

As discussed earlier in this chapter, there are many different genres in the category of nonfiction. Here are some examples that you might see on the test.

## Primary and Secondary Sources

A **primary source** is a text written by someone who witnessed, or was part of, an event. A primary source might be a journal entry, letter, or speech. A primary source is a valuable tool because it might provide details that people did not know because they did not witness the event. However, a primary source can also be colored with the author's feelings and opinions about the event or the people involved.

A **secondary source** is a nonfiction text that collects information from a variety of primary sources. A secondary source might be an encyclopedia entry, textbook excerpt, newspaper article, or dictionary entry. Secondary sources are valuable because they can provide an overview of an event that includes information from a variety of sources.

| Primary Source | Secondary Source |
|---|---|
| journal | dictionary entry |
| diary | textbook |
| newspaper article from a particular year | encyclopedia entry |
| photograph | biography |

When you see primary and secondary sources on the CAHSEE, you may be asked to identify the main idea or supporting details or to evaluate the credibility of the text.

## Workplace Communication

**Workplace communication** is any document that is meant to give information to employees at a workplace. Workplace communication could be a training manual, a memo, or an email.

The test may ask you to determine the main idea or purpose of the workplace communication. There are four main types of author's purposes: to inform, explain, persuade, and entertain. The purpose of most workplace communication is to provide information or explain how to do something.

Examine the following excerpt from a training manual for construction workers.

## Project Dig Guidelines

- Always wear a hard hat when entering the hole.
- Keep a ladder inside the hole.
- Keep a flashlight in the hole.
- Place appropriate blockades around the hole.
- Label the hole with appropriate warning signs.

**What is the purpose of this selection?**

**A**    to explain what clothing to wear to work

**B**    to describe the construction job

**C**    to explain how to dig a hole

**D**    to describe safety in and around a hole at a construction site

When a question asks you to identify the purpose of an excerpt, it is asking you why the passage was written. Although there is a bullet describing what hat to wear, it is not the main idea of the entire excerpt. You can infer that the bullets are discussing a construction site, but it does not describe the job or explain how to dig a hole. In this case, each of the bullets describes safety tips in and around a hole at a construction site, so choice **D** is the correct answer.

The CAHSEE may also ask you to interpret information from a memo, email, or manual and determine how to apply the information in real-life situations. Let's look at an example.

**Read this sentence from a training manual.**

> Your job as a coffee server is to graciously and promptly serve each customer well-made coffee.

**According to this sentence, what must coffee servers do?**

**A**    Warm up old coffee.

**B**    Welcome customers and serve fresh coffee quickly.

**C**    Sweep floors every hour.

**D**    Seat customers at their own table.

You may be familiar with the job description of a coffee server, but the question is asking you to apply only the information from this sentence to the real-life responsibilities of a coffee server. This sentence states only that coffee servers need to be polite and quick as they serve good coffee so choice **B** is correct.

## UNDERSTANDING WHAT YOU READ

All of the reading comprehension skills discussed in this chapter focus on helping you use the passages and tools to understand what you read. The CAHSEE measures your ability to understand what you read by testing individual skills, such as finding the main idea and identifying facts and opinions. However, the larger goal of the CAHSEE is to assess your ability to understand the things you read.

In addition to mastering the individual skills discussed, it is important to evaluate the texts and apply what you read to real-life situations.

### Evaluating Nonfiction Texts

One of the skills that will help you become a more proficient nonfiction reader is learning how to evaluate a nonfiction text. Evaluating a text requires you to be a critical reader and to examine facts, opinions, sources, and statistics in order to determine the credibility of the text.

The **credibility of a text** is the level to which the text can be trusted. Once you determine the credibility of a text, you can decide if the text will be a useful tool for whatever your purposes are. This is an especially useful skill when doing research.

The CAHSEE will not ask you to evaluate an entire text, but it will ask you to identify facts and opinions, understand statistics, and determine the reliability of a source.

For example, a nonfiction text that is attempting to inform the reader should not contain the author's opinions. Likewise, statistics should include a large number of people surveyed and identify who was surveyed.

Sources are also important in evaluating what you read. The source of a passage is where the information comes from and some sources might be trusted more than others. For example, a passage about urban living might include statistics from the New York Department of Housing. Because the article is about city living, these statistics would probably be more useful than urban statistics that came from the Des Moines City Hall.

It is a reader's job not only to understand what information is presented, but also to determine the credibility of the information. As you read, use the following questions to determine the credibility of a passage.

- Does the passage contain mostly facts or opinions?
- What is the source of the information presented in the document?
- How reliable are the statistics? Do they represent a cross section of the general population, or are they limited by number and geography?

## Understand Facts and Opinions

One of the ways to identify supporting details in a passage is to recognize facts and opinions.

A **fact** is a statement that can be proven correct.

**Red-eyed tree frogs live in the rain forest.**

You can verify that red-eyed tree frogs live in the rain forest by looking in an encyclopedia or biology book, so this statement is a fact.

An **opinion** is a statement that is based on a belief or an experience and cannot be proven true or false.

**Red-eyed tree frogs are ugly and scary.**

Some people may find red-eyed tree frogs beautiful and gentle, so this statement is an opinion.

Most nonfiction texts should contain mostly facts in order to explain, inform, or describe. These texts should generally not contain the opinions of their authors.

However, there is an exception. Nonfiction texts that are meant to persuade, such as editorials, should contain opinions supported by facts because their purpose is to convince the reader to do or think something.

The CAHSEE may present you with a passage that has both facts and opinions and ask you to identify the fact or the opinion. Look at the following example.

**Which of the following statements is an opinion?**

**A**   There is often ice in cold weather.

**B**   Extreme cold can be dangerous for children and elderly people.

**C**   Anything below 60 degrees is cold.

**D**   To be safe in cold temperatures, people should dress in layers.

All of the options can be proven true or false except for choice C. People have varying opinions about the weather: Some people may think that any temperature below 60 is cold, while others may think that temperatures in the 40s and 50s are warm. Therefore, the correct answer is choice **C**.

## Real-Life Applications

The purpose of nonfiction is to provide information to a reader so that the reader can apply the information to practical situations. Reading comprehension skills are not just ways of reading to find the main idea. These skills are a set of strategies that help you understand the information that you read and then make connections between that information and your life. Reading comprehension is a group of skills that you will use throughout your life.

On the CAHSEE, some of the questions will ask you to make connections between the real world and what you read.

Let's look at some examples of making connections between reading and the real world.

# The Largest Muscle

The heart is the largest and most important muscle in the body. The function of the human body relies on the regular beating of the heart. It is responsible for pumping blood through the veins in order to reach every part of the body. The heart, unlike leg or arm muscles, is an involuntary muscle. It works without the brain consciously telling it to pump the blood. A healthy heart pumps blood in a rhythmic pattern and beats between 75 and 80 times each minute.

**Which of the following best illustrates the purpose of the heart?**

**A**  a light switch

**B**  the rhythmic cycle of a furnace in the winter

**C**  the beat of a drum in a marching band

**D**  the engine of a car

For this type of question, you must understand the main idea of the passage, and then make connections between what you have read and real life.  In this case, you are asked to make an analogy comparing the purpose of the heart to something unrelated. A light switch, unlike a heart, can be turned on and off at will.  Choices B and C mention the rhythmic cycle of the heart but do not accurately convey the idea that the body needs the heart to pump in order for it to work. The correct answer is choice **D** because both the heart and a car's engine pump liquid throughout their respective bodies.  Both must function properly in order for the body and the car to run.

Reread the excerpt about *Healthy Food Choices*. See how the questions ask you to relate what you have read to what you might experience in real life.

# Healthy Food Choices

The school cafeteria offers a large variety of food. Some of the food has high nutritional content, while other food offers only fat and calories. In order to maintain a healthy diet and weight, people need to understand what they are eating and how to read a label.

Nutritional food offers fewer calories and more vitamins and minerals. Ideal nutritional foods are packed with natural ingredients such as fruit, grains, and proteins. Food that is good for your health contains more protein, folic acid, potassium, fiber, and vitamins than preservatives, salt, and sugar.

Food that is not as nutritional often has a long list of ingredients that are not natural, such as color, high fructose corn syrup, and trans fats. The labels of unhealthy snacks might also list salt and sugar as two of the main ingredients. Unhealthy food is also high in calories and low in nutritional things such as folic acid, fiber, and protein.

Food packaging is required by law to list the calories, fat content, protein, vitamins, and ingredients on the label. Ingredients on a food label are listed from highest to lowest. For example, if salt is the first ingredient on the list, it means that it is the most prominent ingredient in the item. The label also offers a serving guide. The serving guide tells you how many servings are in each package. It is important to multiply the number of servings in the package by each of the food measurements. For example, if there are 110 calories in the snack but three servings per package, you are actually eating 330 calories if you eat the entire package.

**You are looking for a healthy snack at the grocery store. You read the first three ingredients in each of four choices. Which snack would most likely be the healthiest?**

A    raspberries, soy protein, folic acid

B    corn syrup, fructose, lemon flavoring

C    salt, polysaturated fat, yellow #4

D    soy protein, synthetic raspberry flavoring, sugar

This question is asking you to apply what you have learned about food ingredients to a real-life situation. It assumes that you understand the main idea of the passage and can make connections between the passage and real life. You may not have memorized which ingredients are healthy and which are unhealthy, but you probably remember that the passage lists both types of ingredients. Quickly skim paragraphs 2 and 3 to determine that you are looking for natural ingredients that provide protein, vitamins, and minerals. The only option that offers these ingredients is choice **A**.

**According to the passage, you could find information about the number of calories in a bag of potato chips—**

A    in the ingredients list.

B    in the serving size number and the calorie count.

C    on the package.

D    directly under the brand's name.

This question is also asking you to make connections between what you have read and real life. The passage does not specifically discuss a bag of potato chips, so you need to apply what you have learned about labels to a made-up bag of chips. The last paragraph of the passage explains that calories are listed on the label of every food product, but don't be fooled by choice C. Later in the paragraph, the passage explains that serving size also affects the number of calories in an entire package. The only correct answer is choice **B**.

## SUMMARY

You learned a lot of points in this chapter. Let's review some of the points.

- Literary passages offer a message or a theme.
- Nonfiction passages are written for a specific purpose: to inform, explain, or describe.
- Approach reading comprehension questions using these strategies:
  - Read the passage.
  - Decode the questions.
  - Research the details.
  - Predict the answer and check the choices.
- You should know the following types of questions you will be asked:
  - main idea
  - detail
  - inference
- There are many strategies for reading effectively:
  - Look for the main idea.
  - Pay attention to structure.
  - Mark up the passage.
  - Use the paragraph topics.
  - Break it down.
  - Keep moving.
  - Summarize.
  - Research.
  - Make inferences.
- Nonfiction texts have similar features: texts with a lot of information, unfamiliar words, graphics or diagrams, and a specific sequence.
  - A primary source is a text such as a journal that is written by someone who witnessed or was part of an event.
  - A secondary source is a text such as an encyclopedia entry that collects information from a variety of primary sources.
  - Workplace communication is any document that is meant to give information to employees at a workplace.
  - It is important to distinguish facts from opinions.
- To understand what you read, you need to do the following:
  - Evaluate the credibility of the text.
  - Make a real-life connection.

# Chapter 2
# Reading Comprehension Quiz

Read the passage and answer questions 1 through 6.

# Binary Images

A binary image is a digital image that has only two values, black or white, for each pixel. Binary images are also referred to as *bilevel* or *two-level* images. It should be noted that the terms *black-and-white*, *B&W*, and *monochrome* are also often used for this concept, but may also refer to images that are grayscale images. (Binary and grayscale images are different because grayscale images will include a range of gray, a color that binary images do not have.)

A binary image is usually stored in memory as a bitmap, which is a packed array of bits. Binary images often arise in digital-image processing as masks, or as the result of specific operations such as dithering, segmentation, or thresholding. Some laser printers, fax machines, and bilevel computer displays can handle only binary images.

Binary images can also be read mathematically. For instance, white would be read as 0 and black may be read as 1. An entire binary image may read as rows and rows of 0s and 1s. There are several algorithmic techniques that rely on the binary ordering of these pixel values of 0 and 1.

Binary images are often used in many applications, as they are easy to process, but

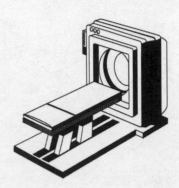

as an illustration, they are somewhat poor. They are most useful where all the information needed is a silhouette of an object, and where the silhouette may be easily obtained. This makes binary images ideal for use in military or medical settings.

1. **Which statement BEST expresses the main idea of the passage?**

   A  Binary images are of limited value.

   B  Binary images have many technical uses.

   C  Laser printers can handle only binary images.

   D  Binary images are limited to grayscale images.

2. **Which statement below is accurate given the information in the passage?**

A   Binary images are formed from algorithmic techniques.

B   Binary images are stored in memory as grayscale images.

C   Binary images are made up of pixels having two possible values.

D   Binary images are the basis for color output for most digital devices.

3. **What type of image might binary images render well?**

A   a weather pattern

B   an identification photo

C   a television show

D   an image of the color spectrum

4. **Which statement is the BEST generalization for the passage?**

A   Recent developments in computation and color output have made binary images outdated.

B   Because of their construction, a binary image is the best choice for digital representation of an object.

C   Binary images should be avoided for digital output in favor of other, more sophisticated images.

D   Despite their limitations, binary images are a simple and effective way to create a digital image of an object.

5. **What is the author's purpose in writing this passage?**

A   to tell an interesting story about the inventor of binary images

B   to persuade the reader to adopt binary images over grayscale images

C   to present factual information about a special kind of digital image

D   to inform the reader about how best to select the image format for a project

6. **Where might you most likely see this type of passage?**

A   in a technology magazine article

B   in an advanced photography textbook

C   in a science fiction novel

D   in an MRI instruction manual

**Read the passage and answer questions 7 through 11.**

# Is Stress Getting to You?

1 The alarm clock rings, we rush out of bed, we throw on our clothes, maybe grab a quick breakfast, and run out the door. Maybe we get stuck in a traffic jam on our way to work or school. As we wait, trapped in the middle of a sea of automobiles, our pulse quickens and our breath becomes shallow. We growl at the other drivers, who we blame for our predicament. This is a typical morning for many Americans. It is not only stressful, but also unhealthy.

2 The constant pressures of everyday life take a toll on the physical and mental well-being of millions of people each year. Medical research indicates that common illnesses such as high blood pressure, heart disease, stomach ulcers, and headaches are related to stress. Stress is also an underlying factor in emotional and behavioral problems including difficulty concentrating, aggressive behavior, and difficulty sleeping or eating. While there are "positive" effects of stress, there are many "negative" ones, which we often fail to link to their true cause. Instead of nervousness and aggression, people who manifest these negative reactions to stress find themselves lethargic, overeating, or avoiding social situations.

3 What's the solution? Relax! It sounds simple, but many people find it incredibly difficult. True relaxation is more than getting away from the regular routine. It is the experience of finding peace of mind, self-awareness, and thoughtful reflection. Find small ways to build relaxation into your day-to-day routine. Exercise to relieve stress. Walk, bicycle, dance, or swim a little bit each day.

4 For physically fit people, strenuous exercise, which allows them to work up a sweat, can give a tremendous feeling of relaxation afterward. The deep breathing necessitated by exercise can help calm the anxious body. Deep breathing in general is a great way to relax. Participate in creative activities such as painting, drawing, knitting, or cooking. Try some mental exercises to relieve stress, such as imagining a special place where you enjoy going. Most importantly, try to build relaxation into every day.

**7. Why is relaxation essential?**

A   It keeps us physically fit.

B   It prevents us from becoming self-aware.

C   It helps us lead healthy lives.

D   It makes the body more stressed.

**8. According to this article, what happens to MOST people who are stressed?**

A   They become aggressive under pressure.

B   They don't eat enough breakfast.

C   They don't accomplish many things.

D   They may develop health problems.

**9. What is one of the negative responses to stress mentioned in paragraph 2?**

A   shallow breathing

B   a quickened pulse

C   lethargy

D   sweating

**10. Which of the following is NOT mentioned as a way to relieve stress?**

A   mental exercise

B   denying worries or concerns

C   physical movement

D   pursuing an artistic endeavor

**11. Why might people find it difficult to relax?**

A   They don't mind the health problems they have.

B   They think that relaxation is good only for children.

C   They enjoy being stressed.

D   They probably think they are too busy to relax.

Read the passage and answer questions 12 through 16.

# A Revolution in French Paintings

The Louvre's annual Salon opened for the last time on June 1, 1848. The Revolutions of 1848 in France had put the Salon's collection at risk, and it was forced into taking steps to secure the safety of its treasures. Jeanron, the Salon director, had barely prevented the rebels from setting the building on fire, and he now insisted on renovating the empty, desolate rooms, and giving the museum a different mission.

To commemorate the museum's founding, Parliament voted a sum of two million francs to cover the cost of the renovation, and it was decided that there would no longer be a hectic round of contemporary exhibitions in the Louvre. The Salon Carré, where exhibitions featuring new works of art had traditionally been held, was transformed into a vast space housing a permanent collection that featured masterpieces from the Louvre's considerable holdings.

Groups of artists opposing this trend feared the museum would therefore be more of a mausoleum than a vital cultural force that would foster discussion and debate. As a result, contemporary French artists would soon form their own oppositional salons, the first of which, the Salon des Refusés, was held in 1863. It exhibited the works of the beginning Impressionist movement, and included key paintings by Eduoard Manet, Henri Fantin-Latour, James McNeill Whistler, and many of their peers. This group formed the nucleus of what would become the proto-modernist avant-garde. By 1881, the French government withdrew support from public exhibitions of art altogether. This led to the formation of the Société des Artistes Français, who took sole responsibility for the exhibition of their works.

12. **According to the passage, which statement is accurate?**

   A   Social upheaval in France threatened to destroy its artistic treasures.

   B   Jeanron was not qualified to be the director of the Salon.

   C   Parliament was exasperated with Jeanron's performance as director.

   D   Contemporary French artists had confidence in government officials in the exhibition of their works.

**13. According to the passage, which statement is accurate?**

A   By the 19th century, the Louvre would withdraw from exhibiting the works of contemporary French artists.

B   Social upheaval in French society destroyed the Louvre's collection.

C   A reorganization of the Louvre's contemporary collection allowed the museum to continue annual salons featuring contemporary art.

D   French artists were pleased with the Paris Salon.

**14. Which of the following could be inferred from the passage?**

A   The Louvre's decision not to exhibit contemporary work was a result of artists' dissatisfaction with the museum.

B   The expertise of the Louvre's director, Jeanron, was in doubt after the museum was nearly burned in the Revolution.

C   The place of contemporary art in mid-19th-century France was an uncertain one.

D   The Louvre was a museum that was in disrepair and had no resources available with which to continue its salon.

**15. Which statement BEST describes the final result of the passage?**

A   Nineteenth-century France was a place of great uncertainty and social turmoil.

B   The legitimacy of French cultural institutions was thrown into doubt by the February Revolutions.

C   French contemporary art ceased to be of any importance after the Salon de Carré.

D   Artists stopped depending on the state for bestowing institutional legitimacy on their works.

**16. Which statement BEST summarizes how the French artists felt about art at this time?**

A   They felt the Louvre was the best place to exhibit all French art.

B   They believed the 1848 Revolution was good for revitalizing art.

C   They worried that the Louvre would lose its significance in the art world.

D   They recognized the Impressionist movement would establish France's place in the art world.

Read the passage and answer questions 17 through 20.

# Nature's Disguise

*Camouflage* is a word derived from the French verb *camoufler*, meaning "to disguise." In nature, it allows an animal to remain indistinguishable from its environment. The most common form of camouflage found in nature is, simply, color. Antelope, deer, or rodents are earth-toned, while fish or crabs may exhibit a combination of aqueous blue or gray bodies with white underbellies. Other animals may develop more intricate patterns based on the complexity of their surroundings and the behavior of the species. Some frogs and salamanders may produce natural microscopic pigments called biochromes, which absorb and reflect certain wavelengths of light, rendering them indiscernible to predators.

Certain physical structures, such as fur, may act as an array of tiny prisms that reflect and scatter light. The polar bear is an excellent example of this phenomenon. Its black skin absorbs light, while its translucent fur diffuses it, making the bear almost disappear in the icy arctic glare. An animal's color may change with the seasons, as with certain foxes, or through diet, depending on the consumption of different organisms, as with the iridescent cuttlefish. But this is less a matter of adaptation than it is an outcome of spe-

cific circumstances. Camouflage is naturally a trait of both predator and prey. A Bengal tiger's quarry, to its detriment, may sometimes be color-blind, in that it cannot distinguish between orange and green. This is clearly beneficial to the tiger with its striped coat. But another large feline, the lion, is also color-blind, and a giraffe may therefore appear as an undifferentiated mass among the foliage, making it difficult for the big cat to fix it as prey.

Military camouflage, as a widespread tactic, was not strategically employed until relatively recent times. The history of military camouflage is a complex one, as the tactics were adopted and modified over years. Up until the 19th century, stealth was not a tactical concern, and many European armies were turned out in striking uniforms of elaborate design. Columns of soldiers were arrayed in handsome tunics of vermillion, emerald green, and sky blue that, when marching under impressive standards accompanied by fife and drum corps, were intended to unnerve and intimidate the enemy. The brightly colored jackets of various regiments also allowed for easy communication on the battlefield before the advent of modern communications systems. But it was in 1857 that British colonial armies, suffering an appalling casualty rate during their occupation of India, were forced to abandon their traditional red coats for those of a more neutral tone. The British adopted a grayish tan called *khaki*, which was derived from the Urdu word for "dusty." This battle dress became standardized by 1902, and is arguably the basis for modern military camouflage. Other armies followed suit with brown, olive, or field gray uniforms, and soon, military garments were tailored to suit their specific environments. During World War II, Soviet riflemen traversed the snowy, frozen steppes in white thermal blouses, while American marines waded ashore on tropical Pacific islands in green and beige featuring abstract jungle patterns. Aircraft and ships alike were painted in elaborate schemes, known as dazzle patterns, that rendered them tough to discern in the skies and on the seas. By the end of the 20th century, the art of concealment had become an important tactic of the armies of many nations, and represented an advance in military strategy.

17. **Based on the passage, which of the following statements is MOST accurate?**

A   Camouflage allows an animal to stand out among its surroundings.

B   The simplest form of camouflage is color.

C   Military camouflage was derived from animal patterns.

D   Camouflage develops as a result of evolution over generations.

18. **What does the passage state about the ways in which camouflage may benefit animals?**

A   Camouflage may prevent prey from being recognized.

B   Predators without natural camouflage are at a disadvantage.

C   Animals without natural camouflage live in danger of becoming instant prey.

D   Animals that adapt to their habitats possess a natural form of camouflage.

19. **What does the passage suggest about the benefits of camouflage for modern armies?**

A   Camouflage aids modern armies by facilitating communications.

B   Camouflage represents an important tactical advantage for modern armies.

C   Camouflage uniforms make it easier for troops to recognize their side in battle.

D   Camouflage uniforms provide a distinct psychological edge.

20. **Which statement BEST summarizes the passage?**

A   Both animals and armies depend on camouflage as a means of concealment.

B   Armies copied animal behavior when they adopted camouflage as a means of concealment.

C   Camouflage is used by both animals and armies, but these uses should be considered separately, as their means and ends are quite different.

D   Animals and armies both depend upon camouflage as a way of alerting their enemies.

# Answers and Explanations

**1. B**

The passage shows us all the ways that binary images are useful, often in technical ways, so choice B is the correct answer. Although binary images are not good illustrations, they do have many uses; therefore, choice A is incorrect. Choice C is incorrect because some laser printers handle images that are not binary, for example, color images. Binary images are not grayscale because they do not have the color gray; therefore, choice D is incorrect.

**2. C**

A binary image is one that has two possible values, black or white, for each pixel, so choice C is correct. Choice A is incorrect because binary images, while useful in algorithmic techniques, are not themselves made up of algorithms. Choice B is incorrect because binary images are stored as bitmaps, not grayscale images. Choice D is incorrect because binary images are only black and white, not color.

**3. A**

Binary images would probably render a weather pattern best because the image would be a silhouette, so the correct answer is choice A. The passage states that binary images are poor illustrations and tend to show silhouettes rather than actual pictures. Therefore, choices B and C would be incorrect because a photo and a television show are more complex images than just silhouettes. Binary images are not color, so an image of the color spectrum would be impossible to produce; therefore, choice D is incorrect.

**4. D**

The passage gives a technical overview of how binary images are simple structures that can usefully represent digital information, but only in a limited way. This makes choice D correct. Despite recent developments in computation and color output, binary digital images are still used by the military and medical fields, so choices A and C are incorrect. Choice B is incorrect because the text says that binary images are not complex in their construction, and it doesn't say that they are the best way to represent objects.

**5. C**

The author is writing about binary images to present a factual understanding to the reader, so choice C is correct. Choice A is incorrect because the author does not mention any inventor in connection with the binary images. Choice B is incorrect because the author is not attempting to persuade the reader of the benefits of binary images over grayscale images—the author's tone is neutral on this subject. While the passage does discuss the best uses for binary images, it is not the author's main purpose in writing the passage. The author's purpose is to present facts about binary images. Therefore, choice D is incorrect.

**6. A**

You would most likely see this type of informational text in a technology magazine article, so choice A is the correct answer. You would be unlikely to see this passage in an advanced photography textbook because binary images are not the best way to capture most photographic images, so choice B is incorrect. Choice C is incorrect because the passage is more informational, rather than narrative. Choice D is incorrect because the passage only focuses on medical imagery in the very last paragraph, so it's unlikely this text would be found in an MRI instructional manual.

**7. C**

According to the passage, relaxation is important for mental and physical well-being and leading a healthy life, so choice C is correct. Choice A is incorrect because the passage does not state, directly or implicitly, that relaxation keeps us physically fit. Choice B is incorrect because relaxation can lead to becoming more self-aware. Choice D is incorrect because relaxation does not make the body more stressed—it actually relieves stress.

## 8. D

Answer choice D is correct because people who are stressed, may indeed, develop health problems. Answer choice A is incorrect because not all people who are stressed become aggressive. Answer choice B is incorrect because people who are stressed may eat an adequate breakfast. Answer choice C is incorrect because people who are stressed may accomplish many things.

## 9. C

The correct answer is choice C. Lethargy is one of the negative responses to stress, according to paragraph 2. Choice A is incorrect because shallow breathing is mentioned in the first paragraph, but it is not mentioned in the second paragraph as a negative response to stress. Choice B is incorrect because a quickened pulse is mentioned in the first paragraph as a reaction to stress, but not in paragraph 2. Choice D is incorrect because sweating is not a negative reaction to stress.

## 10. B

The correct answer is B. Denying worries or concerns is not a good way to relieve stress. Choice A is incorrect because mental exercise such as imagining is a good way to relieve stress, as mentioned in the passage. Choice C is incorrect because physical movement relieves stress. Choice D is incorrect because pursuing art is a good way to relieve stress.

## 11. D

Choice D is correct because people probably think they are too busy to relax. Choice A is incorrect because people do worry about the health problems they have from stress. Choice B is incorrect because people like to relax; they do not think relaxation is only for children. Choice C is incorrect because many people do not enjoy being stressed.

## 12. A

Social upheaval in France did threaten the Louvre, so choice A is correct. Choice B is incorrect because the article makes no mention of, nor does it imply, whether Jeanron was qualified. Choice C is incorrect because there is no mention or implication in the story about whether the Parliament was exasperated with Jeanron. Choice D is incorrect because the passage mentions how some French artists were afraid the government would mute their creative and artistic discussions and debates.

## 13. A

After the Salon of 1848, the Louvre no longer held a salon for contemporary artists. Other salons arose in its place. Choice A is correct. Choice B is incorrect because social upheaval threatened, but did not destroy the Louvre's collections. Choice C is incorrect because the Louvre did not continue the annual salons featuring contemporary art. Choice D is incorrect because the French artists were not pleased with the Paris Salon and formed their own separate salons.

## 14. C

France was a nation that had gone through a series of social upheavals, which culminated in the 1848 Revolutions. The status of many of its institutions had been cast in serious doubt, and the role of contemporary art in France was open to debate. Decisions as to what would constitute a proper place of its exhibition were undecided and open to debate. Although it is not explicitly stated as such, this is the main topic to be inferred from the passage. Choice C is the correct answer. Choice A is incorrect because the artists' dissatisfaction was not the cause of discontinuing exhibitions of contemporary French artists. Choice B is incorrect because Jeanron's expertise is not questioned directly or implicitly in the article. Choice D is incorrect because the museum received aid from the French Parliament.

## 15. D

After the Salon de Carré lost status, artists themselves looked to form their own organizations that would lend their work credibility within these new social circumstances. The correct answer is choice D because artists ceased looking to the state for approval, which best describes the final result of the passage. Choice A is incorrect because even though 19th-century France was a place of uncertainty and turmoil, this does not indicate the final result of the passage. Choice B is incorrect because even though the passage mentions how French cultural institutions were thrown into doubt, this is not the best result to infer from the passage. Choice C is incorrect because French contemporary art continued to be important.

## 16. C

The answer that best summarizes how the French felt about art is choice C. The French artists were extremely worried that the Louvre would lose its significance in the art world. Choice A is incorrect because they soon began to prefer exhibiting art on their own. Choice B is incorrect because the passage makes no mention, directly or implicitly, of whether the 1848 Revolution revitalized the French art world. Choice D is incorrect because the passage does not state that French artists recognized the impact that Impressionism would have on the rest of the art world.

## 17. B

Based on the information in the passage, choice B is correct because the most common form of camouflage found in nature is color. Choice A is incorrect because camouflage allows an animal to conceal itself, not stand out. Choice C is incorrect because, historically, military camouflage was not derived from patterns in nature. Choice D is incorrect because the passage does not mention how camouflage among animals developed evolutionarily.

## 18. A

The correct answer is choice A because camouflage can benefit animals that are not recognized. Choices B and C are incorrect because animals without camouflage reap no benefit from camouflage. Choice D is incorrect because while it is an assumption that may or may not be true, it does not state a benefit that animals derive from camouflage.

### 19. B

Choice B is correct because the passage states that camouflage represents an important tactical advantage for modern armies in that it renders both troops and equipment tough to discern. Choice A is incorrect because camouflage does not aid or ease communications for modern armies. Choice C is incorrect because camouflage does not make it easy for troops to recognize each other. Choice D is incorrect because camouflage uniforms do not provide a distinct psychological edge according to the passage.

### 20. A

Both animals and armies depend on camouflage as a means of concealment, so choice A best summarizes the content of the passage, making it the correct answer. Choice B is incorrect because, based on the passage, it makes no mention, stated or implied, of whether armies copied animal behavior when they adopted camouflage. Choice C is incorrect because it does not summarize the passage, stating that camouflage in animals and armies have nothing in common and should not be discussed together. Choice D is incorrect because animals and armies depend on camouflage to conceal, not to alert their enemies.

# Chapter 3

# Literary Response and Analysis

## RESPONDING TO AND ANALYZING LITERATURE

The Literary Response and Analysis strand of the Reading section of the CAHSEE uses multiple-choice questions to measure comprehension and analytical skills. There are approximately ten passages of varying lengths on the test. The passages are a mixture of genres, including short stories, scenes from plays, poetry, nonfiction articles, and workplace memos and documents.

Each passage is followed by a series of three to six multiple-choice questions that test your comprehension and your ability to analyze a passage. Each question tests a different reading comprehension skill. The skills are adapted from the California High School English-Language Arts Content Standards. Some of these skills are more difficult than others. For example, some questions may simply ask you the main idea, while others will ask you the meaning of a particular metaphor or symbol in a passage. The more complex questions are targeted at assessing your ability to make connections between the themes of the passages and apply the meaning of the passages to real life.

This chapter will help you break down these literary response and analysis skills and practice applying them to passages.

## Kaplan's 4-Step Method for Literary Response and Analysis Questions

In Chapter 2, we taught you to approach Reading Comprehension questions in four steps. You will need to approach Literary Response and Analysis questions following the same method.

**Step 1:** Read the passage. As you read, take notes in the margins of the text, so that you can refer back to the information quickly.

**Step 2:** Decode the questions. Sometimes the question will be worded in such a way that you will need to rephrase it in your own words. Once you understand exactly what the question is asking, you will be better prepared to answer it.

**Step 3:** Research the details. Remember when you took notes in the margins beside the passage? When you are faced with a difficult question, this is the moment when your note-taking abilities will help you.

**Step 4:** Predict the answer, and check the answer choices. When you read, sometimes it is obvious what types of questions the test will ask. If the passage is about a mystery, you will be asked to draw conclusions. If the passage belongs to a specific genre, you can almost bet that there will be a question geared toward asking about that genre.

Like Kaplan's Method for other question types, Kaplan's 4-Step Method for Literary Response and Analysis Questions requires you to do most of your work before you actually look at the answer choices. It's very tempting to read the questions and immediately dive into the answer choices. Don't do this. The work you do beforehand will save you more time in the long run and increase your ability to avoid tempting wrong answer choices.

## ELEMENTS OF FICTION

In order to analyze a literary passage, you need to be able to identify the tools that the author uses to craft the story, poem, or play into a piece of literature.

These elements of fiction, poetry, and drama will serve as the basis for you to break down a story and understand the author's goals and messages.

Fiction is a large category that includes short stories and novels. In fictional texts, authors make up the story in order to entertain and stir emotion in the reader. Authors use tools such as plot, setting, characters, narrator, and theme to craft their story into a work of literature.

## Plot

**Plot** is the sequence of events that make up a story. The plot of a story is the arc that establishes the action of the story.

The beginning of the arc is called the **rising action**. The rising action sets up the characters, situations, and events that lead to the height of the action in the story.

The top of the arc is called the **climax**. The climax is the height of the action where the tension of the conflict comes to a head.

The downswing of the arc is called the **falling action**. The falling action is the events that lead to the resolution of the conflict. The end of the arc is the **resolution** of the conflict and the conclusion of the story.

## Conflict

The action of a fictional story is usually focused on a conflict. A **conflict** is a challenge that the main character faces in a story. There are three types of conflict frequently used in fiction:

1.  a conflict between two characters such as a fight or battle
2.  a conflict between a character and herself such as a struggle for a character to change part of her personality
3.  a conflict between a character and the environment such as a character attempting to climb a glacier or cross the Antarctic

As the plot develops, tension usually builds around the conflict until it reaches the climax. The climax is the moment in the story where there is the most suspense.

Read "Babysitting Adventure" and use it to answer the plot and conflict questions that follow. It may be helpful to use the table below and fill it in after you read the passage and before you answer the questions.

| Plot: | |
|---|---|
| Conflict: | |
| Rising Action: | |
| Climax: | |
| Falling Action: | |

# Babysitting Adventure

Darius and Jose are 13, and they each have two younger siblings. Ever since Darius and Jose can remember, their parents have gone out regularly together and left the kids with a babysitter. Sometimes Darius and his brothers Zach and Owen go over to Jose's house where they order pizza and watch movies with a babysitter. Other times Jose and his sisters Alicia and Eliza go over to Darius's house for the night. No matter which house all the kids congregated at, on these nights all six kids enjoyed staying up late and running their babysitter ragged.

Jose and Darius are saving up to buy new hockey equipment. About a week ago, they asked their parents if they could babysit the kids in order to save up some money. Darius's parents agreed immediately. "I think that is a great idea," said Darius's mom.

Jose's parents were not so eager though. "I'm not sure you can handle all four kids," said Jose's father.

Finally, after days of negotiation, both parents agreed to let the older boys babysit the kids on their own for $20 each.

Darius spent the afternoon finding Disney movies and craft supplies to entertain the kids, while Jose loaded up on chips, popcorn, and soda. The adults left at 6:30, and the house was peaceful for a half an hour as Darius put on a movie for the girls, while Jose played video games with the boys.

"This is not bad at all," said Darius.

"It's great. It's fun to play with Zach and Owen! We should do it more often," said Jose.

"We should get dinner ready. I'll grab the pizza out of the oven."

Jose replied, "Great, I'll bring the kids to the table."

That's when disaster struck. No one seemed to want the pizza the way it was. Alicia needed her cheese taken off, Zach didn't like sausage, Owen burned his lip, and Eliza just plain refused to eat. As Darius and Jose ran around the table trying to help all of the kids get what they wanted, the noise in the kitchen grew louder.

"I don't want to eat!"

"I need some soda!"

"Ooops . . . dropped my cheese!"

Amidst the noise of the whining kids, cups were knocked over and plates smashed to the floor.

"It's a river," Zach exclaimed as he started sliding in a puddle of spilled cola.

"Here's some paint," yelled Alicia as she started rubbing her hands in the pizza sauce that had dripped on the table.

"We've gotta get them under control," yelled Darius as he frantically grabbed some paper towels to mop up the floor.

"All right, all right, all right! Calm down!" screamed Jose.

The kids stopped and looked at him. "What do you think you are doing? Look at this mess. You don't act like this when Mom and Dad are home. Everyone sit down. If anyone even wants to think about ice cream, you better help clean up."

"Alicia, grab the garbage can and bring it to the table. Zach, take this and wipe up the spilled soda. The rest of you, sit still," ordered Darius.

In a few minutes, the kitchen was cleaned up and order was restored.

"Okay, let's go to the living room and start the movie. If you guys can behave yourselves and give us some respect, we will think about making some popcorn."

By the time their parents came home, the house was clean and all of the kids were sitting on the couch watching their movie and politely eating popcorn.

**Which of the following BEST explains Darius and Jose's problem in the story?**

A   They needed money to get hockey equipment.

B   Their brothers and sisters started to get out of control.

C   Jose's parents didn't trust them.

D   They didn't have any confidence in themselves.

*Problem* is a synonym for *conflict.* When the CAHSEE asks you identify a character's problem, it is probably asking you to identify the main conflict of a story. A story can have many conflicts, but the biggest conflict is the one that reaches a peak at the climax of the story and is resolved at the end of the story. In this case, it may have been helpful to sketch out a plot diagram in order to identify which conflict reached a climax in the story.

Although Darius and Jose wanted to babysit in order to save money and Jose's parents weren't immediately ready for them to babysit, that conflict was not played out in the story. Their biggest problem in the story was that their brothers and sisters started to get out of control. In this case, the climax of the story is at dinnertime when food starts flying and the kids start to get out of the control. The conflict is resolved as Darius and Jose start to get control of their siblings. Choice **B** is the only correct answer.

**Which of the following is the BEST inference of what will happen next?**

A   Darius and Jose raise enough money to buy their brothers and sisters new hockey equipment.

B   Their brothers and sisters start to get out of control again.

C   Jose's parents are proud of Jose for his hard work.

D   Jose and Darius's parents ask the boys to babysit again.

The resolution of the story is how the conflict at the climax of the story is resolved. In this story, the climax is the disastrous dinner. Jose and Darius get control of the kids and demonstrate their ability to babysit successfully to their parents. Their parents see the success and they ask them to do it again. Choice **D** is the correct answer.

## Setting

The **setting** is the time and place that a story takes place. The setting can often contribute to the conflict of the story. For example, if the conflict of a story is a character attempting to climb a mountain in a blizzard, the setting is at the center of the conflict.

The setting always relates to the plot because it is where the action occurs. For example, if the conflict of a novel is a battle between two high school football teams, the setting would most likely be a high school football field.

**Which of the following BEST describes the setting of "Babysitting Adventure?"**

A    a school cafeteria

B    a suburban home

C    an isolated farmhouse

D    a restaurant

The setting of a story should include the location that the story's action takes place. In this case, only choice **B** accurately reflects the story's location. Choice A is incorrect because the story is not set in a school cafeteria. Choices C and D do not accurately describe a place where any of the action takes place.

## Character

The people involved in a fictional story are called **characters**. There are often many characters in a particular story. The main character or characters of a story are called **protagonists,** while secondary characters are called **subordinate characters**.

The protagonist of a story is the character who faces the main conflict and is involved in the climax and resolution of the story. The protagonist of a story is often better defined than the subordinate characters because he or she plays a more dominant role in the story.

The protagonist and the subordinate characters interact with each other in order to move the plot of the story along.

For example, in a fictional story about two friends on a journey across the country, the protagonists are the two friends. They might meet ten subordinate characters along the way. These characters provide action at each stop and help inform the reader about the progress of the journey, but they do not face conflicts that create the climax of the story.

**Who are the protagonists in "Babysitting Adventure?"**

Darius and Jose are both the main characters of the story. They both have the same conflicts and goals, and both work together to resolve them. The other characters are subordinate because they interact with Darius and Jose in order to move the action of the story forward.

## Character Motivation

Each main character in a story has reasons for his or her actions. This is called the character's **motivation**. Characters are often motivated by their own conflicts and relationships with other characters.

### INTERNAL MOTIVATION

- A character may be motivated by his goals or internal conflicts.

For example, imagine a story about an athlete training for the hurdles in the Olympics. All of the action is centered on her hours of practice and dedication to her sport. The character's motivation is based on her internal conflict—her drive to win her hurdling races.

## EXTERNAL MOTIVATION

- A character may also be motivated by the actions of the other characters in the story.

For example, imagine a story about a girl who meets her mysterious, long-lost aunt. Her aunt disappears again and the protagonist follows clues to look for her aunt. She ends up in a remote forest where her aunt reveals her secrets. The protagonist learns from her aunt how to make forgotten, ancient medicines discovered in this mysterious forest.

The motivation of a character plays a large role in the development of a story. In order to start thinking about the character and his or her relationship to other characters, you should ask yourself why a character is doing something as you read the story.

To determine a character's motivation, you may want to ask yourself the following questions:

- What is the character's goal?
- Why is the character acting that way?
- What is the character reacting to?

Reread "Babysitting Adventure" to answer the following questions.

**How do you think Darius's and Jose's parents react to the boys' babysitting?**

**A**  Both sets of parents are impressed.

**B**  Jose's parents are upset and Darius's parents are supportive.

**C**  Jose's parents are angry and Darius's parents are sad.

**D**  Darius's parents are happy and Jose's parents are mad.

This question is asking you to identify the reaction of the boys' parents to their babysitting. If Darius and Jose's parents had walked in during dinner, their reaction to the boys' babysitting capabilities may have been different. However, in order to answer this question, you need to look back to the text and reread what the boys' parents actually said and then infer their emotions. Both sets of parents expressed pride and were happy with the job the boys had done. Choice **A** is the correct answer because both sets of parents were impressed with the boys.

**What motivates Darius to seize control of his siblings and start giving orders in "Babysitting Adventure?"**

A He had a bossy nature.

B He wanted his parents to trust his babysitting skills.

C He was angry with his sister.

D Jose didn't seem to care, so he had to do something.

Choice D is incorrect because Jose also takes control alongside Darius. Darius may have been angry, but he was probably angry with more people than just his sister, so choice C is not the best answer. There is nothing in the text to indicate that Darius is bossy, so choice A is incorrect. But Darius's goal in the story is his need to raise money for hockey equipment. He has agreed to babysit in order to do that. So his internal motivation for all of his actions is to save money. In order to do that, he needs to get more babysitting work. So based on the character's internal and external conflicts, you can describe his motivation as choice **B**.

## Characterization

**Characterization** is a series of tools an author uses to introduce the character to the reader. Because a reader cannot meet the character to make his or her own observations, the author needs to describe each character's traits, motivations, and conflicts to reader.

An author can introduce a character to the reader in several ways:

- what the character says about himself
- what the narrator and other characters say about the character
- the character's own actions

For complex characters such as the protagonist of a story, the author will include a lot of characterization. The characterization will give information about the character's background, personality traits, and interactions with other characters.

As you read a story, you should get familiar with how each character acts and anticipate what that character will do next. In many stories, you will even develop a relationship with the characters. You may like some and dislike others. It is the reader's job to formulate a complete picture of the character based on all of the elements of characterization.

To get to know a character as you read a story, you may want to ask the following questions as you read:

- How would I introduce this character to one of my friends?
- Could I be friends with this character? Why or why not?
- What is the character going to do next?

On the test, you may be asked to make a prediction about how a character might act in a particular situation, describe the character's traits, or explain the character's motivation. You will be able to do this because of the characterization that the author has provided.

Read the following excerpt from a story and answer the characterization questions that follow.

# Family Ties

We moved to our apartment when I was two years old. Ms. Gretch has always lived below us. Ms. Gretch was our landlady, but never less than part of our family. She is in her sixties, but as stylish as my mom. While most ladies her age wear dated suits or house dresses, Ms. Gretch dresses like an artist in funky shirts, jeans, and high-heeled boots. My mom once told me, "I hope that I can be half as confident about myself when I am Ms. Gretch's age!"

Ms. Gretch always keeps her door open in case I want to come by and visit. She often cooks dinner for the whole family. She comes upstairs for dinner at our house every Sunday, just as a grandmother might. On Friday afternoons, ever since I can remember, Ms. Gretch and I have baked cookies and discussed the events of the week. She was the first to know about my first boyfriend and the first to know when I was cut from the basketball team. And, of course, she has always been there to give me a hug when I needed it.

She has been such a huge part of our family that I just assumed that we were her only family. But one day, she knocked on our door and talked to my dad. "Mark, I came to ask you a favor. My son, Roger, is in trouble and needs a place to stay. Would you be kind enough to help me fix up the apartment upstairs?"

"Your son?" my dad exclaimed.

"Yes, I have a son, about your age in fact, but he moved out when he was 18 and I have only heard from him about every five or six years since then. I only hear from him when he needs money."

"Oh no, Ms. Gretch, that is so sad," said my mom, and she took Ms. Gretch's hand. "I can't believe you have never rented out the apartment upstairs."

"I guess I have always been saving it for him. He has had a lot of trouble in his life and never understood how a family can help you through it. But maybe now that he is going to move in for a while, I can show him how much I love him and help him turn his life around," sighed Ms. Gretch as she smiled at me.

"Well, considering his history, that is very generous of you. Of course I will help you," Dad said.

Characterization questions may ask you to use all of the information about two characters in the story to describe the relationship between the characters.

**Which of the following BEST describes the relationship between the narrator and Ms. Gretch?**

A    Ms. Gretch is the narrator's grandmother.

B    Ms. Gretch is the narrator's landlady.

C    Ms. Gretch is the narrator's neighbor.

D    Ms. Gretch is the narrator's landlady but acts like her grandmother.

This question is asking how to *best* describe the relationship between two characters, so you need to use the characterization provided and describe their relationship. Although the first choice may seem accurate, Ms. Gretch and the narrator are not really related. The next two choices are technically accurate, but they do not describe how the characters really interact. The narrator has always treated Ms. Gretch like a grandmother even though she was actually her landlady. The only choice that *best* describes the relationship is choice **D**.

The CAHSEE may ask you to make inferences about a character based on indirect information in the story.

**What kind of person is Roger in the story?**

A    Roger is troubled and distant from his family.

B    Roger is a criminal.

C    Roger is a dedicated son.

D    Roger is happy and distant.

Because you never actually meet Roger in the story, you need to rely on what other characters say about him. This question is asking you to make an inference about Roger's character traits based on what you learn about him. Because the narrator's family didn't even know that Ms. Gretch had a son after living with her for all of those years, you can infer that he is distant from his family. Ms. Gretch describes him as troubled when she talks about him with her neighbors, so the only accurate answer is choice **A**.

Sometimes you may be required to describe a character based on indirect information from the text.

**Which of the following characteristics of Ms. Gretch is emphasized most in the passage?**

A   her artistic nature
B   her love and generosity
C   her frugality
D   her confidence

The author has used characterization to describe Ms. Gretch as both artistic and confident, but neither of these character traits is emphasized as much as Ms. Gretch's love and generosity, so the correct answer is choice **B**.

## Point of View

Many authors use a storyteller, or narrator, to tell their story. This is called the **point of view** of the story. A narrator may be a character in the story or an outside observer. There are three main types of narrators in fiction, each providing a different point of view.

The first-person narrator is a narrator who is also a character in the story. A first-person narrator is usually the main character and tells the story as he or she witnesses it. A first-person narrator uses the pronouns *I, me,* and *we* and colors the story with emotions and feelings about what is going on in the story. A first-person narrator provides a personal point of view that tells the reader exactly how he or she feels about the action in the story.

**I got off the train in San Francisco with Julia ready to start our adventure. We weren't sure where we were going to live or how we were going to support ourselves, but we knew we were ready to take on our exciting new life.**

A third-person narrator is a narrator who is an outside observer and not a character in the story. The third-person narrator uses the pronouns *he, she,* and *they* and does not convey the inner thoughts, emotions, and motivations of the characters in the story.

**Jessica and Julia arrived in San Francisco on a Monday morning. They got off the train loaded with suitcases and bags. Their smiles showed excitement and anticipation as they stood in the middle of the train station deciding where to go.**

A third-person omniscient narrator is a narrator who is an outside observer of the action in the story who also has the ability to read the thoughts and the emotions of all of the characters in the story. The third-person omniscient narrator also uses the pronouns *he, she,* and *they* to tell the story.

**Jessica and Julia arrived in San Francisco early in the morning. They were both very excited about starting a new life, but Julia was especially nervous about finding a place to live. Julia had two job interviews set up for the next day, but Jessica had none. As Jessica loaded her arms with luggage, she worried about finding a job in this large new city.**

Reread "Babysitting Adventure" to answer the following question.

**From whose point of view is the story told?**

**A**   Darius

**B**   Jose

**C**   third-person point of view

**D**   third-person omniscient

The story uses third-person pronouns such as *he, she,* and *they,* so you know that the narrator of the story is not a character in the story. The narrator does not look into Jose or Darius's mind during the climax to show how nervous they might be. So you can conclude that the narrator does not offer insight into the inner thoughts and emotions of the characters. Choice **C** is the correct answer because the narrator is not a participant in the action of the story, nor does he or she have access to the inner thoughts and emotions of the characters.

## ELEMENTS OF POETRY

A **poem** is a text that uses words artistically in order to create a mental picture and convey a message. Poems may have many of the same elements of fiction, such as a narrator, setting, theme, and even characters. But because poets focus on manipulating words into an art form, poets also rely on special tools called **poetic devices**.

Here are some common poetic devices. These poetic devices are commonly used by poets, but they can also be found in fictional passages. On the test, you may be required to identify the meaning of figurative language and poetic devices in fictional passages.

### Imagery

**Imagery** is a word or phrase that creates a mental picture in the reader's mind by describing a particular moment or scene in a way that appeals to the reader's five senses. The imagery used by a poet often emphasizes the theme, or message, of the poem. Imagery can be created by using figurative language, such as similes, metaphors, and personification.

Read the following poem and look for the examples of imagery.

# Mending Wall
*by Robert Frost*

Something there is that doesn't love a wall,

That sends the frozen-ground-swell under it,

And spills the upper boulders in the sun,

And makes gaps even two can pass abreast.

The work of hunters is another thing:

I have come after them and made repair

Where they have left not one stone on a
stone,

But they would have the rabbit out of hiding,

To please the yelping dogs. The gaps I mean,

No one has seen them made or heard them made,

But at spring mending-time we find them there.

I let my neighbor know beyond the hill;

And on a day we meet to walk the line

And set the wall between us once again.

We keep the wall between us as we go.

To each the boulders that have fallen to each.

And some are loaves and some so nearly balls

We have to use a spell to make them balance:

'Stay where you are until our backs are turned!'

We wear our fingers rough with handling them.

Oh, just another kind of out-door game,

One on a side. It comes to little more:

There where it is we do not need the wall:

He is all pine and I am apple orchard.

My apple trees will never get across

And eat the cones under his pines, I tell him.

He only says, 'Good fences make good neighbors'.

Spring is the mischief in me, and I wonder

If I could put a notion in his head:

'Why do they make good neighbors? Isn't it

Where there are cows?

But here there are no cows.

Before I built a wall I'd ask to know

What I was walling in or walling out,

And to whom I was like to give offence.

Something there is that doesn't love a wall,

That wants it down.' I could say 'Elves' to him,

But it's not elves exactly, and I'd rather

He said it for himself. I see him there

Bringing a stone grasped firmly by the top

In each hand, like an old-stone savage armed.

He moves in darkness as it seems to me—

Not of woods only and the shade of trees.

He will not go behind his father's saying,

And he likes having thought of it so well

He says again, "Good fences make good neighbors."

A metaphor is a comparison between two things without using the words *like* or *as.*

*And some are loaves and some so nearly balls* compares the boulders to loaves and balls to describe how the wall looks.

A simile is a comparison between two things using the words *like* or *as*

*Like an old-stone savage armed* compares the neighbor to a stone-age man.

Personification is the use of figurative language to give something not human the characteristics of a human.

*Stay where you are until our backs are turned!* gives the wall the ability to follow orders.

## Repetition

Poets often repeat words and phrases in their poems in order to emphasize an idea or the theme of the poem. Poets may even repeat entire lines like the chorus of a song.

In *Mending Wall*, the poet repeats two lines:

"Good fences make good neighbors."

"Something there is that doesn't love a wall."

The theme of the poem is that there is a struggle for boundaries between neighbors. These lines emphasize the theme or the message of the poem.

## Symbolism

**Symbols** are objects that stand for something of greater meaning. For example, poets may include roses and interlocking hands to symbolize love, or a budding flower to symbolize rebirth. Poets use symbols to emphasize the theme of the poem.

In *Mending Wall*, the wall is a symbol for boundaries between neighbors.

Use the poem *Mending Wall* to answer the questions that follow.

Read the following lines from the poem.

He is all pine and I am apple orchard.

My apple trees will never get across

And eat the cones under his pines, I tell him.

**What does the author convey from these sentences?**

A     what each person grows on his land

B     the purpose of the wall

C     that there is no purpose for the wall because the neighbors do not pose a danger
      to each other

D     what each neighbor thinks about the wall

In this excerpt, the poet uses figurative language, and the question is asking you to interpret its meaning. It is not asking you to identify what the figurative language is, but instead, how it adds meaning to the poem. The pine trees and apple orchard are symbols. They stand for something of greater meaning. The two types of trees stand for the differences between the two neighbors and highlight the fact that the neighbors can live together in harmony without the need of the wall because they pose no threat to each other. The correct answer is choice **C**.

**Which of the following lines is an example of personification?**

A    He only says, 'Good fences make good neighbors'

B    Before I built a wall I'd ask to know / What I was walling in or walling out

C    My apple trees will never get across / And eat the cones under his pines

D    The gaps I mean, No one has seen them made or heard them made / But at spring mending-time we find them there

Personification is a type of figurative language or imagery that gives something nonhuman the characteristics of a person. Apples are not human and do not have the ability to eat other things, so the correct answer is choice **C**.

## ALLEGORY

An **allegory** is a work of literature that relies on symbols to get its theme or moral across to the reader. In an allegory, the setting, events, characters, and objects in the story are symbols for something of greater meaning. The characters are often animals or objects that are personified to have the traits of humans.

**Fables**, or stories in which animals, plants, and objects are given human traits in order to illustrate a moral, are examples of allegory.

For example, the story *The Little Engine That Could* is a fable about a small, not well-cared-for train engine that makes it to the top of the mountain through strong will and determination. The story can be an allegory for the American Dream, that hard work and determination offer opportunity for everyone. All of the characters in the story are symbols for different socioeconomic classes in America.

Allegories use animals and objects to symbolize larger ideas in order to make the theme easier to understand or to make the reader laugh at the theme in order to draw attention to it.

## ELEMENTS OF DRAMA

**Drama** is a form of literature that is meant to be performed on stage. Drama usually has many of the same elements of fiction and poetry such as plot, conflict, characters, figurative language, and setting, but the arc of the story is created differently.

When you read drama on the page, it is not organized in paragraphs; instead, it is a series of lines for the actors and directions to the director of the play.

Read the excerpt from the following scene of a play and use the sidebars to identify the elements of drama.

### SCENE I
*(Georgiana and Mr. Harriman sit in Georgiana's kitchen after they have completed a tour of the apartment.)*

>  **Stage Directions: Words in parentheses provide stage directions and describe the scenes. From this short description, the director of the play will make a set for the stage.**

**GEORGIANA:** Have you ever lived with a roommate before?

**MR. HARRIMAN:** Yes, I have had several roommates throughout the years.

>  **Dialogue: The characters' names followed by a colon and a line is the dialogue, or conversation between two characters.**

MR. HARRIMAN: (aside) But they never last long!

 **Aside: An aside is a short remark meant only for the audience to hear. The actor usually turns to face the audience as he says the line to emphasize that the other characters on stage are not meant to hear his thoughts.**

GEORGIANA: Have you found it easy to live with other people?

MR. HARRIMAN: (shifting position nervously) Yes, always. I am very relaxed and enjoy the company of other people.

 **Stage directions also tell the actor how to act on the stage. Most of an actor's actions are determined by the actor's and director's interpretation of the play. But a playwright will often include specific directions in order to emphasize a point. In this case, the playwright is trying to show the audience that Mr. Harriman is uncomfortable and might have something to hide.**

GEORGIANA: I am a nurse, so I work a lot of different shifts. Often, I am home during the day and work at night, so it is likely we won't see each other often.

MR. HARRIMAN: (nods his head) (aside) Thank God! This is a dream come true.

GEORGIANA: With my previous roommate, we split the chores up evenly each week. Here is a sample chore list. (hands him a piece of paper)

MR. HARRIMAN: (takes a moment to read the list as Georgiana excuses herself to go the bathroom) (aside) Cleaning the bathroom will be the least of my housework duties.

GEORGIANA: (addressing the bathroom mirror) He has great references and definitely makes enough money to pay the rent. We will probably rarely see each other, which is ideal. But something seems awkward about him. I just find him unsettling with his mismatched socks and perfectly parted hair. He seems to squirm around even when I ask the simplest of questions. Maybe he is just socially awkward and I am judging him too harshly. But what does he have in that bag? It kind of smells, and I swear it moves around a bit. Oh, I must be imagining it. He is just a little unusual, and there is nothing wrong with that.

 **Soliloquy: a long speech by one character directed toward the audience**

*(Georgiana returns to the kitchen.)*

**MR. HARRIMAN:** (holding up the chore list) This looks fair to me. But I would like to be responsible for our own groceries.

**GEORGIANA:** (smiles) Great, me too. Well there is just one more thing to tell you before you leave and then I'll call you tomorrow and let you know.

**MR. HARRIMAN:** (grabs his satchel and sits up straight in his chair) What's that?

**GEORGIANA:** The landlord doesn't allow any pets. That's not a problem, is it?

**MR. HARRIMAN:** (drops the bag and out scurry 12 white lab mice) Oh excuse me, sorry! Technically, they are not pets. They are part of my work . . .

**GEORGIANA:** (jumping on the chair) What are those? Oh, Mr. Harriman, please pick up those rodents and get out of here!

## Dialogue

**Dialogue** is a conversation between two or more characters on the stage. Playwrights use dialogue to move the plot of the drama forward and create characters.

The interaction on stage moves the plot forward as characters create conflict with each other.

The dialogue also provides characterization for the characters in the play in two ways: allowing the characters to describe themselves through what they say, and allowing characters to talk about each other.

## Soliloquy

A **soliloquy** is a long speech given by a character in a drama that is not directed at anyone in the play. It is meant for the audience and usually gives the audience information about the character's background or motivations.

**What is the purpose of Georgiana's soliloquy in the passage?**

A    to describe how Mr. Harriman looks
B    to let the audience know that Georgiana is uneasy about Mr. Harriman
C    to explain why Georgiana wants a roommate
D    to explain Mr. Harriman's strange behavior

The purpose of a soliloquy is to explain something that has happened in the past or the character's motivations. In the dialogue, up until this point, the audience has no idea that Georgiana has noticed the odd behavior of Mr. Harriman. The purpose of this soliloquy is to express Georgiana's uneasiness about Mr. Harriman, so choice **B** is the correct answer.

## Asides

An **aside** is a short remark in the presence of other characters, but it is meant only for the audience.

**What character traits do Mr. Harriman's asides reveal about him?**

**A**    He is stern and hardworking.

**B**    He is funny and not very serious.

**C**    He is relaxed and warm.

**D**    He is deceitful and uneasy.

Asides are another way for playwrights to provide characterization of their characters. Asides give the audience information that is not available to other characters on stage. All of Mr. Harriman's asides let the audience know that there is more to his character than meets the eye and that he is hoping to hide these things from Georgiana until he moves in. The correct answer is choice **D**.

## THEME

The **theme** of a story or poem is the message that the author is trying to convey. The theme connects all of the elements of the passages together: the setting, plot, characters , dialogue, and figurative language and gives them a single purpose of conveying a message to the reader.

For example, an author might write a poem about spring. The main idea of the poem is spring, but the theme might be about new beginnings or a fresh start. In order to convey the theme of new beginnings in the poem, the author uses all of the elements of a poem to help create the theme. The similes and metaphors might compare the blooming flowers to birth, while the spring setting helps the reader visualize birth and new beginnings in the natural blooming of trees and flowers.

The following questions may help you identify the theme of a passage:

- How do the characters act? Do they set a good example or a bad example, and what can a reader learn from their actions and consequences?
- Does the action in the story highlight a particular message?
- How does the figurative language emphasize a message?
- Is the setting gloomy or happy?

Reread "Family Ties" to answer the question.

**Which of the following themes is developed in the story?**

A   Neighbors should be friendly.

B   Family are the people who are closest to you rather than people related by blood.

C   Renting an apartment is better than living in a house.

D   Landladies should be generous.

The theme of a story or a poem is the message the author is trying to convey. In this story, the author spends a lot of time comparing the relationship between a family and their landlady to a family. The tenants are not related to her, but they are more like a family to their landlady than her own son is. Therefore, the theme of the story is choice **B**.

## TONE AND MOOD

In addition to the elements in fiction, poetry, and drama introduced earlier, an author uses other tools to convey the theme of a story or a poem. Two of the puzzle pieces that can help you understand the message of a story, play, or poem are tone and mood.

**Mood** is the feeling that is conveyed to a reader while reading a story or poem. The mood of a work of literature is created by the words that an author uses to tell the story.

For example, what is the mood of the following sentence? How do the words help create the mood?

**The gleeful kids sang with delight as they danced around the radiant campfire and roasted scrumptious marshmallows.**

The mood of the sentence is happy. The words *gleeful, delight, radiant,* and *scrumptious* describe the action and characters in a positive way.

**Tone** is the attitude that a piece of writing expresses to the reader. It is also created by the author's word choice. Authors often adopt a *voice* for their writing to help them or their characters express themselves.

For example, the voice may be angry and defensive if the author is writing a letter to the editor to complain about inadequate garbage pickup.

Tone is often used to describe the attitude of the character in the story. By examining the words a character uses in dialogue, you can identify the attitude of the character.

For example, what is the character's tone in the following sentence? How do the words help create the tone?

**"I knew you would lose the keys! I never should have trusted you! What do you expect me to do now?"**

The tone of the sentence indicates that this is an argument. The words *never* and *trusted* (as used in this example) plus the exclamation points help the author express a frustrated attitude.

Tone and mood are very similar concepts and, in a story or a poem, are often related. One way to distinguish between the two devices is to ask yourself the following questions:

- What is the author trying to tell me about her attitude? This is the tone.
- What emotions does this poem make me feel? This is the mood.

Reread *Mending Wall* and answer the following question.

**Which pair of words BEST describes the tone of this poem?**

A   happy and carefree

B   awe and amazement

C   frustration and annoyance

D   anger and distrust

The author of the poem is not happy about the wall and spends much of the time questioning the need for a wall at all. He compares his neighbor to a savage and expresses frustration at having to repair the wall each spring even though it doesn't seem to serve a purpose. The speaker wants to tell his neighbor but is frustrated. Although he might be angry about repairing the wall, it is the neighbor who is distrustful, so choice D is not correct. The speaker's attitude about the wall is clearly one of frustration and annoyance, choice **C**.

## AUTHOR'S PURPOSE

Authors usually write with a particular goal in mind. This goal is what the author intends the reader to take away from the text. Perhaps the author wants to tell the reader about a recent discovery, describe a beautiful moment in nature, or persuade the reader to root for a particular football team. This goal, or reason, is called the **author's purpose**.

There are four main purposes: to inform, explain, persuade, and entertain. Texts written with each purpose have their own particular characteristics that help authors achieve their goal.

Identifying the author's purpose will help you make predictions about what you will read in the passage. It will also help you focus on the things that the author wants you to take away from the text. For example, a writer who is writing to entertain might include exaggerations and jokes in the text, while an author writing to inform might include statistics and facts.

Examine the chart to identify the characteristics, examples, and author's goal for each of the distinct purposes.

| Author's Purpose | Example | Characteristics | Author's Goal |
|---|---|---|---|
| inform or describe | instruction manuals, newspaper articles, biographies | nonfiction, facts, statistics, data | to tell the reader about a particular topic |
| persuade | newspaper editorials, speeches, advertisements | opinions, examples, supporting facts and data | to convince the reader to do or believe something |
| narrate | fiction, poetry | figurative language, hyperbole | to create emotion within the reader |

In addition to looking for the characteristics outlined in the chart, you can ask the following questions as you read a text in order to identify the author's purpose:

- What does the author want me to take away from the text?
- Why is the author writing this?
- What characteristics of the specific purpose does the author include?

Reread *Mending Wall* to answer the following question.

**What is the author's main purpose in the poem?**

**A**   to entertain his neighbor
**B**   to describe the relationship between two neighbors
**C**   to inform his neighbor about building a wall
**D**   to persuade people to build walls

The poem *Mending Wall* uses imagery to describe the relationship between two neighbors and convey a theme of boundaries between these neighbors. It does not contain instructions or a persuasive argument. Although the purpose of a poem might be to entertain, the purpose would be to entertain the reader, not a character in the poem. The only choice that describes the purpose of the poem is choice **B**. The purpose of a poem or a story is often related to the theme of the poem.

## SUMMARY

You learned a lot in this chapter. Let's review some of the most important points.

- Fiction is a genre that includes short stories and novels.
- Plot is the sequence of events that makes up a story.
  - Plot consists of rising action that leads up to a climax and is resolved by the resolution.
- The plot of the story revolves around the conflict, or problem, in the story.
- The conflict is the problem that the main character faces in the story. There are three types of conflicts:
  - a conflict between two characters such as a fight or battle
  - a conflict between a character and herself such as a struggle for a character to change part of her personality
  - a conflict between a character and the environment such as a character attempting to climb a mountain in a snowstorm
- The setting of the story is where and when the action takes place.
- Characters are the people who participate in the action of a story.
  - The protagonist is the main character of a story.
  - Subordinate characters are less-developed characters in a story who interact with the protagonist to create action.
- The reason why a character acts a certain way in a story is called character motivation.
  - Internal motivation: a character might be motivated by his internal goals or conflicts
  - External motivation: a character might be motivated by the actions of other characters in the story
- Characterization is the methods that an author uses to introduce a character to the readers. There are three types of characterization:
  - what the character says about himself or herself
  - what the narrator and other characters say about the character
  - the character's own actions
- Point of view is the perspective from which the author chooses to tell the story.

- o   The first-person narrator is also a character in the story.
- o   The third-person narrator is an outside observer of the action in the story who does not have access to the other characters' inner thoughts and emotions.
- o   The third-person omniscient narrator is an outside observer of the action who also knows what each character is thinking.
- Poets use poetic devices and word play to create a mental picture and convey a message to the reader.
- Imagery creates a mental image in the reader's mind by appealing to the reader's five senses.
- Metaphor is a comparison between two things without using the words *like* or *as.*
- Simile is a comparison between two things using the words *like* or *as.*
- Personification is figurative language that gives something nonhuman the character traits of a human.
- Poets use repetition (repeated lines or phrases) to emphasize the message of their poem.
- Symbols are objects that stand for some greater meaning in order to emphasize the theme.
- An allegory is a work of literature that relies on symbols to get its theme or moral across to the reader.
- Drama is literature that is meant to be performed on stage.
- Stage directions are parenthetical words in the script of a play that provide directions for the actors and directors on stage.
- Dialogue is a conversation between two or more characters in a drama or story.
- An aside is a short remark meant only for the audience to hear.
- A soliloquy is a long speech by one actor alone on the stage meant only for the audience's ears.
- The theme of a story, poem, or play is the message that the author is trying to convey.

I am the descendant of a race whose imaginative and easily excitable temperament has at all times rendered them remarkable; and, in my earliest infancy, I gave evidence of having fully inherited the family character. As I advanced in years it was more strongly developed; becoming, for many reasons, a cause of serious disquietude to my friends, and of positive injury to myself. I grew self-willed, addicted to the wildest caprices, and a prey to the most ungovernable passions. Weak-minded, and beset with constitutional infirmities akin to my own, my parents could do but little to check the evil propensities which distinguished me. Some feeble and ill-directed efforts resulted in complete failure on their part, and, of course, in total triumph on mine. Thenceforward my voice was a household law; and at an age when few children have abandoned their leading strings, I was left to the guidance of my will, and became, in all but name, the master of my actions.

1. **This passage is BEST described as which of the following?**

   A   fiction

   B   biography

   C   news article

   D   informational essay

2. **Why does the narrator choose to use a pseudonym?**

   A   He is relating the memory of a dream that he finds embarrassing.

   B   He is a modest and quiet man, and wishes to call no attention to himself.

   C   He is an outcast to be scorned, and has caused unspeakable misery.

   D   He has left his family for another land, and has become his own master.

3. **When does the narrator realize that he has a special character?**

   A   after a long journey to foreign lands

   B   almost from birth

   C   upon returning from Elah-Galabus

   D   after waking from a dream

4. **How does the narrator claim to have acquired such terrible habits?**

   A   They are inherited qualities that are a part of his character.

   B   They were learned in the uttermost reaches of the globe.

   C   They are the result of a haunting fear of the shadow of death.

   D   He is the unfortunate victim of an incredibly weak will.

Read the following passage and answer questions 5 through 9.

# The Tell-Tale Heart
### by Edgar Allan Poe

It is impossible to say how first the idea entered my brain; but once conceived, it haunted me day and night. Object there was none. Passion there was none. I loved the old man. He had never wronged me. He had never given me insult. For his gold I had no desire. I think it was his eye! Yes, it was this! One of his eyes resembled that of a vulture—a pale blue eye, with a film over it. Whenever it fell upon me, my blood ran cold; and so by degrees—very gradually—I made up my mind to take the life of the old man, and thus rid myself of the eye forever.

Now this is the point. You fancy me mad. Madmen know nothing. But you should have seen me. You should have seen how wisely I proceeded—with what caution—with what foresight—with what dissimulation I went to work! I was never kinder to the old man than during the whole week before I killed him. And every night, about midnight, I turned the latch of his door and opened it—oh so gently! And then, when I had made an opening sufficient for my head, I put in a dark lantern, all closed, closed so that no light shone in, and then I thrust in my head. Oh, you would have laughed to see how cunningly I thrust it in! I moved it slowly—very slowly, so that I might not disturb the old man's sleep. It took me an hour to place my whole head within the opening so far that I could see him as he lay upon his bed. Ha!—would a madman have been so wise as this? And then, when my head was well in the room, I undid the lantern cautiously—oh

so cautiously—cautiously (for the hinges creaked)—I undid it just so much that a single thin ray fell upon the vulture eye. And this I did for seven long nights—every night just at midnight—but I found the eye always closed; and so it was impossible to do the work; for it was not the man who vexed me, but his evil eye.

5. This passage is BEST described as which of the following?

A  biography

B  history

C  fiction

D  essay

6. What exactly is it about the old man that torments the narrator so?

A  his incredible wealth

B  his evil eye

C  his beating heart

D  his condescending tone

7. How do the multiple exclamation points function in the passage?

A  They indicate an expression of the narrator's surprise at being unprepared.

B  They indicate an expression of the narrator's agitation.

C  They indicate that the narrator is very impatient.

D  They indicate that the narrator is a reckless man.

8. Why does the narrator postpone the murder of the old man?

A  He loses his nerve from fear of the old man.

B  He is not upset when the old man's vulture eye is closed.

C  He thinks the old man may be suspicious of his motives.

D  He decides after a week to change his plan to murder the old man.

9. What do the exaggerated actions and words of the narrator signify?

A  He doesn't want to wake the old man.

B  He hopes to avoid detection.

C  He is paranoid.

D  He cannot see in the darkness.

Read the following passage and answer questions 10 through 14.

# The Premature Burial
## by Edgar Allan Poe

There are certain themes of which the interest is all-absorbing, but which are too entirely horrible for the purposes of legitimate fiction. These the mere romanticist must eschew, if he does not wish to offend, or to disgust. They are with propriety handled only when the severity and majesty of truth sanctify and sustain them. We thrill, for example, with the most intense of the 'pleasurable pain' over the accounts of the Passage of the Beresina, of the Earthquake at Lisbon, of the Plague of London, of the Massacre of Saint Bartholomew, of the stifling of the hundred and twenty-three prisoners in the Black Hole of Calcutta. But, in these accounts, it is the fact—it is the reality—it is the history which excites. As inventions, we should regard them with simple abhorrence.

I have mentioned some few of the more prominent and august calamities on record; but in these it is the extent, not less than the character of the calamity, which so vividly impresses the fancy. I need not remind the reader that, from the long and weird catalogue of human miseries, I might have selected many individual instances more replete with essential suffering than any of these vast generalities of disaster. The true wretchedness, indeed—the ultimate woe—is particular, not diffuse. That the ghastly extremes of agony are endured by man the unit, and never by man the mass—for this let us thank a merciful God.

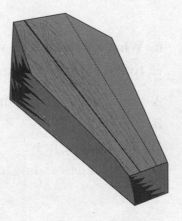

To be buried while alive is, beyond question, the most terrific of these extremes which has ever fallen to the lot of mere mortality. That it has frequently, very frequently, so fallen will scarcely be denied by those who think. The boundaries which divide Life from Death are at best shadowy and vague. Who shall say where the one ends, and where the other begins? We know there are diseases in which occur total cessations of all the apparent functions of vitality, and yet in which these cessations are merely suspensions, properly so called. They are only temporary pauses in the incomprehensible mechanism. A certain period elapses, and some unseen mysterious principle again sets in motion the magic pinions and the wizard wheels. The silver cord was not meant forever loosed, nor the golden bowl irreparably broken. But, where, meantime, was the soul?

10. **What is the narrator's attitude in the passage?**

A   light

B   keen

C   uplifting

D   calm

11. **In this passage, which topic does the narrator think is entirely unfit for fiction?**

A   questions of life and death

B   literary accounts of actual disaster

C   the wretched suffering of multitudes

D   ghastly agony endured by a single soul

12. **How does the reader know that Poe intends this work to be comic?**

A   He makes his narrator suffer a tragedy.

B   He turns the narrator into a bold, daring hero.

C   His narrator makes unintended, ironic comments.

D   His narrator finds premature burial funny.

13. **Which element does Poe send up as a true horror in this piece of fiction?**

A   the Massacre of Saint Bartholomew

B   the concept of being buried alive

C   legitimate or romantic fiction

D   the narrator's sensationalist character

14. **How does Poe make the reader a willing collaborator to his narrator?**

A   The reader is aligned with the narrator by the use of *we*.

B   The reader buries the narrator following his instruction.

C   The reader sees through the narrator's story.

D   The reader asks the narrator to tell him a story.

Read the following passage and answer questions 15 through 20.

# The Masque of the Red Death
### by Edgar Allan Poe

1 It was a voluptuous scene, that masquerade. But first let me tell of the rooms in which it was held. There were seven—an imperial suite. In many palaces, however, such suites form a long and straight vista, while the folding doors slide back nearly to the walls on either hand, so that the view of the whole extent is scarcely impeded. Here the case was very different; as might have been expected from the duke's love of the bizarre.

2 The apartments were so irregularly disposed that the vision embraced but little more than one at a time. There was a sharp turn at every twenty or thirty yards, and at each turn a novel effect. To the right and left, in the middle of each wall, a tall and narrow Gothic looked out upon a closed corridor which pursued the windings of the suite. These windows were of stained glass whose color varied in accordance with the prevailing hue of the decorations of the chamber into which it opened. That at the eastern extremity, was hung, for example, in blue—and vividly blue were its windows. The second chamber was purple in its ornaments and tapestries, and here its panes were purple. The third was green throughout, and so were the casements. The fourth was furnished and lighted with orange—the fifth was white—the sixth with violet.

3 The seventh apartment was closely shrouded in black velvet tapestries that hung all over the ceiling and down the walls, falling in heavy folds upon a carpet of the same material and hue. But in this chamber only, the color of the windows failed to correspond with the decorations. The panes here were scarlet—a deep blood color. Now in no one of the seven apartments was there any lamp or candelabrum, amid the profusion of golden ornaments that lay scattered to and fro or depended from the roof. There was no light of any kind emanating from lamp or candle within the suite of chambers. But in the corridors that followed the suite, there stood, opposite to each window, a heavy tripod bearing a brazier of fire that projected its many rays through the tinted glass and thus illumined the room. And thus were produced a multitude of gaudy and fantastic appearances. But in the western or black chamber the effect of the fire-light that streamed upon the dark hangings through the blood-tinted panes was ghastly in the extreme, and produced so wild a look upon the countenances of those who entered, that there were few of the company bold enough to set foot within its precincts at all.

4   It was in this apartment, also, that there stood against the western wall, a gigantic clock of ebony. Its pendulum swung to and fro with a dull, heavy, monotonous clang; and when the minute-hand made the circuit of the face, and the hour was to be stricken, there came from the brazen lungs of the clock a sound which was clear and loud and deep and exceedingly musical, but of so peculiar a note and emphasis that, at each lapse of an hour, the musicians of the orchestra were constrained to pause, momentarily, in their performance, to hearken to the sound; and thus the waltzers perforce ceased their evolutions; and there was a brief disconcert of the whole gay company; and, while the chimes of the clock yet rang, it was observed that the giddiest grew pale, and the more aged and sedate passed their hands over their brows as if in confused reverie or meditation. But when the echoes has fully ceased, a light laughter at once pervaded the assembly; the musicians looked at each other and smiled, as if at their own nervousness and folly, and made whispering vows, each to the other, that the next chiming of the clock should produce in them no similar emotion; and then, after the lapse of sixty minutes (which embrace three thousand and six hundred seconds of the Time that flies), there came yet another chiming of the clock, and then were the same disconcert and tremulousness and meditation as before.

15. **Under which category of fiction might this story BEST fall?**

A   horror

B   realistic

C   mystery

D   fantasy

16. **Why does Poe go into great detail about the apartments?**

A   to describe the evening's factual events

B   to set a specific mood and tone

C   to take delight in describing a lavish setting

D   to introduce the revelers at a banquet

17. **Which of the choices BEST describes the configuration of the duke's rooms?**

A   The duke's rooms are connected by a long, straight hallway.

B   The duke's rooms are laid out like a difficult maze.

C   The duke's rooms are all visible to one another through brightly colored windows.

D   The duke's rooms each open to a center chamber.

18. Read the following quotation from paragraph 4.

> . . . after the lapse of sixty minutes (which embrace three thousand and six hundred seconds of the Time that flies), there came yet another chiming of the clock . . .

**What do the detailed descriptions of time and the clock signify?**

A   an accurate portrayal of the time that is elapsing

B   an indication of the duke's wealth

C   a countdown to something dreadful ahead

D   a nuisance that interrupts the musicians

19. **What clue tells the reader that harsh judgment will be passed?**

A   The duke has built a lavish palace full of grotesque images.

B   Most of guests are unable to step into the black chamber.

C   The partygoers ignore their sense of unease in favor of entertainment.

D   The people are dressed up for a masquerade ball.

20. **What purpose do the decadent rooms serve in the story?**

A   They are intended to amaze and awe the reader.

B   They give the story a heightened sense of reality.

C   They are intended to make the guests feel comfortable.

D   They lend the story a nightmarish quality.

# Answers and Explanations

## 1. A

Choice A is the correct answer because in the first paragraph, the narrator introduces himself not as a real person, but as a persona. The events of the story are also too exaggerated and unreal, which suggests that the passage is fiction. The passage has overtones of a biography, choice B, but the overblown language and unbelievable events lead the reader to suspect this biography is not 100 percent accurate; therefore, this choice is incorrect. Choices C and D are incorrect because the passage is not formatted as a news article nor an informational essay, and the facts that are recorded in the story are impossible to verify.

## 2. C

The narrator claims that his behavior has caused unspeakable misery, so he doesn't want to give his real name; therefore, choice C is correct. Choice A is incorrect because the narrator is not relating a memory of a dream that embarrasses him. Choice B is incorrect because the narrator is not a modest or quiet man who wishes to call no attention to himself. Choice D is incorrect because leaving his family and becoming his own master are not the reasons the narrator hides his name.

## 3. B

The narrator claims that he was aware of his special character from the days of his earliest infancy, so choice B is the correct answer. Choices A and C are incorrect because the narrator recognized his special character long before he made his long journey or returned from Elah-Galabus. Choice D is incorrect because the author recognized his special character as a child, not after waking from a dream.

**4. A**

Choice A is the correct answer because the narrator claims to have inherited an imaginative and excitable temperament from his descendants, which caused him to develop terrible habits. Choices B, C, and D are incorrect because the narrator does not claim these are reasons he acquired terrible habits.

**5. C**

The exaggerated description of his tormented mind that the man offers implies the passage is a work of fiction, so choice C is correct. Choices A and B are incorrect because biography and history avoid this style and tone in favor of the objective presentation of facts. Choice D is incorrect because the passage makes no use of citation, as essays do to support their arguments.

**6. B**

The old man's blue eye, covered with a film, like that of a vulture, torments the narrator and drives him to murder. Choice B is correct. The narrator does not covet the old man's wealth, nor does he despise his character; in fact, he states that he loves him. Choices A and D are incorrect. The story's title, "The Tell-Tale Heart," refers to a climactic episode that occurs later in the story, but is not part of this passage. Choice D is incorrect.

**7. B**

Poe uses the exclamation points as a literary device to show that his narrator is extremely agitated, with the marks frequently interrupting the narrator's train of thoughts, so choice B is correct. Choices C and D are incorrect because the narrator is neither reckless nor impatient; he is quite careful and methodical in planning the old man's murder. Choice A is incorrect, for although the narrator is agitated, nothing in the passage transpires that surprises him; in his paranoia, he tries to plan extensively.

## 8. B

When he enters the old man's bedroom, the narrator finds the old man's eye closed, and cannot bring himself to murder him, so choice B is the correct answer. Choice A is incorrect because the narrator does not lose his nerve from fear. Choice C is incorrect because the narrator does not mention whether the old man is suspicious. Choice D is incorrect because the narrator does not decide to change his plans.

## 9. C

The exaggerated words and actions of the narrator signify his tortured mental state and paranoia, so choice C is correct. While the narrator wants to avoid detection and waking the man, his exaggerated actions and words have little to do with these answers, so choices A and B are incorrect. Choice D is incorrect because his exaggerated actions and words have nothing to do with his inability to see in the dark.

## 10. B

The narrator is quite keen and eager to discuss premature burial, so choice B is correct. Choices A, C, and D are incorrect because the narrator's attitude is not light, uplifting, or calm because he is actually excited and fascinated by the concept he's discussing.

## 11. D

The one topic the narrator deems unsuitable for fiction is the suffering of a single person, so choice D is correct. Choices A, B, and C are incorrect because the narrator introduces a number of subjects that deal with death and human suffering, such as earthquakes and disease. The narrator admits that although some of these accounts may be distasteful, they nonetheless may make for legitimate fiction, if handled properly. The fact that these disasters affect many, and not one, make them acceptable to the narrator.

## 12. C

The narrator is a writer who declares a subject taboo and then proceeds to discuss the taboo in great detail, which Poe knew was both ironic and funny. Choice C is correct. Choice A is incorrect because nowhere in the passage does the narrator suffer a tragedy. Choice B is incorrect because the narrator is not a bold, daring hero. Choice D is incorrect because the narrator does not find premature burial funny, but he is fascinated by it.

## 13. D

Poe sends up the narrator's sensationalist character as a true horror because Poe wants to mock people who are curious and excited by other people's misery. Choice D is correct. Choice A is incorrect because the Massacre of Saint Bartholomew is just a detail, but not the true horror in the story. Choice B is incorrect because while the narrator is horrified by the idea of being buried alive, Poe uses this concept to distract from the true horror. Choice C is incorrect because Poe's main focus is the narrator's character, not legitimate or romantic fiction.

## 14. A

Choice A is correct because the narrator draws the reader in by the use of the word *we*, thus drawing even the most unwilling reader in as his collaborator. Choice B is incorrect because the reader doesn't actually bury the narrator. Choice C is incorrect because whether or not the reader sees through the narrator's story, the narrator has already yoked the reader to him by use of the word *we*. Choice D is incorrect because the narrator does not mention that the reader asked him to tell a story.

## 15. A

The correct answer is choice A because the description is intended to be macabre and chilling. Choice B is incorrect because the passage is not intended to be realistic fiction. Choices C and D are incorrect because even though it is unclear why the events are taking place and the description of the events are unreal, the purpose of the passage is not to mystify the reader or provide them with a fantasy of escape, but to shock and terrify the reader.

## 16. B

Poe's detailed description of the duke's apartments sets the mood and tone for the strange events that unfold later in the story, so choice B is correct. Choices A and C are incorrect because Poe is not interested in providing a factual account of the evening's events nor does he delight in describing a lavish setting. The passage does not give much word about the guests at the party, so choice D is incorrect.

**17. B**

By reading the passage very closely, the reader is able to ascertain that the rooms of the duke's apartments are laid out like a maze, with each room reached by taking a sharp turn every 20 or 30 yards along a corridor. Choice B is correct. Choice A is incorrect because the hallway from which the rooms are reached is not straight, as is usually the case in such palaces. Choice C is incorrect because the rooms are visible only one at a time, not altogether. Choice D is incorrect because there is no mention of the rooms opening to a center chamber.

**18. C**

The detailed and poetic description of the clock and the time it keeps signify a countdown to something dreadful ahead, so choice C is correct. Poe is not concerned with providing an accurate portrayal of events, so choice A is incorrect. Choice B is incorrect because the clock is less an illustration of the duke's wealth, than of passing time and impending doom. Choice D is incorrect because the clock represents more than a nuisance to the musicians—it represents death.

**19. C**

When characters in a story ignore their inner conscience in favor of entertainment, this often indicates that they will be punished, so choice C is correct. Choice A is incorrect because a harsh judgment will be handed down. Choice B is incorrect because even though most guests are not bold enough to face the black room, this in itself is not enough to warrant harsh judgment. Choice D is incorrect because dressing up for a masquerade ball is not a reason to be harshly judged.

**20. D**

The decadent descriptions of the rooms are intended to give the story a nightmarish quality, so the correct answer is D. Choice A is incorrect because even though the rooms may amaze and awe the readers, the primary purpose of the description is to scare the reader and the partygoers. Choice B is incorrect because the description of the rooms is not intended to give the reader a heightened sense of reality, but rather unreality. Choice C is incorrect because the rooms are not intended to make the guests feel comfortable.

# Section 2
# Writing

# Chapter 4

# Writing Conventions

## UNDERSTANDING WRITING CONVENTIONS

The Writing section of the CAHSEE assesses your ability to understand writing conventions by asking you 15 multiple-choice questions. The test will ask you to identify main and subordinate clauses and correctly use them; identify gerund, infinitive, and participial phrases; and understand punctuation mechanics. You will need to understand the parts of a sentence, as well as how to construct and use proper sentences. You will also need to be familiar with proper English usage, grammar, diction, and syntax.

This chapter will help you master writing conventions and rules to follow when taking the CAHSEE. It will help you identify correct and incorrect writing conventions and grammar. It will provide practice tips and strategies for using proper writing conventions. Finally, this chapter will offer you a chance to practice the skills and strategies you have learned with a quiz based on CAHSEE-type questions.

## Kaplan's 4-Step Method for Writing Conventions Questions

**Step 1:** Read each sentence one time carefully, looking for identifiable mistakes. (We'll point out some common mistakes as we go through the punctuation, grammar, and usage review that follows.)

**Step 2:** Substitute all the answer choices into questions that have fill-in-the-blank answers. In most cases, it will be obvious which answers you can eliminate quickly.

**Step 3:** Circle the mistake within the incorrect answer choice if there is one. If there is no error, circle choice D, "Leave as is." Fill in the appropriate box on your answer sheet and move on.

**Step 4:** If the question really confuses you, put a check mark next to it and come back to it later, only if you have more time after finishing the entire section.

To do your best on CAHSEE's Writing Conventions questions, you'll have to work at a steady pace, zero in on the error, and have confidence in your chosen answer. You must have a firm grasp of correct punctuation, grammar, spelling, capitalization, and usage. You also need to be able to recognize common errors.

This chapter will give you the skill review you need to succeed in these areas. We'll review sentences, clauses and phrases, sentence structure errors, modifiers, and parallel structure. In addition, we will cover grammar and usage, punctuation, and capitalization. Even if you think you've seen the material in English class, avoid the temptation to rush through it.

## SENTENCES

A **sentence** is a group of words that expresses a complete thought. Most people write in sentences but often think in pieces of sentences, or fragments. A basic sentence has two parts: a subject and a verb.

**He ran.** (*He* is the subject; *ran* is the verb.)
**The dog ate.** (The *dog* is the subject; *ate* is the verb.)

You will need to be able to identify a sentence on the test. In order to do this, you need to understand two parts of a sentence: the subject and verb.

The **subject** is who or what the sentence is about. It is the "naming" word in the sentence. *Carol*, *house*, and *fish* are noun naming words. *He*, *you*, *me*, *she*, and *it* are pronoun naming words. To find the subject, ask, "Who or what is acting in this sentence? Who or what is this sentence about?"

The **verb** can be an action word, such as walk, sing, or laugh. To find the action verb, ask, "What did the subject do?"

A **linking verb** is a bit different. It shows a state of being rather than a state of action. Any form of the verb to be (is, am, was, will be, will have been, etc.) is a linking verb. Other verbs can be either a linking verb or an action verb depending on how they are used (seem, look, smell, taste, sound, turn, feel, grow, appear, get, remain, etc.).

**The boy looks sleepy. (linking verb)**
**The doctor looks at the X-ray. (action verb)**

A **helping verb** does just what it says: It helps other verbs be complete. For example, an *-ing* verb cannot stand alone as the only verb in a sentence. When an *-ing* word is the ONLY verb, you know immediately that you are looking at a sentence fragment!

**Marissa talking with her friends.**
**Corrected: Marissa is talking with her friends.**

Helping verbs include forms of *be*, *have*, and *do*, as well as *can* and *could*, among others.

## CLAUSES, PHRASES, AND SENTENCES

A **clause** is a group of words with a subject and a verb. Another name for a sentence is **independent clause**. That is, it is a clause that can stand alone as a complete thought.

On the other hand, a **dependent clause** is what the name suggests. It cannot stand alone; it must "lean" on another sentence to make it a complete thought. Dependent clauses frequently begin with subordinating conjunctions such as *after*, *since*, or *because*.

**Miguel plays the trumpet. (independent clause)**

**Because Meg enjoyed science fiction movies. (dependent clause. It cannot stand alone and needs another sentence.)**

**Because Meg enjoyed science fiction movies, <u>she decided to study science in college.</u> (The dependent clause is "leaning" on the underlined sentence.)**

A **phrase** is simply a group of words without a subject and a verb. The words are related but do not form a complete thought. A phrase has many jobs in a sentence.

**The guide put our canoe in the river. (prepositional phrase)**

**Paddling our canoe upstream would be difficult. (noun phrase)**

**I wanted to float downstream instead. (infinitive phrase; an infinitive = to + a verb)**

## Types of Sentences

A **simple sentence** contains a subject and a verb. Knowing some patterns found in simple sentences will help you identify and write complete sentences.

### PATTERN 1: (SUBJECT-VERB) [S-V]

| Michelle | ate. |
|----------|------|
| subject  | verb |

Who is acting in this sentence? *Michelle* (subject)
What did Michelle do? *ate* (verb)

## PATTERN 2: (SUBJECT-VERB-DIRECT OBJECT) [S-V-DO]

A **direct object** is a noun or pronoun that receives the action of the verb. In other words, the verb is an action verb, and the direct object is the target of that action.

| Jonah | hit | the ball. |
|-------|-----|-----------|
| subject | verb | direct object |

Who is acting in this sentence? *Jonah* (subject)

What did Jonah do? *hit* (verb)

What did Jonah hit? *a ball* (direct object)

## PATTERN 3: (SUBJECT-VERB-INDIRECT OBJECT-DIRECT OBJECT) [S-V-IO-DO]

An **indirect object** tells to whom or for whom something is done. The direct and indirect objects can also change places in this pattern.

| Kim | gave | Karl | a slice of pie. |
|-----|------|------|-----------------|
| subject | verb | indirect object | direct object |
| Kim | gave | a slice of pie | to Karl. |
| subject | verb | direct object | indirect object |

Who is acting in this sentence? *Kim* (subject)

What did Kim do? *gave* (verb)

What did Kim give? *a slice of pie* (direct object)

To whom did Kim give a slice of pie? *Karl* (indirect object)

## PATTERN 4: (SUBJECT-LINKING VERB-NOUN) [S-LV-N] OR (SUBJECT-LINKING VERB-ADJECTIVE) [S-LV-A]

| Ms. Bowers | is | the teacher. |
|------------|-----|--------------|
| subject | linking verb | noun |
| The milk | tasted | sour. |
| subject | linking verb | adjective |

### PATTERN 5: (WORD OR PHRASE-SUBJECT-VERB-WORD OR PHRASE) [W/PH-S-V-W/PH]

Words or phrases can be added to any of these patterns in almost any place that makes sense. Here are some examples.

| Fortunately, | Mai | sings | with our band. |
|---|---|---|---|
| word | subject | verb | prepositional phrase |

| In the morning, | Alexandra | put | the supplies | in the back of the truck. |
|---|---|---|---|---|
| prepositional phrase | subject | verb | direct object | two prepositional phrases |

| At the beginning of the move, | one character | gave | Rachel | a rose. |
|---|---|---|---|---|
| two prepositional phrases | subject | verb | indirect object | direct object |

| Now, | the computer | seems | inexpensive | to me. |
|---|---|---|---|---|
| word | subject | linking verb | adjective | prepositional phrase |

A **compound sentence** consists of two simple sentences joined by a connecting word called a **coordinating conjunction** (*for, and, nor, but, or, yet, so*).

**She met Tom** at the high school, **and they drove to the campground** near the river.

The two simple sentences are underlined. The other parts in the sentence are phrases. Phrases are like the sprinkles on cupcakes. They add information and interest to a sentence but do not have a lot to do with the basic structure.

A **complex sentence** consists of an independent clause or simple sentence plus a dependent clause. The clause can come before the first sentence or at the end of the first sentence.

| After they set up their tents, | Tom and Susan talked with the river guide. |
|---|---|
| dependent clause | independent clause (sentence) |
| Tom and Susan talked with the river guide | after they set up their tents. |
| independent clause (sentence) | dependent clause |

## SENTENCE STRUCTURE ERRORS

The purpose of writing is to communicate ideas. Sentence structure errors make your ideas hard to follow, which is why they are frequently tested on the CAHSEE. It is vital to be able to recognize and write coherent, well-structured sentences.

## Fragments

A **fragment** is a sentence part. It needs something more to make it complete.

| Types of Fragments | Example | Problem |
|---|---|---|
| dependent clause | Because we got into the boat. | A dependent word or subordinating conjunction such as *because*, when placed before a subject and verb, creates a dependent clause. |
| relative pronoun clause | Who was elected to the new position. | A relative pronoun such as *who* can introduce a question but creates a fragment when simply placed before a verb. |
| *-ing* word | The girl running in the street. | The verb in a sentence cannot be only an *-ing* word. It needs a helping verb such as *is* or *was*. |

| prepositional phrase | At the grocery store. | If the word group starts with a preposition and does not have a subject and verb added, it is a fragment. |
| to + verb | To swim in the ocean. | This word group does not have a subject or a verb. |
| explaining words | For example, a big, three-person tent. | Sentences beginning with words such as *for example*, *for instance*, or *like* must have a subject and verb. It is wise not to begin a sentence with *such as* because this almost always results in a fragment. |

## HOW TO FIND A FRAGMENT AND FIX IT

Look at the word group carefully and find the subject.

Look again and find the verb. If it is an *-ing* word, make sure it has a helper like *is* or *was*.

**Austin helping his aunt.**

**Austin was helping his aunt.**

If the word group begins with a dependent word (subordinating conjunction), such as because, after, or since, be certain there is a second word group containing both a second subject and verb.

**Because we were late.**

**Because we were late, we missed the bus.**

If the word group begins with explaining words like for example, for instance, or like, check closely to be sure there is BOTH a subject and a verb.

**For example, yesterday the pet store sold a cat, two dogs, and a parrot.**

**Which sentence is correctly written?**

A   At the beginning of the concert, sitting in the second row of the balcony.

B   Since the official letter had failed to arrive at the house on time.

C   For example, a big yellow bus with bright red lettering on the side.

D   Sakura and Kendrick study at the library every day after school.

| A | incorrect | This group has no subject. |
|---|-----------|---------------------------|
| B | incorrect | This word group is a dependent clause. It needs another subject and verb to make it a complete sentence. |
| C | incorrect | This word group has no verb. |
| **D** | **correct** | |

## RUN-ON SENTENCES AND COMMA SPLICES

A **run-on sentence** is exactly what it sounds like. One sentence "runs" into a second sentence, and there is no punctuation or conjunction in between.

**We finished fixing the baked beans John began frying the chicken.**

A **comma splice** joins two sentences with nothing but a comma.

**We finished fixing the baked beans, John began frying the chicken.**

Both of these errors make a sentence difficult to read and the idea difficult to understand.

## FINDING A RUN-ON SENTENCE OR A COMMA SPLICE

1. Find the subject and verb in a sentence.

2. If there are two sets of subjects and verbs, you might have two sentences incorrectly put together.

3. Are the sentences joined by a connecting word or subordinating conjunction? If so, you do NOT have a run-on sentence or comma splice. You can stop here.

4. Is there a subordinating conjunction before either the first or second sentence? If so, you do NOT have a run-on sentence or comma splice. You can stop here. If there is no subordinating conjunction or coordinating conjunction, continue.

5. Is there any punctuation between the two sentences? If not, you DO have a run-on sentence.

6. Is there only a comma between these two sentences? If so, you DO have a comma splice.

7. Is there only a conjunctive adverb (*however, nevertheless, therefore,* etc.) between the sentences with NO semicolon? If so, you DO have either a run-on (no punctuation) or a comma splice (only a comma).

## FIXING A RUN-ON SENTENCE OR COMMA SPLICE

| Put a period between the sentences. | We finished fixing the baked beans. John began frying the chicken. |
|---|---|
| Add a connecting word and a comma between the sentences. | We finished fixing the baked beans, **and** John began frying the chicken. |
| Add a subordinating conjunction or dependent word between the sentences. | We finished fixing the baked beans **when** John began frying the chicken. |
| Put a semicolon between the sentences. | We finished fixing the baked beans; John began frying the chicken. |

| Add a conjunctive adverb (*however, nevertheless, therefore,* etc.) and a semicolon. | We finished fixing the baked beans; **therefore,** John began frying the chicken. |
|---|---|
| Add a subordinating conjunction or dependent word before the first sentence. | **When** we finished fixing the baked beans, John began frying the chicken. |

Read the following sentence.

> Ramone is an excellent football player, however, his sister, Latoya, is a better athlete.

**Which option corrects the error in the sentence?**

**A**  football player however his sister, Latoya

**B**  football player; however, his sister, Latoya

**C**  football player however, his sister, Latoya

**D**  Leave as is.

| A | incorrect | Removing the commas makes this comma splice a run-on sentence. |
|---|---|---|
| **B** | **correct** | The semicolon separates the two sentences; the word *however* is a conjunctive adverb that connects the ideas. |
| C | incorrect | Removing the comma after *player* makes this a run-on sentence. |
| D | incorrect | The sentence contains a comma splice. |

## MODIFIERS

**Modifiers** are words or phrases that give more information in a sentence. The most common are adjectives and adverbs.

**Adjectives** are colorful words that give more information about nouns or pronouns. An adjective answers one of these questions:

- How many?
- Which one?
- What kind?

**With her long red hair blowing in the wind, Camille stood on the deck of her father's only, elaborate yacht and waved at her seven cousins on shore.**

There are several adjectives here. *Long* and *red* tell us about Camille's hair; *only* and *elaborate* explain her father's yacht, and *seven* tells us about the cousins who were not sailing with Camille.

**Be careful:** Some adjectives have *-ing* or *-ed* endings that make them look like verbs.

**The talented actor just finished an exciting film.**

In this sentence, *talented* and *exciting* are adjectives even though they look like they might be verbs. The trick is to see what the word is doing in the sentence. In this case, *talented* is telling us about the actor, and *exciting* is telling us about the film. Adjectives provide more information about nouns; they do not describe an action.

**Adverbs** are words that provide information about verbs, adjectives, or other adverbs.

An adverb can answer these questions:

- Where? (here, there, everywhere)
- When? (now, later, yesterday)
- How much? (very, too, more)
- How? (quickly, slowly)
- How often? (never, sometimes)

**Remember:** An ad verb can never modify a noun. Many, but not all, adverbs end in *-ly*.

Do not use a negative adverb such as *hardly, scarcely, rarely,* or *never* when there is another negative in the sentence.

**I do not hardly know anyone at that school.**

**Corrected: I do not know anyone at that school.**

## Comparing

Adjectives and adverbs are used to show or compare quality or amount.

- The positive form is the word itself; it is found in the dictionary: *smart.*
- The comparative form compares something with ONE other: *smarter.*
- The superlative form compares something with TWO OR MORE others: *smartest.*

**My turtle is smart.**

**My turtle is smarter than Madge's turtle. (Madge has only one turtle.)**

**My turtle is the smartest turtle in our neighborhood. (Presumably, there are several turtles in the neighborhood.)**

Generally, one-syllable adjectives and adverbs use the *-er* or *-est* endings. Some two-syllable adjectives do so as well (*lucky, luckier, luckiest*). *More* or *most* are always used for adjectives of three syllables or more (*more beautiful, most beautiful*).

Use either *-er, -est,* OR *more, most.* Do NOT use both.

**Yuki is the most smartest student in class.**

**Corrected: Yuki is the smartest student in class.**

A few adjectives and adverbs change form.

**Adjectives**

| good | better | best |
|------|--------|------|
| bad | worse | worst |
| many | more | most |

**Adverbs**

| well | better | best |
|------|--------|------|
| badly | worse | worst |

Do NOT add -er or -est to these words.

**That is the bestest movie I've seen all year.**

**Corrected: That is the best movie I've seen all year.**

Choose the correct word to fill in the blank.

**Samuel thinks my mom's cake tastes _____ than mine.**

**A**  best

**B**  better

**C**  more better

**D**  most bestest

| A | incorrect | *Best* is the positive form. It is not the comparative form of the word. |
|---|-----------|-------------------------------------------------------------------------|
| **B** | **correct** | *Better* is the comparative form, which is used to compare two different elements—in this case, my mom's cake and mine. |
| C | incorrect | The adverb *better* never uses *more* or *most*. |
| D | incorrect | The adverb *best* compares several things. It is never used with *most* or *more*. |

## Common Modifier Mishaps

To express ideas correctly, words or phrases must be close to whatever they are modifying. When a modifier is incorrect, the sentence does not express the idea correctly. On the CAHSEE, read each sentence carefully to see if the modifier is incorrectly placed.

A **misplaced modifier** is in the wrong place in a sentence.

I went to get the mail eating an ice cream cone.
(The mail is not eating an ice cream cone.)

Corrected: Eating an ice cream cone, I went to get the mail.

A **dangling modifier** occurs when part of a sentence is implied rather than stated.

Hurrying home, my bag dropped on the sidewalk. (A person is hurrying home, not a bag.)

Corrected: My bag dropped on the sidewalk while I was hurrying home.

### FIXING INCORRECT MODIFIERS

Look for "limiting words" such as *only, a few, almost, hardly, nearly, just, almost, even,* or *scarcely*. These must be placed right before the words they modify.

Kaitlyn found only two unusual shells at the beach. (She found a lot of shells, only two of which were unusual.)

Look for a missing word—often the "real" subject of a sentence (the person or thing doing the action). If the subject is absent, add it.

Walking slowly down the street, the school bus passed me. (The school bus was not walking slowly down the street. I was.)

Corrected: The school bus passed me as I was walking slowly down the street.

Read the following sentence.

> Sitting in the cafeteria, the fire alarm went off.

**Choose the best way to express the thought.**

**A**     In the cafeteria, sitting, the fire alarm went off.

**B**     The fire alarm went off sitting in the cafeteria.

**C**     While I was in the cafeteria, the fire alarm went off.

**D**     Leave as is.

| A | incorrect | The fire alarm is not sitting in the cafeteria. |
|---|-----------|--------------------------------------------------|
| B | incorrect | The fire alarm is not sitting in the cafeteria. |
| C | **correct** | The implied subject corrects the modifier. |
| D | incorrect | This is a dangling modifier. |

## PARALLEL SENTENCES

Parallel sentences are often tested on the CAHSEE. In a correctly written parallel sentence, similar parts of a sentence are in the same part of speech.

**At the festival, students from different countries marched, danced, and were playing musical instruments.**

The words *marched* and *danced* are both past tense forms of verbs. The final verb is not in the simple past tense.

**Corrected: At the festival, students from different countries marched, danced, and played musical instruments.**

### Other Parallel Structure Problems

All the verbs in a sentence must be in the same tense.

**She started to make lasagna but decides to make spaghetti instead. (*Started* is past tense, but *decides* is present tense.)**

**Corrected: She started to make lasagna but decided to make spaghetti instead.**

When two things are compared, both should be in the same grammatical form.

**I think walking home is easier than to take the bus. (The verb walking should match the verb taking.)**

**Corrected: I think walking home is easier than taking the bus.**

Certain paired words are called *correlative conjunctions* (both . . . and, neither . . . nor, either . . . or, rather . . . than, etc.) and need to be followed by parallel words or phrases. Look at the example. Determine whether or not the verbs are parallel in structure.

**I think he should either study regularly or quitting his job is another possibility.**

**Corrected: I think he should either study regularly or quit his job.**

## GRAMMAR AND USAGE

### Verb Tense

Verb tenses are important because the tense tells when something takes place.

**Nikki goes to the library. (The verb tells us this is happening in the present. Therefore, the verb is in the present tense.)**

**Nikki went to the library. (The verb tells us that this happened some time in the past. Therefore, the verb is in the past tense.)**
**Nikki will go to the library. (The verb tells us that this will happen in the future. Therefore, the verb is in the future tense.)**

Test questions may contain verbs in two different, incorrect tenses.

Verb forms can be confusing. The trick is to think of the time expressed in the sentence.

| Verb Form | Time | Example |
|---|---|---|
| present | now | Julia **watches** movies every day. |
| past | yesterday | Julia **watched** movies last night. |
| future | tomorrow and beyond | Julia **will watch** movies next week. |
| present perfect | action begun in the past and still going on OR completed at some time in the past | Julia **has watched** movies for hours at a time. |
| past perfect | action begun in the past and completed before a second action took place | Julia **had watched** movies on her VCR before she got a DVD player. |
| future perfect | action that is ongoing and will take place in the future | Julia **will have watched** 500 movies by the end of this month. |

## Subject-Verb Agreement

A singular subject must have a singular verb just as a plural subject must have a plural verb.

**The cat sits by the window every day.**

*Cat* is singular, and the verb *sits* is also singular.

Look at the verb in the following chart.

| singular | first person | *I* | **mop** |
|---|---|---|---|
| | second person | *you* | **mop** |
| | third person | *he*, *she*, *it* or any singular noun | **mops** |
| **plural** | first person | *we* | **mop** |
| | second person | *you* | **mop** |
| | third person | *they* or any plural noun | **mop** |

Notice that only the third-person singular form of the verb is different. With "regular verbs," that is, verbs that do not change form, you add an *-s* to the third-person singular verb.

## Irregular Verbs

You can find out whether a verb is regular or irregular by looking in the dictionary. Irregular forms are listed directly after the part of speech.

go (gō) v. went, going, going, goes

Irregular verbs change form and become different words.

| Verb Form | Example |
|---|---|
| present | begin |
| past | began |
| future | will begin |
| present perfect | has begun |
| past perfect | had begun |
| future perfect | will have begun |

The irregular verbs *be*, *do*, and *have* seem to cause the most problems.

| | | be | do | have |
|---|---|---|---|---|
| **singular present and past** | *I* | am/was | do/did | have/had |
| | *you* | are/were | do/did | have/had |
| | *he, she, it* | is/was | does/did | has/had |
| **plural present and past** | *we* | are/were | do/did | have/had |
| | *you* | are/were | do/did | have/had |
| | *they* | are/were | do/did | have/had |

## Possible Verb Problems

Compound subject occurs when a sentence has two or more subjects. The verb in this type of sentence is always plural.

**Timmy and Tashi like peanut butter and banana sandwiches.**

Often, a phrase separates the subject from the verb. The easiest way to deal with this is to mentally cross out the interrupting phrase. Then you can identify the subject and verb.

**The pots and pans ~~in the kitchen~~ need to be washed.**
    subject                    verb

Some words make the subject seem plural when it is not. These words include *along with*, *including*, *together with*, *in addition to*, and *as well as*.

**William, together with his cousins, goes to the park every day.**
subject                            verb

*William* is the singular subject of the sentence. The verb must be singular as well.

Collective nouns are nouns that refer to groups of people or things that act as a unit are collective nouns. They are always singular.

**My family always has a big picnic in July.**
  subject          verb

The family, as a unit, has the big picnic. The individual members act as one.

If both subjects in the sentence are singular, the verb is singular.

**Either Ted or Kailee has a copy of the class notes.**

If one subject is singular and the other is plural, the verb agrees with the closest subject.

**Neither Michele nor her sisters have arrived.**

In questions, the subject follows the verb.

**Who owns that beautiful dress?**

When *There are* or *There were* begins a sentence, the subject always follows.

**There are many trees in the park.**

To locate the subject and make sure the subject-verb agreement is correct, rephrase the sentence.

**Many trees are in the park.**

An indefinite pronoun points to an unnamed person or thing. Any word ending in *-body*, *-one*, or *-thing* is singular and needs a singular verb. Words beginning with *any-*, *no-*, *every-*, and *some* are also singular.
**Everybody is welcome at the library.**

**Somebody always leaves a book on the bus.**

**Everything at the garage sale is inexpensive.**

## Other Indefinite Pronouns

| Singular | Plural | Either (depending on the rest of the sentence) |
|---|---|---|
| another | both | all |
| each | few | any |
| one | many | enough |
| | most | most |
| | several | none |
| | | some |

The indefinite pronouns that can be either singular or plural are unusual. This is the only case in which a prepositional phrase determines whether the verb is singular or plural.

Remember: We usually cross out the phrase that comes between the subject and the verb. This is not true in the case of these special indefinite pronouns.

**All of the pie is burnt.**

In this case, the noun *pie* in the prepositional phrase tells us that we need a singular verb because we are writing about a single pie.

**All of the pies are delicious.**

Here, the prepositional phrase contains a plural noun, *pies*, and as a result, the verb must be plural.

## Still More about Pronouns

Pronouns can be subjects or objects in a sentence.

**She gave him the bicycle.**

It is very important to be able to recognize whether a subject or object pronoun should be used in a sentence. This is tested frequently on the CAHSEE.

| Subject Pronouns | Object Pronouns | Possessive Pronouns (show ownership) |
|---|---|---|
| I | me | my, mine |
| you | you | your, yours |
| he, she, it | him, her, it | his, her, hers, its |
| | | |
| we | us | our, ours |
| you | you | your, yours |
| they | them | their, theirs |

Look at this sentence.

**Denzel and _____ go to the soccer game every Friday.**

Which word belongs in the blank?

For a moment, cross out *Denzel and*. Would you write "Me go to the football game every Friday"? Probably not. *Me* is an object pronoun. It either receives the action of the verb or tells us to whom or for whom something was done. *I* is a subject pronoun. It would fit correctly in the sentence, as would *he* and *she* as well as *we* and *they*. Yes, it sounds strange, but it is grammatically correct.

Look at another sentence.

**The coach handed the trophy to Takako and _____.**

What word would fit in the blank?

Take out Takako's name. Now read the sentence.

**The coach handed to the trophy to _____.**

What would you put in this sentence?

Any objective pronoun would fit correctly in terms of grammar: *me, him, her, us, them.*

Another pronoun trouble spot involves *who* and *whom.* Actually, this one is easy to solve.

**_____is in charge?**

Clearly, the pronoun *who* is the subject here: "Who is in charge?" *Who* is always used as a subject. To check, substitute a singular subjective pronoun such as *he.*

**He is in charge. (*Him* would not be correct.)**

That leaves only *whom*, which is always used as an object.

**To whom are you writing?**

The subject of this sentence is *you.* Turn it around. "You are writing to whom?" *To* can act as a preposition. When it does, the word that follows is ALWAYS in the objective case. To check, turn the question around and substitute *him.*

**You are writing to him?**

## Pronoun Agreement

When a pronoun occurs in a sentence, it must agree with the noun.

**When you go into that store, the clerks always offer to help her.**

Clearly, *you* should be changed to *she*, and the verb *go* should be changed to *goes.*

Indefinite pronouns can be a bit trickier.

**Everyone should bring their ideas to the meeting.**

**Corrected: Everyone should bring his or her ideas to the meeting.**

*Everyone* is a singular indefinite pronoun. It must be matched by another singular pronoun.

## PUNCTUATION AND CAPITALIZATION
### Quotation Marks

Quotation marks are used in pairs. Quotation marks indicate that someone else's words are being used exactly in a direct quotation:

**"To strive, to seek, to find, and not to yield" is the best line ever written by Tennyson.**

Quotation marks are used to refer to a short work like an article, a poem, a short story, or a song.

**Tennyson's poem "Ulysses" is my favorite.**

Quotation marks are used to refer to sayings, words, or unusual words.

**Is "two heads are better than one" a reliable saying?**
Do NOT use quotation marks for indirect quotes.

**Emiko said "that she did not want to visit the museum today."**

**Corrected: Emiko said that she did not want to visit the museum today.**

**Remember:** Periods and commas always go inside quote marks; semicolons and colons go outside.

## Apostrophes

There are only TWO main uses of apostrophes.

Apostrophes should be used with contractions.

**I don't want to read any more tonight.**

Apostrophes should be used to show ownership.

**That stereo is Dalia's.**

Plurals never use an apostrophe.

**The boy sold many cup's of lemonade.**

**Corrected: The boy sold many cups of lemonade.**

## A Useful Apostrophe Rule

Apostrophes are used only with nouns to show ownership. They are never used with pronouns.

**That coat is her's.**

**Corrected: That coat is hers.**

This is especially important with the *it's/its* problem.

*It's* is a contraction meaning "it is."

**It's a long drive to California.**

*Its* is a possessive pronoun:

**The mouse thinks that the cheese is its.**

If you are not sure whether to use an apostrophe or not, remove the contraction and substitute the words. In this sentence, put in *it is*. If the sentence makes no sense, then do not use the apostrophe.

**The mouse thinks that the cheese it is. (This sentence makes no sense.)**

**Corrected: The mouse thinks that the cheese is its.**

## Commas

Often, students think comma rules are hard to understand. This is not true. Commas are very easy to deal with once you think about the way they are used.

### RULE #1: COMMAS ARE USED WITH CERTAIN SENTENCE CONNECTORS

When two sentences are joined by a coordinating conjunction, put a comma after the word that comes before the conjunction.

**We made a salad, and we knew in 20 minutes that we had made the right decision.**

A comma can be used only if a sentence (or independent clause) is on either side of the coordinating conjunction.

Read this sentence.

**We decided to make a salad and were happy with it.**

Look at the words following the coordinating conjunction. Is *were happy* a sentence? Does it have a subject? Because the subject is *we*, which is in the first clause and there is no subject in this second clause, we do not use a comma.

**Important:** If two sentences are connected with a subordinating conjunction, do not use a comma.

**Rachel went skating even though a storm was approaching.**

*Even though* is a subordinating conjunction; no comma is required.

## RULE #2: USE COMMAS TO SET OFF UNESSENTIAL INFORMATION

Sometimes information is added to a sentence that is not absolutely vital to the meaning of the sentence. This includes words or phrases such as "*Oh, you might be interested in knowing that. . .*" words or phrases.

**Mr. Gonzalez, who is nearly 90 years old, will attend my graduation.**

If we remove the phrase *who is nearly 90 years old*, the sentence still communicates the same thought: Mr. Gonzalez will be at graduation.

Sometimes, however, if we remove the clause or phrase, the sentence does not communicate the same thought. When this happens, we do not use commas.

**Milk that is left on the kitchen counter sours quickly.**

All milk does not sour quickly. Milk that is left at room temperature, however, is likely to sour quickly. In this case, we do not use commas.
Sometimes, the subject will be renamed in a sentence. This is called an **appositive**.

**My teacher, Ms. Stelve, assigned a science project.**

In this sentence, *Ms. Stelve* renames the subject, *My teacher*. Again, the same rule applies. We could remove the name from the sentence and not affect the meaning. Therefore, it is surrounded by commas.

**My teacher assigned a science project.**

## RULE #3: USE COMMAS AFTER INTRODUCTORY WORDS, PHRASES, AND CLAUSES

Phrases (groups of related words) and dependent clauses (groups of words with a subject and verb that need another sentence to "lean on") are followed by a comma when they begin the sentence.

Examples of introductory words.

**Nonetheless, Mrs. Ruiz thinks we should continue working on the project.**

**Incidentally, I thought the class would be easy.**

Examples of introductory phrases.

**In the meantime, I have a lot of work to do.**

**By the way, coats are on sale at the mall.**

Examples of introductory clauses:

**Because I studied all week, I did well on the test.**

**When we went hiking, I used Noah's backpack.**

## RULE #4: USE COMMAS WITH ITEMS IN A SERIES

In a sentence listing three or more parallel elements, commas are used between the elements. Therefore, look for the individual parts in the list and separate them with commas. The comma before the *and* in this type of sentence is not tested.

**Raymone ordered pizza with mushrooms, olives, and pepperoni.**

Sometimes, the list will be longer and be made up of phrases.

**I like hiking in the mountains, fishing in the ocean, and running in the park.**

## Other Comma Uses

### CONJUNCTIVE ADVERBS

When a conjunctive adverb is used in a sentence, use a comma. The trick is to know exactly *where* to place the comma.

Read these two sentences.

**I believe, however, in your ability to learn how to dance.**

**Karlene ordered roast chicken; however, everyone else ordered grilled fish.**

In the first sentence, *however* is simply an added word that could be removed without changing the meaning of the sentence. When this happens, surround the word with commas just as we did in Rule #2.

In the second sentence, *however* separates two independent clauses. What would happen if we used commas around the word?

**Karlene ordered roast chicken, however, everyone else ordered grilled fish.**

That's right! If you separate two sentences with a comma, you create a comma splice. That is why we need the semicolon before the word *however*. Why is there a comma after the word? Look at Rule #3. An introductory word in a sentence is followed by a comma.

### DIRECT ADDRESS

When someone is addressed directly at the beginning of a sentence, a comma follows the name.

**Micah, please feed the goldfish.**

If a person is addressed in the middle of the sentence, the name is surrounded by commas.

**I want you, Rosetta, to bake muffins for the sale.**

## CONSECUTIVE ADJECTIVES

If two or more adjectives can be separated by the word *and*, use commas.

**I found some comfortable, inexpensive shoes on sale.**

Could you say "comfortable and inexpensive shoes"? Yes. Therefore, you use commas.

**Nellie's yellow silk shirt was ruined in the wash.**

Could you say "yellow and silk shirt"? No. Therefore, no comma is used.

Another trick is to reverse the adjectives. Are these sentences correct?

**I found some inexpensive, comfortable shoes on sale.**

**Nellie's silk, yellow shirt was ruined in the wash. (This sentence sounds awkward.)**

## DATES, PLACES, AND NUMBERS

Commas are used to separate dates:

**Edgar arrived in New York on Thursday, November 9, 2006.**

If only a month and year are given, you do not need to use a comma:

**Edgar arrived in New York in November 2006.**

Use commas with addresses, but do NOT use commas before the zip code:

**Alma has an apartment at ABC Road, Sometown, Ohio 12345.**

A comma separates the city and state AND follows the state name in a sentence:

**She went to Aiken, South Carolina, to visit relatives.**

Commas are used for numbers greater than 999.

**The warehouse contained 3,765 boxes of cereal.**

## DIRECT QUOTATIONS

Commas set off the words inside quotation marks. Place a comma after the first words of a quotation if it is interrupted by the "attribution" (*Cara said*) or other words of explanation (*Niko wrote in her journal*).

**"I offered to help out," Cara said sadly, "but they didn't need me."**

**Samuel said, "I will meet you at the stadium in an hour."**

**"To learn to sing," Niko wrote in her journal, "is my first goal."**

Commas also follow the attribution or words of explanation when these words are at the beginning or in the middle of a sentence.

## Semicolons

Use a semicolon to join two closely related sentences. You do NOT need to use a coordinating or subordinating conjunction when you use a semicolon.

**When you write an essay, look at the question carefully; it is important to answer all the parts of the question.**

Semicolons are also used with conjunctive adverbs such as *however, moreover, therefore,* or *nevertheless* when the adverb separates two sentences.

**I have a very limited budget; therefore, I cannot go to the concert.**

When lists have a lot of commas, semicolons are used to separate the parts in order to make the sentence easier to read.

The menu at the restaurant featured chicken lasagna with extra cheese, a salad, and bread; sirloin steak with baked potato, green beans, and breadsticks; grilled tuna, steamed vegetables, and saffron rice; and a cheese plate with fruit.

## Colons

When an independent clause is followed by a list, use a colon to separate the clause and list.

The sports store sells many different products: skateboards, helmets, soccer balls, bikes, and running shoes.

Notice that the list itself has commas just as if it were an actual part of a sentence instead of a list.

Certain phrases give you a clue that a colon is required, such as: *the following* or *as follows*.

Colons are also used in formal letters. The salutation is followed by a colon.

Dear Senator Smith:

### COLONS AND QUOTATIONS

Colons are often used in dramas. A colon follows the name of the speaker.

BOB: I think we should ask Marcella about this box.

OMAR: Let's not bother her. Open it yourself.

Colons are also used to introduce long quotations.

Famed director Kiera Smith described her latest film to her adoring fans: "In this film, I have created a masterpiece. Never before have vegetables been used as characters to express the true feelings of vegetarians. I believe that my film sets a new standard for the industry in terms of imagination."

Finally, colons are used to set off an explanation or important information.

**Driving a golf ball on the range requires one important tactic: concentration.**

**I finally found what I'd been looking for: a reasonably priced computer.**

## Capitalization

Knowing when to capitalize a word is easy if you follow the rules.

Capitalize the first word in a sentence.

**Steak is his favorite food.**

**Miki said, "This book has beautiful illustrations."**

Capitalize proper nouns, that is, the names of specific people, places, and things (Tom, Texas, Spanish, Big Bend Park). This is often tested on the CAHSEE. A tricky part: Regions such as *the South* are capitalized, but directions are not.

**Ines has always wanted to live in the South.**

**Go south on 281 until you get to Theo Street.**

(To check if a word is a common noun that is not capitalized, put *a*, *an*, or *the* in front of it: *a house*, *the fish*.)

Capitalize titles Dr., Ms., Dad, Mom, or Uncle Charles. You would NOT capitalize a family title if it is preceded by a possessive word.

**I asked my mom if I could have a second piece of cake.**

**Like always, Mom said no.**

Capitalize the pronoun *I*, days of the week, names of the months, and holidays. Capitalize the first word AND important words in titles of books, movies, television programs, newspapers, stories, songs, essays, etc. Do NOT capitalize articles (*a, an, the*), coordinating conjunctions, or prepositions (*to, from, with, by,* etc.) unless that word is the first word in a sentence or title.

**Gary just finished reading *The Best Guide to Travel in the United States.***

## SUMMARY

You learned a lot in this chapter. Let's review the most important points:

- A sentence consists of a subject and a verb.
- A subordinating conjunction can make a sentence turn into a fragment.
- A fragment is an incomplete thought. You can fix a fragment in one of two ways:
  - by adding a subject or verb
  - by attaching it to the previous or following sentence
- A run-on sentence consists of two sentences with no punctuation or conjunction between.
- You can fix a run-on sentence in several ways:
  - by adding a comma and coordinating conjunction
  - by inserting a period
  - by inserting a semicolon
  - by inserting a semicolon and an adverbial connective followed by a comma
- A comma splice consists of two sentences joined by only a comma. To fix a comma splice, use one of these methods:
  - add a coordinating conjunction
  - remove the comma and add a subordinating conjunction
  - replace the comma with a semicolon
  - replace the comma with a semicolon and add an adverbial connective followed by a comma
- Sentences must use parallel:
  - items in a series
  - verb tenses
  - similar comparisons
  - parts of speech in correlative conjunctions
- Subjects and verbs MUST agree in both tense and number (singular or plural).
- Only pronouns in the subjective case (I, you, he, she, it, we, they) can be used as subjects.
- Only objective pronouns (me, you, him, her, it, us, them) can be used as objects.

- Possessive pronouns do NOT use apostrophes.
- Periods and commas go inside quotation marks; semicolons and colons go outside.
- Apostrophes are used to show possession and indicate a contraction.
- Commas are used:
  - with a coordinating conjunction to join two sentences
  - to separate extra information that is not vital to the sentence
  - to follow introductory words, phrases, or clauses
  - to separate items in a series
  - with a conjunctive adverb if it is simply an added word
  - to follow a conjunctive adverb (which has been preceded by a semicolon) to separate two sentences
  - to separate dates, places, and numbers
- Semicolons are used to:
  - separate closely related sentences
  - separate parts of a list that contain multiple, confusing commas
- Colons are used to:
  - separate a clause from a list
  - introduce long quotations
  - set off an important piece of information

# Chapter 4
# Writing Conventions Quiz

Read the following questions and select the best answer for each question.

1. Bradley is the best player on the <u>soccer team, and is</u> the leading scorer.

   A   soccer team; and is
   B   soccer team and is
   C   soccer team. And is
   D   Leave as is.

2. The orbit of Saturn around the Sun takes 25 <u>Earth years, it has</u> 56 moons.

   A   Earth years. It has
   B   Earth years: it has
   C   Earth years it has
   D   Leave as is.

3. Our dog has a <u>brown belly; however, his</u> fur is black.

   A   brown belly, however, his
   B   brown belly however; his
   C   brown belly; however his
   D   Leave as is.

4. <u>Despite her upbringing; Grandma</u> likes to eat with her fingers.

   A   Despite, her upbringing Grandma
   B   Despite her upbringing, Grandma
   C   Despite her upbringing Grandma
   D   Leave as is.

5. When my sister starts the first grade in the fall, <u>she will have been going to my school.</u>

   A   she will go to my school.
   B   she has been going to my school.
   C   she had been going to my school.
   D   Leave as is.

6. The doctor said that after I take a bath, <u>I have lied down to rest.</u>

   A   I have laid down to rest.
   B   I should lie down to rest.
   C   I should lay down to rest.
   D   Leave as is.

7. Whenever my father took us fishing, <u>he always stopped for ice cream on the way home.</u>

   A   he always stops for ice cream on the way home.
   B   he had always stopped for ice cream on the way home.
   C   he has been stopping for ice cream on the way home.
   D   Leave as is.

8. <u>When my parents go to Mexico</u>, it was their first vacation in ten years.

A  When my parents will go to Mexico
B  When my parents have gone to Mexico
C  When my parents went to Mexico
D  Leave as is.

9. Because he is in a rock band, we _____ that he likes loud music.

A  inferred
B  implied
C  infer
D  imply

10. My spaghetti sauce is as good as or _____ than hers.

A  better
B  best
C  greatest
D  greater

11. My mom told me that if I eat my peas and beans, I _____ have a banana split for dessert.

A  could
B  can
C  might
D  may

12. My cousins have to go to the barn in the mornings to see if the chickens have _____ any eggs.

A  lain
B  laid
C  lay
D  lied

13. Sherry told me to mind my own business, even though she said she didn't mind _____ questions about her job.

A  me
B  myself
C  my
D  I

14. Marcel tried to explain the rules to me as they were told to _____.

A  him
B  he
C  I
D  us

15. The teacher mandated that _____ ride the bus together to the play.

A  us
B  our
C  we
D  him

16. Although it doesn't thrill me, Shanice and _____ are going to the ballet tomorrow.

A  us
B  him
C  me
D  I

17. My mom said, "Grandma always told me, <u>'It is polite to serve others before serving yourself,' so that's why I fill my plate last."

A  "It is polite to serve others before serving yourself," so
B  'It is polite to serve others before serving yourself' so
C  "It is polite to serve others before serving yourself" so
D  Leave as is.

18. Meeting a movie star is a <u>once in-a-lifetime opportunity, and</u> I don't want to miss it.

A  once in a lifetime opportunity, and
B  once-in-a-lifetime opportunity, and
C  once in a lifetime-opportunity, and
D  Leave as is.

19. The speaker told the audience about her experiences <u>(she had traveled the world quite extensively.)</u> in Asia and South America.

A  (She had traveled the world quite extensively.)
B  (she had traveled the world quite extensively),
C  (she had traveled the world quite extensively)
D  Leave as is.

20. If no bears exist in the forest, <u>why would she say "watch out for bears".</u>

A  why would she say "watch out for bears?"
B  why would she say "watch out for bears"?
C  why would she say "watch out for bears."?
D  Leave as is.

# Answers and Explanations

## 1. B

Choice B is correct because the second clause is dependent on the first clause, so there would be no punctuation dividing them. Choice A is incorrect because the second clause cannot stand alone after the semicolon as an independent clause. Choice C is also incorrect for the same reason. As written, choice D, the comma is used incorrectly.

## 2. A

Choice A is correct because the second clause is a separate thought and complete sentence. The period is required for this distinction. Choice B is incorrect because a colon is used to indicate a list or series. Choice C results in a run-on sentence, which is the joining of two independent clauses without any punctuation. If a comma was going to be used, as in choice D, then a coordinating conjunction such as *and* is needed.

## 3. D

The sentence is correct as written, so choice D is correct. A semicolon separates the two independent clauses, and a comma comes after the introductory element *however*. Choice A is incorrect because closing punctuation is needed after *belly* before the sentence can move on to the second thought. Choice B is incorrect because *however* is part of the second clause, not the first clause. In choice C, a comma is needed after the introductory element.

### 4. B

The introductory phrase *Despite her upbringing* requires a comma to separate from the remainder of the sentence, so choice B is correct. Choice A places the comma in the wrong spot. *Despite* does not stand alone in this sentence as the introductory element. Furthermore, choice C requires punctuation because although it is part of the total meaning, the introductory phrase is modifying the independent clause *Grandma likes to eat with her fingers*. It is not an independent clause, as is written in the original sentence, choice D.

### 5. A

Choice A is the correct answer because it accurately describes when the action will take place, which in this case is the future, so the sentence uses the correct future tense. Choice B is incorrect because the action takes place in the future, but by using the present perfect tense *has been*, that action is incorrectly placed in the past. Choice C is incorrect because the action takes place in the future, but the phrase *had been* is in the past perfect tense and implies that the action was completed in the past. Choice D is incorrect because the phrase *will have been going* is in the future perfect tense and describes a future, ongoing action that is impossible to perform in this case.

### 6. B

The speaker is *going to take* a bath, so the ensuing action must also be in the progressive present tense. Choice B is the correct answer, because *lie* is used to describe an action toward yourself. Choice A describes an action that took place before the bath, which is not the desired meaning. Choice C uses the present tense *lay*, but *lay* is used to mean an action taken toward another object. You *lay* something down. Choice D, again, suggests action that took place in the past.

### 7. D

In this sentence, the father took them fishing, and afterward, he always did the same thing. The verb agreement in this sentence is in the past tense. Choice D, *leave as is*, is correct because *stopped* uses the past tense. Choice A is incorrect because it changes the tense in the second clause to the present tense. Choice B changes the tense to the past perfect, which describes an action that ended before another past action had started. Choice C changes the tense to the present perfect, which is opposite of what is desired.

## 8. C

The second clause in this sentence is speaking of the past, *it was their first. . .* Thus, the first clause must agree with this tense. Only choice C, *went to Mexico*, is correct because it describes a single event that already took place. Choice A describes a vacation the parents haven't taken yet and may not be planned. Choice B is set in the past, but the description is not specifically for one trip but possibly many. Only one trip can be their *first vacation in ten years*. Choice D describes a trip that will happen in the future.

## 9. C

To *infer* is to come to a belief based on evidence. To *imply* is to suggest or indicate something that has not been proven. The *because* expressed in the sentence assumed he liked loud music based on the fact that he was in a band that typically plays loud music. Thus, they *infer* this belief because of the evidence. Choice A is incorrect because the verb tense should be in the present tense.

## 10. A

This blank is looking for a word that means "of higher quality." This can be inferred from the phrase *as good as or*. If the sauce were the *best*, choice B, then the speaker wouldn't take the time to compare her sauce to the other with *as good*. *Greater* signifies a higher quantity, not quality; thus, choices C and D are incorrect. If the sauce surpasses being just *as good as* the other, then it is *better*, choice A.

## 11. D

The difference between *can* and *may* lies in ability. *Can* means that something or someone is able to complete an action. *May* means that someone is allowed to do something. In this sentence, the speaker will be allowed to have a banana split if she eats her peas and beans. Thus, *may*, choice D, is the correct choice. The speaker is able to have a banana split, but her mom

CAHSEE ENGLISH-LANGUAGE ARTS

might not let her. *Could* and *might* both bring an element of question to the action, which is not the intended meaning.

## 12. B

A person lies down. But, a person lays an object down. The chickens *lay* eggs, but in this question we are looking for the present perfect tense *have laid*, which is choice B. Choice A is the past perfect for lie. Choice C is present tense *lay*, and choice D is past tense for the word *lie*, as in being dishonest.

## 13. C

Choice C is correct because the word *my* shows ownership of the questions. Choice A is incorrect because *me* is a noun, not a possessive adjective. Choices B and D don't make sense in the sentence.

## 14. A

Someone told the rules to Marcel, or someone told *him* the rules, so choice A is correct. He wouldn't have had the rules told to *he*, choice B. The speaker *I* (choice C) was not there the first time, so *us* (choice D) is also eliminated.

## 15. C

The correct answer is C because *we* is the subject of the dependent clause. Choice A is incorrect because *us* is the object of a verb, not a subject pronoun. Choice B is incorrect because *our* shows possession of something. Choice D is incorrect because the teacher is addressing a group, not a single person.

## 16. D

Choice D is correct because *I* is a subject pronoun and can work as the subject of the sentence. Choice A is incorrect because *us* is a pronoun that receives the action of the verb; it is not a subject pronoun. Choice B is incorrect because the sentence refers to *me* and requires a first-person pronoun, not a third-person pronoun. Choice C is incorrect because *me* cannot be the subject, only the object of a verb or preposition.

**17. D**

When a quote is used inside another quote, single quotation marks are used. In the sentence provided, the mother is providing a quote from Grandma. The single quotation marks are used correctly. There is also a comma after Grandma's quote to set off the independent clause that follows.

**18. B**

The phrase *once in a lifetime* is being used to modify *opportunity* in this sentence. Thus, it is hyphenated as a compound adjective, so choice B is correct. All of the other choices misuse the hyphens or leave them out altogether.

**19. C**

When an independent clause is used in parentheses, it is capitalized and punctuated only if it stands alone outside another sentence. However, if it is contained inside another sentence, the punctuation and capitalized first word are left out, so choice C is correct. Choice B punctuates the sentence appropriately, but the added comma after the parentheses is not needed because the rest of the sentence is a dependent clause.

**20. B**

The phrase *watch out for bears* is a quoted statement within a sentence that asks a question. However, the quoted statement is not a question in itself, so the question mark should go outside the quotes, which means answer choice B is correct. Choice A is incorrect because the quoted statement is incorrectly punctuated as a question. In choice C, the period is not necessary after the quoted phrase. Choice D is incorrect because the sentence is not a statement, it is a question.

Chapter 5
# Writing Strategies

## HOW TO WRITE STRATEGICALLY

When you reread your writing, do you often change words, move sentences, and rewrite paragraphs? Well-written essays have many things in common, such as a controlling thesis, supporting details, precise language, and an active voice—basic writing strategies that make essays clearer, easier to understand, and more effective.

The Writing section of the CAHSEE will ask you to write an essay, but it will also ask you to read passages and make choices about how to strengthen the writing. In this chapter, you will learn how to apply these writing strategies to passages similar to what you will see on the test.

Although this chapter focuses on helping you strengthen other people's writing, you should also keep these writing strategies in mind when you work on your own essays.

Use our systematic approach to focus on the questions and the points.

## Kaplan's 3-Step Method for Writing Strategies Questions

**Step 1:** Read the passage.
**Step 2:** Read each question and answer choice carefully.
**Step 3:** Eliminate the answers you know won't work.

Let's examine Kaplan's 3-Step Method for Writing Questions in more depth.

**Step 1: Read the passage.**

Look for areas where the writing could be improved. Perhaps a paragraph has two main topics. Can you split the paragraph into two paragraphs? Are there enough supporting details for two paragraphs? Make notes next to the writing about improvements you would make.

**Step 2: Read each question and answer choice carefully.**

You will most likely need to refer back to the passage to determine which answer fits best.

**Step 3: Eliminate the answers you know won't work.**

Cross out those options and concentrate on determining which of the remaining answers is correct.

## MAIN IDEA AND THESIS

The first paragraph of an essay is called an **introduction**. It usually grabs the reader's attention and introduces the topic of the essay. The most important part of an introduction is the thesis. The **thesis** is the sentence that provides the main idea of the essay and the writer's perspective on the topic.

John was a brilliant singer who also wrote lyrics about social consciousness themes.

This sample thesis tells you the main idea, but it also explains what perspective on the topic the author will develop:

- Main idea: The essay will focus on songwriter John.
- Perspective on the topic: John has a social conscience that he expresses through his music.

In traditional five-paragraph essays, the thesis sentence is usually the last sentence of the first paragraph. However, the CAHSEE sample passages are generally just a few paragraphs long, so the thesis can usually be found in the first sentence of the passage.

Some questions on the CAHSEE will ask you to choose the best thesis or topic sentence for a passage from a list of four choices. In order to do that, you may want to ask yourself the following questions:

- Which sentence establishes the main idea of the passage?
- Which sentence explains the author's perspective on the main idea?
- Does this sentence express the main idea of a single paragraph or the entire essay?
- Does this sentence state a specific main idea?

Read the following passage to answer a main idea question.

# Esperanto

(1) While most languages were developed from people speaking in a common way for hundreds of years and then writing the language down over time, Esperanto was created on purpose. (2) A polish man, named Dr. Ludovic Lazarus Zamenhof, developed the language in the 1870s and 1880s  in order to create a language that people across the world could use to communicate. (3) Although Esperanto is more popular in some parts of the world than others, it is now spoken by almost two million people across the globe.

(4) Esperanto has helped bridge cultural divisions between people from different countries. (5) Many journal articles, pieces of literature, and political essays have been written in Esperanto so that people from different countries can read and then discuss the ideas. (6) The language has also been used for radio broadcasts in order to make the programs available to a wider audience. (7) Esperanto has also been used in wartime as a way to communicate with people who don't speak a common language. (8) While the language is not that popular in the United States, many members of the armed forces can speak it in order to get information about their enemies.

(9) Esperanto has a set vocabulary with specific rules that allow new words to be introduced into the language in a way that people will understand. (10) When the language started, there were 900 vocabulary words and countless prefixes and suffixes. (11) The

prefixes and suffixes all follow regular rules and can be used to introduce new words into the language. (12) For example, the word for *computer* had to be added to the language because computers were not around in the late 1800s.

(13) With only two million speakers, Esperanto is not the best option for an international language. (14) Maybe Chinese will one day be the international language because it has the most native speakers worldwide.

**Which sentence would BEST begin the essay?**

**A**  This paper is about a new language.

**B**  Esperanto is a language used by people fighting in modern warfare.

**C**  Esperanto is an invented language that has helped bridge cultural and language barriers for 150 years.

**D**  There are a lot of interesting things about Esperanto.

Although the question stem does not specifically ask for it, this question is asking you to identify a good thesis for the passage. A thesis presents the topic and the author's perspective on the topic. Choice A does not give enough detail about the topic of the passage. Choice B is a supporting detail, and choice D is too general to be a thesis statement. The best answer is choice **C** because it provides a detailed description of the topic as well as a perspective on the topic.

## Topic Sentence

In addition to the thesis sentence, well-written essays also have a **topic sentence** in each paragraph. This sentence states the main idea of the paragraph. The rest of the sentences in the paragraph should provide the supporting details for that topic.

The topic sentence is usually the first sentence of a paragraph. Each topic sentence should support the thesis of the essay in order to ensure that the author includes only details that are related to the topic in the essay.

The CAHSEE may ask you to identify appropriate topic sentences for individual paragraphs within in the passage. Questions may also ask you to identify a sentence that does not belong in a particular paragraph because it does not relate to the topic sentence.

Use the passage "Esperanto" to answer the main idea question that follows.

**Which of the following sentences, if inserted before sentence 9, would make the MOST effective opening sentence for paragraph 3?**

**A**   There are 26 letters in the Esperanto alphabet.

**B**   Esperanto has specific rules to make the language easy to learn and understand.

**C**   Esperanto is easy to type.

**D**   There are a lot of difficult grammar rules for Esperanto.

This question is asking you to identify a good topic sentence for paragraph 3. Choices A and C are supporting details for the paragraph. Choice D reads like a topic sentence, but it is the opposite of the main idea that the details in paragraph 3 are trying to present. Choice **B** is the best answer because it provides a topic that all of the sentences in the paragraph can support.

## SUPPORTING EVIDENCE

Although the main idea is a key component of an essay, an essay is only as strong as its supporting evidence. **Supporting evidence** includes the facts and details that are used to develop and explain the main ideas.

**Facts**, statements that can be proven true, are powerful pieces of supporting evidence because they can be used by a reader who wishes to do further investigation. But there are other kinds of supporting evidence that can provide effective proof of a main idea.

Examine the following chart for examples.

| Supporting Evidence | Definition | Example |
| --- | --- | --- |
| commonly held beliefs | ideas accepted to be true by a large group of people | The Internet has changed the way people communicate. |

| Supporting Evidence | Definition | Example |
|---|---|---|
| definitions | explanations of terms and concepts | A computer network is two or more computers connected together in order to communicate and share resources. |
| examples | specific instances illustrating a main idea | Many college classes are already offered online. In these classes, students communicate with each other and their instructors via email, live chats, and video. |
| hypotheses | ideas or theories that are being investigated in order to find proof of their truth | The Internet will provide a venue for online collaboration so that future students will be learning from a variety of experts in every field. |
| scenarios | descriptions of events that are *likely* to happen at some point in the future | Medical students living in different parts of the world will use the same computer networks to observe a complicated brain surgery and learn from the best doctor in the field, even if the doctor is thousands of miles away. |

The CAHSEE will probably not ask you to identify the different kinds of supporting evidence presented in a passage. But it will ask you to identify which pieces of supporting evidence are relevant to a paragraph. In these scenarios, you need to identify the main idea on your own and then the supporting evidence that relates to the main idea.

The test will also ask you to identify which pieces of evidence most strongly support the main idea, and which main idea is best supported by the evidence provided.

Let's look at some sample questions. Use the examples from the chart to answer the following question.

**Which of the following ideas is supported by the details or evidence in the example column of the chart?**

**A**   The Internet allows friends across the country to talk to each other.

**B**   The Internet will not affect education.

**C**   Computer networks will improve education by allowing students to communicate with experts in every field.

**D**   Everyone should have access to the Internet.

This question is asking you to generate a main idea for a list of supporting evidence. You need to read and assess all of the evidence presented in order to identify the best topic sentence. Once you settle on your choice, you should reread each piece of evidence to make sure that it offers support for the main idea.

Although the evidence talks about communication online, two of the pieces of evidence specifically mention positive effects of Internet communication on education, so choices A and B are not the best options. Choice D is a general statement that could be supported by the evidence, but choice **C** provides a main idea and a perspective that is supported by all five pieces of evidence.

Reread "Esperanto" to answer the question below.

**Which sentence would BEST conclude the passage?**

**A**   Perhaps someone will invent an even easier and more universal language that will be more popular than its predecessor.

**B**   Chinese is difficult for everyone in the world to learn.

**C**   Esperanto should have been advertised better.

**D**   An international language is not important.

This question is asking you to provide a piece of evidence to support the main idea of the last paragraph in the passage. The topic sentence is sentence 13: *With only two million speakers, Esperanto is not the best option for an international language.*

Choice B provides evidence that supports sentence 14, but it would not support the topic sentence of the paragraph. Choices C and D are opinions and do not offer concrete evidence to support the main idea. Choice **A** is a scenario that suggests that a new universal language might be developed, so it is the best answer.

Read the following paragraph to answer the question that follows.

(1) Esperanto has helped bridge cultural divisions between people from different countries. (2) Many journal articles, pieces of literature, and political essays have been written in Esperanto so that people from different countries can read and then discuss the ideas. (3) The language has also been used for radio broadcasts in order to make the programs available to a wider audience. (4) Esperanto has also been used in wartime as a way to communicate with people who don't speak a common language. (5) Pig Latin is another language that kids use to keep secrets.

**Which sentence is NOT related to the main idea of the paragraph?**

**A**  sentence 2
**B**  sentence 3
**C**  sentence 4
**D**  sentence 5

This question is asking you to identify the piece of supporting evidence that is not relevant, or related, to the main idea of the paragraph. The main idea is sentence 1. All of the sentences provide evidence that supports the idea that Esperanto has helped bridge cultural divides except sentence 5. Choice **D** talks about an unrelated language, so it does not provide supporting evidence for the paragraph.

## WORD CHOICE

Presenting a main idea and offering relevant supporting details are important strategies for getting across *what* an author is trying to say. But *how* the author communicates those ideas is equally important. **Word choice** refers to the decisions that an author makes about how to state an idea to most effectively explain the thesis.

### Precise Language

Authors need to use clear and precise language in order to help the reader understand the topic. **Precise language** is language that specifically tells the reader about a subject by using vivid, concrete details or physical images. Which sentence is clearer?

**A: Watch out for that over there.**

**B: Be careful of that murky puddle on the sidewalk three feet in front of you.**

The second sentence uses precise language to describe *what* to be careful of and *where* to look out for it. Precise language is most useful to express an author's main idea. Precise language uses details instead of words such as *that, those, them,* and *there.*

Read the following paragraph and answer the questions that follow.

Clara Barton was a (1) <u>nice</u> woman who bravely risked her life in the American Civil War. In the early months of the Civil War, Ms. Barton collected (2) <u>stuff</u> to distribute to the wounded soldiers on the battlefield. But she didn't stop there. Ms. Barton was one of the few women who entered the battlefield in order to help her countrymen. She personally delivered the medical supplies and then immediately started to help the wounded soldiers. She did not stop her service even when she was almost hit by a bullet. In fact, she left the field only when she was stricken by typhoid fever. Even after her bout with typhoid, she returned to the battlefield to supply first aid to soldiers on both sides of the war.

**In order to achieve a more precise meaning, the underlined word labeled (2) could be changed to—**

A    supplies.

B    medical supplies.

C    bags.

D    equipment.

This question is asking you to provide a more specific description of what Clara Barton distributed to the soldiers in the Civil War by making the language more precise. In choice C, the word *bags* is just as vague as *stuff* and does not provide a vivid description of what Ms. Barton delivered. *Supplies* and *equipment* in choices A and D provide slightly more detail, but they are general and might include anything from food to weapons to music. You know from the context of the paragraph that Barton delivered medical supplies, so choice **B** is the most precise description.

**To more accurately describe the type of woman that Clara Barton was, the underlined word labeled (1) could be changed to—**

A    brave.

B    courageous.

C    happy.

D    shy.

To provide a more precise description of Clara Barton, you need to read the whole paragraph first. Though *brave* would be an accurate description of Ms. Barton, the word *bravely* already appears in sentence one. The words *happy* and *shy* do not provide an accurate or vivid description of her. So choice **B**, *courageous*, is the best answer because it describes her bravery without using the same word twice in the sentence.

## Sensory Details

Have you ever read an essay that put you to sleep? Even if essays have clear main ideas and supporting details, they can fail to deliver the message to the reader because their word choice is so dry. To express the ideas effectively, an author also needs to keep a reader interested.

One of the ways writers can captivate their audience is to use sensory details. **Sensory details** are details that make the reader feel like part of the action by appealing to the five senses—taste, touch, smell, sight, and sound.

**Which sentence is more captivating to the reader?**

**A: The coffee was bad.**

**B: The scalding coffee burnt my tongue and left a bitter taste in my mouth.**

While both sentences describe a bad cup of coffee, the second sentence uses sensory details to make the reader participate in how bad the coffee is. Sentence B appeals to the reader's sense of touch with the words *scalding* and *burnt*. It also appeals to the reader's sense of taste with the word *bitter*. Sensory details offer a way to engage the readers by making them feel as if they are part of the action by participating in the descriptions.

The CAHSEE may ask you to revise sentences by adding more sensory details to make them more interesting and vivid to the reader.

## Appropriate Modifiers

Word choice not only makes an essay livelier, but also helps an author more accurately describe the events.

**Modifiers** are adjectives, adverbs, and prepositional phrases that help an author add description to a work. Let's examine some modifiers and how they work.

### ADJECTIVES
**Adjectives** are words that describe people, places, or things.

The following italicized words describe a person, place, and thing:

*talented* woman

*bustling* Main Street

*heavy* textbook

## ADVERBS

An **adverb** is a word that describes an action by explaining how it was done. Adverbs usually end with the letters *-ly*.

The following italicized words are adverbs describing *how* actions were done.

ran *quickly*

worked *efficiently*

hurt *badly*

## PREPOSITIONAL PHRASES

**Prepositional phrases** describe where something is in relation to something else.

The following italicized words are prepositional phrases describing the location of an object or person.

She was *in the back of the line.*

The bicycles were *loaded on top of the car.*

He sat *beside the girl he knows.*

You will probably not be asked to identify a particular kind of modifier on the test. But questions on the CAHSEE may ask you rewrite a sentence by adding an appropriate modifier. This type of question is similar to adding sensory details.

**What is the BEST way to rewrite the following sentence?**

> Clara Barton worked to heal soldiers.

**A**   Clara Barton worked devotedly to heal soldiers.
**B**   Clara Barton worked hard.
**C**   Clara Barton worked devotedly to heal wounded soldiers.
**D**   Clara Barton worked a lot.

Choices A and **C** both add modifiers to make the sentence more descriptive. But choice **C** adds an adverb to describe how Clara worked as well as an adjective to describe the soldiers. So choice **C** adds the most clarity and description to the sentence.

Other questions may ask you to correct the modifier. In questions like this, you first need to identify what kind of modifier is being used and then revise the sentence in order to use it appropriately.

**What is the BEST way to rewrite the following sentence?**

> The badly soldier was hurt.

**A**   The soldier badly, was hurt.
**B**   Badly, the soldier was hurt.
**C**   The soldier was hurt.
**D**   The soldier was hurt badly.

In the original sentence, the adverb *badly* is incorrectly modifying a noun. Adverbs describe an action and modify a verb. Adjectives modify a noun. In order to rewrite the sentence, you need to correct the adverb. Choices A and B still use the adverb incorrectly, so they should be eliminated. While choice C is technically correct, it eliminates the modifier altogether, making the sentence drier. The best choice is **D**, which makes the adverb *badly* modify the verb *hurt*.

## THE ACTIVE VOICE

What is the difference between active people and passive people? Active people are always in motion and taking charge of a situation, while passive people are usually calmer and wait for things to happen to them. There are also active and passive personalities in writing. This personality affects the strength and the clarity of an essay.

Sentences can either be written in the active voice or the passive voice. The active voice is generally considered to be the strongest, most concise way to state an idea. The **active voice** in a sentence is when the subject of the sentence is performing the action.

**Clara Barton protected the country's soldiers.**

The **passive voice** in a sentence is when the subject of the sentence is receiving the action.

**The country's soldiers were protected by Clara Barton.**

*Clara Barton* is the subject is both sentences. The subject in the first sentence is the most prominent part of the sentence because it is taking an active role in the action of the sentence. In the second example, the subject is not stressed because it takes a backseat to the action.

If it is difficult for you to identify the subject and object of a sentence, there are other clues to the passive voice.

- Sentences in the passive voice always use forms of the verb *to be* such as *am, are, was, were, be, being,* or *been.* In the passive voice example, the verb *were* is a form of the verb *to be* and signals the passive voice.
- Sentences in the passive voice frequently use the word *by* to name the subject doing the action.

On the CAHSEE, you will most likely be asked to identify a sentence in passive voice and rewrite it in the active voice. Let's look at some sample questions.

**Which revision of the following sentence uses ONLY the active voice?**

> The new technique for dressing wounds that Clara Barton found was something that she stumbled upon.

A The technique that Clara was using was discovered by accident.

B Clara Barton invented a new way of dressing wounds.

C Dressing wounds in a new way was Clara's discovery.

D With the new invention of dressing wounds, something new was Clara's claim to fame.

Sentences in the passive voice do not emphasize the subject of the sentence, which is Clara Barton. The only sentence that emphasizes the subject is choice **B**. You can also tell that choice **B** is the best answer because the other choices have the two telltale signs of the passive voice: the verb *was* and the word *by*.

**Which is the BEST way to state the action in the sentence?**

> The soothing rhythm of her work on the field was broken only by the soldiers' cries of pain.

A On the field, her soothing rhythm of work was broken only by the soldiers' cries of pain.

B Her rhythm of work, which was soothing, was broken only by the soldiers' cries of pain.

C Soothing on the field, her rhythm was broken only by the soldiers' cries of pain.

D Only the soldiers' cries of pain broke the soothing rhythm of her work on the field.

This question is asking you to revise a sentence written in the passive voice into the active voice. In order to identify the only sentence in the active voice, you need to identify the signs of the passive voice. Choices A, B, and C all use the verb *to be* and the word *by*, so the only correct option is choice D. If you cannot identify the signs of the passive voice, you should try to read the sentences aloud. The sentence in choice **D** is the most clear and concise option.

## COMBINING SENTENCES

Short, stubby sentences or long, rambling sentences can also cause a reader to lose interest in the essay and miss the main idea. Sentence combining is one way to spice up an essay and help the reader focus on the main idea rather than on the word choice and structure of the essay.

### When to Combine Sentences

You should combine sentences when the essay or paragraph consists of simple, short sentences of the same pattern.

**The boy fell down. The boy needed an X-ray. He went to the doctor. The X-ray showed a fracture. The doctor gave the boy a cast.**

You should combine sentences that contain the same subject or the same verb.

**The doctor examined the patient. The doctor diagnosed the patient with fatigue.**

You can combine sentences that contain ideas of equal importance.

**The championship game unified the city. The game also demonstrated people's ability to work together.**

### HOW TO COMBINE SIMPLE SENTENCES

Combine the sentences by leaving out the repeated subject. Combine the sentences by leaving out the repeated subjects and verbs and by using adjectives or adverbs.

**Original: The boy fell down. The boy needed an X-ray.**

**Revised: The boy fell down and needed an X-ray.**

To combine these two sentences, you can leave out the second *the boy* and connect the two ideas with the word *and*.

**Original: Juanita was a sophomore. Juanita was dedicated to school. Juanita worked hard.**
**Revised: Juanita was a dedicated and hardworking sophomore.**

To combine these two simple sentences, you can leave out the repeated subject *Juanita* and the repeated verb *was*; then, include the adjectives *hardworking* and *dedicated* to convey the information of the other sentences.

## Coordinating Conjunctions

To combine sentences with ideas of equal importance, you can use **coordinating conjunctions**.

Each coordinating conjunction serves a different purpose. Examine the following chart to understand the ways to use each conjunction.

| Conjunction | Purpose | Example |
|---|---|---|
| and | connects two similar ideas | I like ice cream **and** pie. |
| but | connects two opposite ideas | Jose likes chocolate ice cream, **but** Vanessa likes vanilla ice cream. |
| so | demonstrates that the second idea is the result of the first idea | Samantha was hungry, **so** she cooked a big breakfast. |
| nor | demonstrates the addition of a negative point | Leo does not eat meat, **nor** does he eat fish. |

| or | Connects two inter-changeable ideas | We could go to the Italian restaurant, **or** we could try that new Chinese one. |
| yet | demonstrates contrast | Jessica is a vegetarian, **yet** she is not a vegan. |

In order to combine sentences with coordinating conjunctions correctly, use the following guidelines:

- Make sure each phrase is a complete thought.
- Put the conjunction in the middle of the sentence.
- Insert a comma before the conjunction when you have independent clauses.

Read the following paragraph and answer the question.

(1) Ladybugs are small bugs. (2) They are usually red, orange, or yellow. (3) They have black spots. (4) There are more than 5,000 species of ladybugs in the world. (5) They are all a type of beetle.

**What is the BEST way to combine sentences 4 and 5?**

A    There are more than 5,000 species of ladybugs and they are all a type of beetle.

B    There are more than 5,000 species of ladybugs, but they are all a type of beetle.

C    So there are more than 5,000 species of ladybugs, they are all a type of beetle.

D    There are more than 5,000 species of ladybugs, and they are all a type of beetle.

This question is asking you to combine two sentences of similar importance. In this case, you'll need to add a coordinating conjunction. Choice C is incorrect because its coordinating conjunction is at the beginning of the sentence rather than in the middle. The coordinating conjunction in choice B changes the meaning of the sentence. Choice A uses an appropriate coordinating conjunction, but excludes a comma. Therefore, the correct answer is choice **D**.

If you had difficulty identifying the correct way to combine these sentences, you may want to study the coordinating conjunctions chart and memorize each conjunction's purpose. You may also want to memorize the three rules of using coordinating conjunctions.

## SYNTHESIZING INFORMATION

In order to write an essay, authors need to research their topic, which involves much more than simply looking up a subject on the Internet and copying the information into essay form.

Research for an essay should come from a variety of sources because each source offers a different perspective on the topic. The writer's job is then to synthesize the information into an integrated essay that explains the topic and provides a unique angle. A writer must also be able to read documents and determine whether the information from the source is credible.

Types of sources vary, each offering information for different purposes. Examine the following chart for information about various sources, as well as their pros and cons.

| Source | Description | Benefits | Downfalls |
|---|---|---|---|
| autobiography | a story of a person's life recounted in his or her own words | firsthand information; opinions and feelings | facts may be distorted by memory or desire to cast a viewpoint on a topic |
| biography | an account of a person's life written by someone else | comprehensive information on the life and times of a person | no information on the person's mindset |
| encyclopedia | a book of articles on various topics | general and accurate information on a variety of topics | lacks in-depth detail because space is limited |

| Internet | a global system of information accessed by personal computers | a large quantity of information on almost every topic; personal and easily updated information | sometimes inaccurate because not sufficiently documented |
| --- | --- | --- | --- |
| journal | a periodical text in which researchers publish the results of their studies | specific facts, data, and details about a particular topic | details can be overwhelming and hard to get through |
| speech | a formal address delivered to a live audience and often published in print | details and often opinions on a specific topic | facts can be slanted to support an argument |
| textbook | a book used for its authority on a particular topic | definitive resource for a particular topic; accompanying graphics | information on topics related to only one subject |

For the test, you will need to know how to research and synthesize information effectively, but the CAHSEE will not ask you to research information. It may ask you where you might find appropriate information to support a main idea or enhance a passage.

Let's look at some sample questions.

**What source is BEST for finding out what happens when you mix sodium and carbon?**

A    an encyclopedia entry on the periodic table of elements

B    a chemistry textbook

C    a biography of a famous chemist

D    a journal article about carbon monoxide

This question is asking you to identify the BEST source for a piece of information. To answer this question, you need to know that sodium and carbon are elements in the periodic table, which is part of chemistry. While choices A and D might have some discussion on each of the elements, they probably wouldn't specifically address the question. Choice C would probably not offer any information about the two elements. Choice **B** is the best answer because it would most likely offer information about both of the elements, as well as what happens when you mix them.

## REVISING FOR AUDIENCE, PURPOSE, AND ORGANIZATION

The Writing Strategies strand of the Writing section of the CAHSEE measures your ability to make a passage stronger and more effective. In addition to the specific strategies such as a thesis, supporting details, and word choice, there are general concepts that you should look for in the revision process.

These broader concepts will help you focus on the audience, logic, and purpose of the writing in order to present a skillful and respectable essay. The Writing Strategies strand of the test will ask you to apply these strategies in order to strengthen the passages you read.

### Audience and Formality

The **audience** of a composition is the people who will read the work. Each piece of writing should have a targeted audience. If the audience is professional, the author's tone and word choice should be formal to reflect the education and needs of the audience.

For example, the audience of a textbook is generally students. The audience for a persuasive essay about the construction of a new town pool is the people who live in the town.

To tailor the composition to the audience, writers should follow several guidelines:

- Use an appropriate tone for the intended audience.
- Use appropriate vocabulary for the intended audience.
- Include relevant graphics and examples for the intended audience.

For example, an excerpt from a fourth-grade history textbook should use a serious tone, simple language, and concrete maps and examples. However, an article for a weekly entertainment magazine should have a lighthearted tone, vibrant word choice, and a lot of pictures.

## Purpose

In addition to paying close attention to their intended audience, writers also need to tailor their writing to their purpose. As discussed in Chapter 3, the author's purpose is his or her goal for the text.

For example, if authors want to entertain the reader, they need to include vibrant words, vivid descriptions, and write in a humorous tone. On the other hand, if writers wish to inform, they need to included concrete examples and definitions, and write in a serious and easy-to-understand tone.

Questions on the test may ask you to revise an author's word choice or supporting details in order to make the passage fit better with the author's purpose or intended audience. To answer these questions, you should first identify the audience and the purpose.

In the directions, passages will often imply the audience and purpose of the composition. For instance, "Read this passage from a high school chemistry textbook and answer the questions that follow." In this case, you would know that the purpose of the passage is to inform and the intended audience is high school students.

However, you can also identify the purpose and intended audience by asking yourself questions about the essay.

- Is the essay attempting to entertain? What words and tone would be relevant?
- What did I learn from this essay? How does the tone reflect the information being offered?
- Is the essay trying to persuade me to do something? What type of vocabulary is appropriate?

## Organization

In the final revision process, writers should also examine their essays for logic, coherence, and organization. When revising for organization, look for the following things:

- Does the essay present a clear thesis?
- Do the main ideas of each paragraph support the thesis?
- Are all of the details relevant to the main idea?
- Do the ideas flow logically?
- Does the essay make sense?
- 

The Writing Strategies strand of the test will not ask you to rewrite the draft or move paragraphs, but it may ask you to identify details that do not belong or to reorder paragraphs.

Let's examine some sample questions. Read this excerpt from a passage and answer the questions that follow.

(1) Okapis are magnificent mammals that come from the Ituri Rain Forest in Africa. (2) They are striking with chocolate-brown coats and zebra-striped legs. (3) The okapis' unique coat served as excellent camouflage from their predators, but it also <u>kept away the scientists</u>. (4) They were not discovered until the early 1900s. (5) Okapis also have a long, sticky, blue tongue that is similar to a giraffe's tongue and useful for eating leaves, grass, ferns, and buds.

(6) Although okapis resemble zebras, they are most closely related to giraffes. (7) They are much shorter than their cousins, but they have a long neck and similar facial features to giraffes.

**Which is the MOST effective substitution for the underlined part of sentence 3?**

**A**   made them difficult for scientists to discover
**B**   helped them lose the scientists on their trail
**C**   helped them hide out
**D**   made them seem made-up

This question is asking you to revise the word choice in sentence 3 by considering the purpose and the audience of the essay. Although you don't know the exact audience of the essay, its purpose is most likely to inform the reader about okapis.  Most informational essays use a formal tone.  The only choice that offers a more formal revision of the original sentence is choice **A**.

**Where would sentence 5 fit better?**

A    before sentence 2

B    after sentence 7

C    after sentence 2

D    before sentence 1

This question is asking you to revise the essay for coherence and logic.  Sentence 5 is a detail that supports the idea that okapis are closely related to giraffes.  Paragraph 2 deals with the relationship between okapis and giraffes.  The only choice that places sentence 5 in paragraph 2 is choice **B**.

## SUMMARY

You learned a lot in this chapter. Let's review the most important points.

- Writing strategies strengthen an essay by providing focus.
- The thesis is the sentence that provides the main idea of the essay and the writer's perspective on the topic.
- The topic sentence states the main idea of a paragraph.
    - Topic sentences should directly support the thesis of the essay.
- Supporting evidence is the facts and details used to develop and explain the main ideas.
    - Supporting evidence can be facts, commonly held beliefs, definitions, examples, hypotheses, or scenarios.
    - The test will not ask you to identify the different kinds of supporting evidence presented in a passage, but it might ask you to identify which pieces of supporting evidence are relevant to a paragraph.
- Authors use relevant and specific word choice to present their ideas.
    - Authors should use precise language that offers vivid, concrete details or physical images.
    - Sensory details are details that make readers feel as if they are part of the action by appealing to the five senses—taste, touch, smell, sight, and sound.
    - Modifiers are adjectives, adverbs, and prepositional phrases that help authors add description to their writing.
    - An adjective is a word that describes a person, place, or thing.
    - An adverb is a word that describes an action by explaining how it was done. Adverbs usually end in the letters -ly.
    - A prepositional phrase describes where something is in relation to something else.
- The active voice in a sentence is when the subject of the sentence is performing the action.
- The passive voice in a sentence is when the subject of the sentence is receiving the action.
    - Sentences in the passive voice always use forms of the verb *to be*, such as *am, are, was, were, be, being,* or *been.*

- o Sentences in the passive voice frequently use the word *by* to name the subject doing the action.
- You should combine sentences when the essay or paragraph consists of simple, short sentences of the same pattern AND combine sentences that contain the same subject or the same verb. You can also combine sentences that contain ideas of equal importance.
  - o Combine sentences by leaving out the repeated subject.
  - o Combine sentences by leaving out the repeated subjects and verbs and by using adjectives or adverbs.
- To combine sentences with ideas of equal importance, you can use coordinating conjunctions such as *and, but, so, nor, or,* and *yet.*
  - o Make sure each phrase is a complete thought.
  - o Put the conjunction in the middle of the sentence.
  - o Insert a comma before the conjunction when combining independent clauses
- Research for an essay should come from a variety of sources. Each source offers different perspectives on the topic, and the writer must synthesize the information into an integrated essay that explains the topic and provides a unique angle.
- The audience of a composition is the people who will read the work.
- The author's purpose is a writer's goal for the text.
- In the final revision process, writers should examine their essays for logic, coherence, and organization.

# Chapter 5
# Writing Strategies Quiz

The following passage is a rough draft. It may contain errors in grammar, punctuation, sentence structure, or organization. Read the passage and answer questions 1 through 4.

(1) Fluorine, chlorine, bromine, and iodine are chemicals that lack only one electron in their outer shells. Thus, they are never found free in nature. (2) Instead, because they have a natural <u>inclination</u> toward forming compounds (such as sodium chloride, known as table salt), they are called halogens. (3) Chlorine ions are essential to the body for several bodily functions. (4) In fact, without it, people would die because certain organs would fail to function. (5) Iodine is necessary for the thyroid gland to function correctly.

(6) Fluorine, found in its various forms in toothpaste and in fluorinated water, works against tooth decay. (7) Water supplies throughout the country are cleaned with chlorine. (8) Chlorine is used in swimming pools as a way to kill the bacteria that enter into the pool. (9) It is also used in washing machines to clean what people call their "whites." (10) Bromine, seen most often in its silver salt form, is used in photographic processes. (11) A silver halide emulsion covers photographic film. (12) When that film is exposed to light, the areas that receive the most light will have the densest concentration of metallic silver. (13) A negative of a picture is produced. (14) From this, a print reflecting the opposite is made.

(15) The negative side of halogens cause them to be understandably feared. (16) They are an integral part of many toxic compounds. (17) Dioxins and chlorofluorocarbons, used in refrigeration and the rocket sciences, are now known to be a major contributor to the depletion of the ozone layer. (18) In addition, when people have been directly exposed to them, illnesses—and, in some cases, deaths—have occurred.

1. Where would be the BEST place to break paragraph 2 into two paragraphs?

   A   between sentences labeled as 7 and 8
   B   between sentences labeled as 8 and 9
   C   between sentences labeled as 9 and 10
   D   between sentences labeled as 11 and 12

2. Where would one MOST likely find this type of passage?

   A   in a college admissions guide
   B   in a college catalog
   C   in the preface to a college-level textbook
   D   in an article in a science magazine

3. Which word be low can be replaced with the underlined word in the passage and retain its meaning?

   A   taste
   B   tendency
   C   incline
   D   decline

4. If you were going to add a concluding sentence after the current one, which of the following would be the BEST sentence?

   A   Therefore, halogens are dangerous and should be banned.
   B   The government should regulate the use of the more dangerous compounds.
   C   Most halogens are more dangerous than useful.
   D   Thus, we must recognize that while halogens can be useful, we must always use caution around them.

The following passage is a rough draft. It may contain errors in grammar, punctuation, sentence structure, or organization. Read the passage and answer questions 5 through 9.

(1) When Abraham Lincoln spoke at the Republican Convention in 1860, the crowd was so exuberant that the awning above the stage collapsed. (2) One person was notably not exuberant. (3) Lincoln himself. (4) In a newspaper account, a man who had observed Lincoln up close said, contrary to a man who would be expected to be triumphant or ecstatic, he appeared diffident and aloof. (5) Of course, history informs us that Lincoln was nominated at that convention to be the Republican candidate for president. (6) He won the election and took office in 1861. (7) During his years in office, prior to being assassinated in 1865, he had to oversee the U.S. Civil War.

(8) As the convention continued, there were reports that Lincoln was often found sitting alone, sometimes with his head in his hands. (9) When approached, he would always state that he didn't feel well. (10) Now that history has written its tale, the truth is that for most of Lincoln's life, he did not feel well. (11) In which today would have been a political liability, he suffered from what was then termed melancholy. (12) He was often maudlin, spoke occasionally of suicide, and, as he grew older, saw the world as a miserable place. (13) In modern terms, he was clinically depressed.

(14) However, one historian states that there are three stages of <u>melancholy, fear, engagement, and transcendence, and they actually worked</u> to give the man tools to be the successful leader that he was. (15) The fear spurred him to examine the core not only of his life, but also of life in the republic. (16) To overcome the fear, he engaged in hard work in every aspect of his life. (17) Finally, in the final stage, he developed an inimitable character based on determination. (18) Depression made him who he was, and it made him perfect for the job he ended up having to do.

**5. How can you edit sentence 7 to help the flow of the passage?**

A   Replace it with a sentence that further discusses Lincoln's duties in office.

B   Remove sentence 7 completely.

C   Have sentence 7 mention the outcome of the Civil War.

D   Combine sentence 7 with sentence 6.

**6. Which of the following words are used as synonyms in the passage?**

A   Convention and Republicans

B   melancholy and depression

C   history and historians

D   suicide and depression

**7. Which of the following would be the MOST precise way to state the underlined phrase in sentence 14?**

A   melancholy. They are fear, engagement, and transcendence, and they actually worked

B   melancholy, which might be fear, engagement, and transcendence, and actually worked

C   melancholy: fear, engagement, and transcendence, and they actually worked

D   melancholy and fear, engagement, and transcendence, which actually worked

**8. How would an editor revise the sentence labeled as 17?**

A   There would be no revision because it is well written.

B   Remove either the word *Finally* or the phrase *in the final stage* because of redundancy.

C   Move the phrase *in the final stage* to the end of the sentence.

D   Move the sentence to the end of the paragraph.

**9. How is the passage organized?**

A   A thesis is presented and defended.

B   Opposite views are presented and found to oppose each other.

C   An argument is presented and then refuted.

D   Various historians present varying views about Lincoln.

The following passage is a rough draft. It may contain errors in grammar, punctuation, sentence structure, or organization. Read the passage and answer questions 10 through 14.

(1) Kansas City is not limited to Kansas. (2) It is also in Missouri, a state adjoining Kansas. (3) Arkansas City is not in the state of Arkansas. (4) It is in Kansas, which also adjoins the state for which it is named. (5) Texas City, however, is in Texas, but it, too, is confusing. (6) It is in Galveston County, which makes people think it must be on Galveston Island, an island just off the coast of Houston, Texas. (7) Texas City, while in Galveston County, is actually on the mainland.

(8) When one heads north, the cities are less confusing. (9) Iowa City is in Iowa. (10) Nebraska City, the home of Arbor Day, is in Nebraska. (11) Minneapolis is in Minnesota, but the capital of Minnesota is not Minneapolis. (12) On the contrary, it is St. Paul.

(13) Why would someone name a city located in a different state the name of its sister state? (14) In some cases, the name occurs accidentally, rather than actually being named after the other state, because of a geographical commonality, as with Arkansas City, which is located on the banks of the Arkansas River. (15) In other cases, settlers named the city after the place from which they originated. (16) Sometimes, a place is named because the residents are dreaming of an idealized version of the place with the original moniker. 17 ) If I were naming a city, I'd name it after my mom.

**10.** Which of the following statements, if added to the beginning of the passage, would introduce it appropriately?

**A** Some towns make sense; some don't.

**B** In the South, there are confusing names.

**C** When it comes to naming places, inconsistency abounds.

**D** Have you ever been to Kansas City?

**11.** If the assignment is to compare inconsistencies and consistencies the student has observed, how should sentence 10 be edited to meet the purpose of the assignment?

**A** Discuss how Nebraska City got its name.

**B** Delete it altogether.

**C** Change it to "Nebraska City is, indeed, in Nebraska."

**D** Change it to "Nebraska City is the home of Arbor Day."

**12.** Which of the following sentences is an extraneous piece of information that should be removed?

**A** Sentence 12

**B** Sentence 14

**C** Sentence 15

**D** Sentence 17

**13.** In sentence 16, the word *place* is used twice. Which of the following words or phrases could replace one instance without changing the meaning of the sentence?

**A** to set down

**B** home

**C** location

**D** park

**14.** To expand the essay, what source would be the BEST one for finding more information on names of places?

**A** a world map

**B** an online dictionary

**C** a literature book

**D** an almanac

The following passage is a rough draft. It may contain errors in grammar, punctuation, sentence structure, or organization. Read the passage and answer questions 15 through 20.

(1) Mary Anne was an excellent writer. (2) She enjoyed plot twists that surprised readers and kept them turning the pages. (3) Just as soon as readers decided that it was the next-door neighbor who stole the apple pie, Mary Anne threw them a curve ball. (4) She would disclose that the neighbor had moved to Florida two weeks before. (5) A reader's heart would pound as a young man walked down a dark alley. (6) When he saw a dark figure coming toward him.  (7) Mary Anne would end the passage with him running into, not away from, the arms of his long-lost buddy.

(8) Mary Anne, herself, had grown up in a Mexican neighborhood. (9) Her family was poor. (10) Her teachers looked down up on her because she was from the "barrio." (11) Her parents, exhausted from working all the time, had little time for their daughter. (12) When Mary Anne would ask for her mother's help with her homework, her mother shushed her away. (13) "It's your homework," she'd say. (14) The truth was probably a mixture of her mother being too tired to concentrate and being afraid she wouldn't understand it enough to offer any help.

(15) Today, she is working on her second novel for a national publisher. (16) The publisher accepted and published her first novel, which became a best-seller. (17) The publisher has given her a big advance to write the second one.

15. Which of the following titles would appropriately name the passage?

A   Mary Anne, Queen of the Writers

B   Who Is Mary Anne?

C   From Poor, Lonely Child to Wealthy, Well-Known Writer

D   Anyone Can if Only They Try

16. Which of the following versions would improve sentence 15?

A   Because Mary Anne is an excellent writer, she is working . . .

B   With the past in mind, Mary Anne is working . . .

C   Despite many past obstacles, Mary Anne is working . . .

D   Without her experience, Mary Anne would not be working . . .

17. Which of the following words could BEST replace the underlined word in sentence 2?

A   liked

B   employed

C   endowed

D   injured

18. Which sentences should be combined to eliminate a fragment?

A   Sentences 1 and 2

B   Sentences 2 and 3

C   Sentences 3 and 4

D   Sentences 5 and 6

19. Which sentences could be switched to BEST improve the paragraph's continuity?

A   Sentences 3 and 4

B   Sentences 6 and 7

C   Sentences 8 and 9

D   Sentences 9 and 10

20. What assumption did Mary Anne's publisher make about her?

A   Mary Anne would go to another publisher.

B   Mary Anne's second novel would be as successful as the first.

C   Mary Anne would write another novel about her life in the barrio.

D   Mary Anne would never write about the barrio in her novels.

# Answers and Explanations

## 1. C

Sentences 6, 7, 8, and 9 are about the cleaning uses of these highly reactive chemicals, while sentence 10 starts discussing a new subject. Sentences 10, 11, 12, 13, and 14 discuss the use of highly reactive chemicals in the photographic processes. Choice C is the correct answer because the paragraph should break between the paragraph topics "cleaning uses" and "photographic uses."

## 2. D

Choice D is correct because an article in a science magazine about the good and the bad aspects of halogens would be a completely appropriate place for this type of writing. Choice A is not correct because, while the information being discussed would most likely be discussed in college, a college admissions guide would discuss the admissions process, not the content taught. College catalogs, likewise, might have a course description of a chemistry course that teaches this information about halogens, but they would not go into this much detail about a single concept in that course. Choice C is the second-best answer, but it is incorrect because content that is this specific would not be in the preface of a book. The preface usually introduces ideas that will be discussed in the book.

## 3. B

Choice B is the correct answer because an *inclination* is a *tendency* toward something. Choice A is not correct because highly reactive chemicals can't develop a *taste* for other compounds; this is too colloquial and informal. Choice C is not correct because an *incline* (while a related word to *inclination*) does fit in this setting. Choice D, *decline*, is the opposite of *incline* and would change the meaning of the sentence.

**4. D**

Choice D is the correct answer because the sentence summarizes the advantages and disadvantages covered in the preceding paragraphs and concludes the paragraph with *we must always use caution*. Choice A is incorrect because it draws a conclusion that fails to address the advantages and benefits of halogens. Choice B is incorrect because it makes the same mistake of addressing only the negatives, and not the positives, of using halogens. Choice C is incorrect because the conclusion drawn directly conflicts with the arguments made in the preceding three paragraphs, all of which discuss the positive uses of halogen.

**5. B**

Sentence 7 shifts from the topic of the convention and the fact that Lincoln had depression, so removing the sentence (choice B) is best. Choice A is incorrect because it suggests that sentence 7 should add a discussion of Lincoln's duties in office, which further removes the reader from the topic of Lincoln's depression. Choice C suggests another off-topic sentence. Combining sentence 7 with sentence 6 would still make the discussion off topic, so choice D is also incorrect.

**6. B**

Choice B is the correct one. In the passage, it states that Lincoln's condition was called *melancholy* at the time, but would today be called *depression*. Choice A is incorrect because the word *convention* means the meeting that was taking place, while *Republican* refers to the people who were attending the meeting. Choice C is incorrect because *history* is the field of study while *historians* are the people who study history. Finally, choice D is not correct because *suicide* is the act of taking one's life, while *depression* is a medical condition from which a person suffers while alive.

**7. C**

The way the underlined phrase is presented is confusing to the reader because it appears as though *melancholy*, *fear*, *engagement*, and *transcendence* were equal ideas. The reality is that melancholy is an independent clause that precedes its list of stages. Therefore, the correct answer is C because it separates the independent clause from the list.

**8. B**

The sentence, as written, contains redundancy, so choice A is not correct, but choice B is. Moving either the phrase (as in choice C) or the sentence (as in choice D) would make the passage flow poorly.

**9. A**

This question asks you to determine how the author organized the essay. Although the author never directly states the thesis (that Lincoln lived a life of depression) in the first sentence, he does present a thesis and defends it thoroughly. Choice B is incorrect because the opposite view (that Lincoln was not depressed) is not presented in the passage. Choice C would indicate that the author's view was wrong (refuted) at the end, when, in fact, it was not. Choice D is incorrect because only one author is presenting facts and opinions.

**10. C**

Choice C is correct because the entire passage is about inconsistencies. Choice A is incorrect because it speaks about towns themselves, not their names. Choice B relates to only the first paragraph, so it does not introduce the passage as a whole. Choice D is incorrect because, like choice A, it is talking about the town itself, not its name.

**11. C**

The correct answer is C because the preceding sentence introduced consistencies in contrast to the inconsistencies in the first paragraph. Choice A is not correct because it is obvious how Nebraska City got its name. The only part that needs deleting is the Arbor Day clause, so choice B is not correct. Choice D is also incorrect because the information about the town being in Nebraska is relevant.

## 12. D

Sentence 17 is an extraneous sentence and unnecessary to the discussion of inconsistent city names. The tone of the passage is informational rather than personal. Choice A is intended to follow the argument about inconsistencies in place names. Choices C and D continue the passage's discussion of how places were named.

## 13. C

Choice C, *location*, could replace the word *place* in either reference without changing the meaning. Although choice A is a meaning for the word *place*, it would not work in this context. Choices B and D would change the meaning of the sentence if either were inserted as a replacement.

## 14. D

Choice D would include the names of a variety of places and specific information for them. Therefore, the correct answer is D. Although choices A and C might have some information about the names of places, they do not provide specific information about the places. Choice B only defines words without providing extra information.

## 15. C

Choice C is the correct answer because it both introduces what the passage is about and catches a reader's attention. Choice A is not accurate because the passage does not include anything about her being superior (as *Queen* suggests). Choice B is not attention-grabbing. Choice D, while a common proverb exemplified by the passage, does not really fully name the passage.

## 16. C

Sentence 15 begins a new paragraph that concludes the passage. In the paragraph just preceding it, the hard life she had growing up is described. Choice C suggests a change of direction in thought, making the sentence's meaning clear. The use of *Because* in choice A would indicate that the previous sentences were supporting the new paragraph. Choice B would change the meaning of the sentence in a way that is not supported. Choice D is incorrect for the same reason as choice B.

## 17. B

The word in choice B would strengthen the argument. The topic sentence states that Mary Anne wrote well-crafted stories. Therefore, if she *employed plot twists* it would support that. Choice A is a synonym of *enjoyed*, but it wouldn't strengthen the argument. Choices C and D are distracters with similar phonetic structures to *enjoyed*, but they would not make sense in the sentence.

## 18. D

Choice D is the best answer because sentence 5 and sentence 6 both relate to the same thought. Sentence 6 is a fragment, which sounds as if the writer had continued a thought carried over from sentence 5, but had not completed it. Combining these two sentences would eliminate the fragment and still maintain the same thought for the sentence. Choice A is incorrect because even though both sentences could be combined, neither are fragments. Choice B is incorrect because sentences 2 and 3 do have fragments. Choice C is incorrect because the thoughts expressed in both sentences are not fragments.

## 19. D

Choice D is the best choice because sentence 10 continues the thoughts of sentence 8, which is about Mary Anne's experience growing up in a Mexican neighborhood. Sentence 9 is about her family's poverty and would best work with sentence 11, which describes how tired her parents were from working all the time. Choices A and B are incorrect because the sequence of the sentences would be disrupted and they wouldn't make sense to the reader. Choice C is incorrect because sentence 9 would have to be rewritten to start paragraph 2. By itself, it's not strong enough to be a lead sentence for a paragraph.

## 20. B

Choice B is correct because the publisher is assuming that Mary Anne's second novel will be as successful as the first, thus she was offered a big advance. Choice A, while it could be correct, is not as strong an argument about why the publisher offered the big advance. Choices C and D are incorrect because there is no mention of what subject matter Mary Anne addressed in her first novel.

# Chapter 6

# The Writing Process

The Writing Applications part of the CAHSEE will test your ability to write a clear and organized response to a writing task or reading passage.

If you're presented with a writing task, you will need to draw on your own personal experience, knowledge, and viewpoint to respond. The writing topic will be broad and most likely something you've thought about before, so don't worry about needing to be an expert on the subject! If you're presented with a reading passage, you will need to read the passage, evaluate it, and then write an essay.

You will be scored on a 4-point scale, which is based on the California Department of Education's content standards. Your essay will be scored by two people, who will assign your writing a score from 1 to 4. If the two scores are different, then your score will be based on an average of the two scores. Make sure you write a readable, logical essay to receive all the points you deserve!

## THE CAHSEE ESSAY

On the CAHSEE, you might be asked to write a biographical narrative of a person who learned about in school. Or the CAHSEE may ask you to read a piece of scientific research and have you determine the most important facts, ideas, or opinions. You may have to write a persuasive essay or business letter. Most likely you will be given a topic, which might look like this.

# REMINDER

✓ Write a response to the writing prompt shown.

✓ You may title your passage if you like, but it is not required.

✓ Dictionaries are NOT allowed. If you cannot spell a word, try sounding out the word. Then write the word in the best way you can.

✓ You may write in either print or cursive.

✓ Make sure you write clearly! Any erasures or strike-outs should be as neat as possible.

## Writing Task

A person who does brave or extraordinary things is often called a "hero" by news media or individuals. People view this person as a role model. Think about a person you have read about who has been called a hero. What makes this person heroic?

Write an essay in which you discuss a person you have read about. Explain why this person is considered a hero. Use details and examples to support your ideas.

# Writing Checklist

This writing checklist will help you strengthen your essay.  Make sure you check the following:

☐ Read the description of the prompt carefully.

☐ Organize your essay with a strong introduction, body, and conclusion.

☐ Support your ideas with specific, detailed examples.

☐ Use words that your audience can understand and that fit the purpose of the writing task.

☐ Use different types of sentences to make your writing interesting.

☐ Check for errors in grammar, spelling, punctuation, capitalization, and sentence formation.

## UNDERSTAND THE WRITING TOPIC

Making sense of what you read isn't always easy or quick. You may need some time to understand and digest what you've read. With a writing task, you want to be sure that you're clear about the direction your essay should take. If you don't understand what the writing task asks you to do, you may end up writing an essay that doesn't make much sense. And as everyone knows, an essay where the author isn't in control of the topic is pretty much a mess. Understanding the writing task is crucial to scoring points on the CAHSEE and in real life.

### Kaplan's 4-Step Method for Writing

**Step 1:** Think.
**Step 2:** Organize.
**Step 3:** Write.
**Step 4:** Fix.

Writing is a process, but if you follow certain steps, it will make your writing process easier and also increase your likelihood of success. The CAHSEE practically gives you all the instructions and structure you need to think about to write your essay. Then if you use Kaplan's 4-Step Method for Writing, half the battle of writing an essay is already accomplished. Aside from writing the essay for you, all the writing mechanics you'll need to cover are included in the writing checklist on the CAHSEE and in Kaplan's 4-Step Method for Writing. Let's consider the steps in terms of the "hero" writing prompt.

### Step 1: THINK

To begin, you must read carefully to be sure that you understand the topic. Do this at least twice.

First, read the words after *Think about . . .*, which tell you the general direction of the topic. In this prompt, you are to think about a person you've learned about who is considered a hero.

Second, look at the question: *What makes this person heroic?*

Next, you must think again, even though the words *think again* are not written. What are the qualities of a hero? Your essay must answer this question.

Finally, read the writing task itself.

**Write an essay in which you discuss a person you have read about. Explain why this person is considered a hero.**

Should you start writing now? Not yet. You need to think a bit more. Ask yourself what the topic really means. There are several possibilities, and the way you write your essay is dictated by the kind of topic stated in the writing task. Therefore, it is crucial that you know exactly how to respond to the task. Look at the following types of essays you could be asked to write:

- biographical narrative: states a sequence of events and explains why those events are significant
- response to literature: shows an understanding of the significant ideas in a literary work
- expository composition: uses evidence to support a thesis and related claims; can include information on different approaches to the idea
- persuasive composition: presents an argument in a logical way and uses rhetorical devices and relevant evidence to support the ideas
- business letter: provides clear information and correctly addresses the intended audience

Let's go back to the sample writing task. Read the topic one more time and see if you can determine what type of writing it is.

If you guessed "expository," you were right! The sample writing task asks for an expository essay because it asks you to explain something.

Now what? The words after *Write* tell you exactly what to do next: You will identify someone you think is a hero and explain why that person is considered heroic.

# ORGANIZE IDEAS WITH PREWRITING

## Step 2: ORGANIZE

Do *not* begin writing immediately, assuming that ideas will come. They won't.

There are many approaches to prewriting, and each approach is directly linked to the writing task.

The very first step is to think about your purpose. Is it to explain? Describe? Inform? Entertain? Persuade? Knowing the purpose helps you decide the best way to organize the essay.

| Purpose | Organization | Methods of Developing Ideas |
|---|---|---|
| explain | logical | deductive or inductive reasoning, cause and effect, comparison and contrast, analysis, problem solution, time sequence, definition, order of importance |
| describe | spatial or chronological | top to bottom, left to right, front to back; time sequence |
| persuade | logical | deductive or inductive reasoning, cause and effect, comparison and contrast, analysis, problem solution, definition, pro/con, order of importance |

In the sample prompt from the beginning of the chapter, the writing task specifies an explanation. Therefore, the essay will be developed logically, using analysis and definition.

Now that the topic has been identified specifically, it is time to gather ideas. Without sufficient ideas, you won't have a paper at all.

For this particular writing task, an analysis chart is a quick and appropriate way to begin.

First, make a quick list of people you've read about who were considered heroes. How much do you know about each one? Let's say your list looks like this:

| Heroes I have read about | What did this person do? | How much do I know? |
|---|---|---|
| George Washington | great general, president | I recall a few facts from an American history class. |
| Eleanor Roosevelt | first lady, social activist | I remember a lot from my history class. |
| Anne Frank | journal writer in WWII | I read her book a while ago. |
| Winston Churchill | prime minister of England | I read about him in class, but there wasn't much information. |
| Martin Luther King, Jr. | Civil Rights leader, winner of Nobel Peace Prize | I know some of what he did, but I'm not sure about all of the facts. |

By looking at the list, it seems as if Eleanor Roosevelt is the logical choice because you probably remember sufficient information.

Now, having decided on a specific topic, you'll need some specific ideas.

First, think about the general topic. Remember, you should think about what makes a person heroic.

What are some qualities of a hero? Write down what you think are the most important. You might think of the following:

- courage
- commitment
- strength
- determination
- optimism

Now make another list and title it "Reasons Eleanor Roosevelt should be considered a hero," or something to that effect. (Notice that the topic is repeated. This will help you focus on examples.)

It is essential to write down thoughts quickly. Do not stop, do not wonder if the response will work, and above all, do not get stalled. No matter what, just keep going.

1. had respect

2. shy

3. first lady

4. helped people and served food at a soup kitchen

5. campaigned for her husband and helped him when he became president

6. visited troops

7. brought home letters and gave them to soldiers' families

8. called First Lady of the World by Truman

9. worked for underprivileged

10. delegate to United Nations

11. spoke up for Marian Anderson, an African American singer

12. helped draft the Universal Declaration of Human Rights for the U.N.

13. wrote a newspaper column during the war, and did other groundbreaking things

14. niece of Teddy Roosevelt

Ideally, generating this list took only a minute or two. Now, think again about the purpose of the essay. You are going to explain why you think this person is regarded as heroic. Remember again what you wrote down about the qualities of a hero. Now look at this list again and cross out ideas that don't seem closely linked to those qualities. Star those that seem appropriate.

1. ~~had respect~~ (This indicates a quality about her that is likable, but it does not support the idea that she is heroic.)

★2. shy as a child

3. ~~first lady~~ (Does this really support the idea that she was heroic?)

★4. helped people and served food at a soup kitchen

★5. campaigned for her husband and helped him when he became president

★6. visited troops

★7. brought home letters and gave them to soldiers' families

8. ~~called First Lady of the World by Truman~~ (This is significant, but it does not support why she is considered heroic.)

★9. worked for the underprivileged

★10. delegate to United Nations

★11. spoke up for Marian Anderson, an African American singer

★12. helped draft the Universal Declaration of Human Rights for the U.N.

★13. wrote a newspaper column during the war, and did other groundbreaking things

14. ~~niece of Teddy Roosevelt~~ (This has nothing to do with Eleanor's heroic status.)

Look at what's left and think about grouping the ideas based upon your list of heroic qualities.

Which qualities of a hero seem to apply to Eleanor Roosevelt?

## Chart Your Essay

You can make another quick chart that will help you fill in the ideas and details—placing the ideas you are trying to prove at the top. Underneath, you will support those ideas by writing details. Charting your ideas before you write saves you time.

First, you have to look at your list and decide if it is too long. You may not have time to write about each and every one of the qualities of a hero that you wrote down initially.

- courage
- commitment
- strength
- determination
- optimism

Because *determination* is part of *commitment,* you can cross it off the list. Is *optimism* a quality that makes a hero? Do you remember enough about Eleanor Roosevelt to support the idea that she was optimistic? If you cannot, you should cross those last two qualities off the list.

Now let's organize your ideas. You can create a rough outline or use a chart. You may find it is easier to see the relationships of ideas in a chart.

| Courage | Commitment | Strength |
|---------|------------|----------|
| visited troops | campaigned for her husband and helped him when he became president | shy as a child, but overcame it as first lady |
| spoke up for Marian Anderson, an African American singer | delegate to United Nations; helped draft the Universal Declaration of Human Rights for the U.N. | |
| | wrote a newspaper column during the war, and did other groundbreaking things | |
| | helped people and served food at a soup kitchen | |
| | worked for underprivileged | |
| | brought home letters and gave them to soldiers' families | |

Based on the chart, your essay will discuss Eleanor Roosevelt's courage and her deep commitment to helping people worldwide. You might see that you do not have enough information to use "strength" in your essay.

You probably know that different writing tasks need different types of charts. A persuasive topic or business letter would most likely need an "argument" chart. When you list the arguments or reasons why something should happen, you are building and supporting your case or main idea.

## DRAFT THE ESSAY

### Step 3: WRITE

Once you decide the purpose and organizational approach you want to take, you must first write a thesis sentence to help guide your writing. Your thesis sentence must directly address the writing prompt. Look at the task again.

---

## Writing Task

**A person who does brave or extraordinary things is often called a "hero" by news media or individuals. People view this person as a role model. Think about a person you have read about who has been called a hero. What makes this person heroic?**

**Write an essay in which you discuss a person you have read about. Explain why this person is considered a hero. Use details and examples to support your ideas.**

---

You are asked to identify a person you have read about and explain why this person is considered a hero. A possible thesis statement might look like this:

*Eleanor Roosevelt was a real hero because of her courage and commitment.*

This thesis statement makes it clear that the first point you will talk about in the essay will be Eleanor's courage, and your second point will be her commitment.

## The Introduction

The first paragraph of the essay is the **introduction**. You want to grab the reader's attention in the first sentence. You can use this energy and excitement to lead up to the thesis sentence.

In the introduction to this writing task, you could use the idea that you did not have enough support for as an attention-getter (Eleanor was shy as child).

Imagine a painfully shy girl who felt awkward and unattractive. Years later, this very same girl became one of the most respected women in the United States. She overcame her personal fears to be an outspoken advocate for human rights. She helped her husband, disabled by polio, succeed as president for four terms. History recalls many political heroes, and that once-shy girl belongs on the list. Eleanor Roosevelt was a real hero because of her courage and commitment.

Notice how this introduction draws the reader in with an interesting facts. Engaging the reader is very important, and beginning an essay without a powerful introduction is one way to lose the reader's interest. As a writer, you should avoid purposeless, general statements such as the following:

In this paper, I will tell you about Eleanor Roosevelt.

This paper is about Eleanor Roosevelt.

Eleanor Roosevelt is a very famous person.

## The Body Paragraphs

Following the introduction is your essay's first body paragraph. Notice that you should elaborate on the thesis statement by discussing its first point (in our example, *courage*). Then you want to support this first point with specific details.

The first sentence of your first body paragraph is the topic sentence. This sentence tells what your paragraph is about. The second sentence supports your topic sentence and provides more information to your readers. You want to answer the question raised in the reader's mind: "What makes Eleanor Roosevelt courageous?"

No one can dispute the courage of this first lady. At a time when the nation faced serious problems, her actions encouraged and supported the American people. She was determined to uphold the nation's courage during World War II. She presented lectures, wrote a daily newspaper column, and spoke on the radio—things no first lady had ever done. She visited troops around the world, encouraging the men and ignoring the possibility of personal danger. She also firmly stood by her personal beliefs that all people were created equal regardless of their race or religion. When the Daughters of the American Revolution prohibited Marian Anderson, a famous African American singer, from performing at Constitution Hall, Mrs. Roosevelt took action. She resigned her membership from the group and arranged a concert for Marian Anderson at the Lincoln Memorial. Because the United States was still in the throes of segregation, this was a heroic and courageous stand indeed. Americans still remember her remarkable determination.

Notice that one piece of information was moved from the topic *commitment* to *courage*. Sometimes, as you're writing a paper, you might find it logical to shuffle ideas, which is perfectly acceptable.

The second body paragraph begins with a transition, *Also*. This tells the reader that the second point, Eleanor Roosevelt's commitment, will be discussed.

Also, Eleanor Roosevelt, like all heroes, was strongly committed to helping others. Her husband, who used crutches and a wheelchair, needed help campaigning. She did not hesitate to jump into the political arena despite her shy nature. During the war, she personally brought back letters from soldiers and made sure that the letters were delivered to the men's families. She felt great sympathy for the poor and helped serve food at a soup kitchen in New York City. Later, President Truman made her a delegate to the United Nations, where she continued her commitment to humankind. Dedicated to the preservation of human rights, Eleanor Roosevelt helped draft the Universal Declaration of Human Rights for the United Nations. Her commitment earned her a respected place in our history.

## The Conclusion

In the last paragraph of the paper, you want to give a satisfactory conclusion. When writing a conclusion, you do NOT want to do any of the following:

- introduce a new topic
- write *Now I'm going to end this essay*
- rewrite the introduction
- add random ideas that didn't seem to fit anywhere else
- apologize for writing a weak/poor essay

A simple summary will work well for this particular essay. Notice that your conclusion reminds the reader of the points you have already discussed.

In conclusion, our country has been blessed by many heroes, both famous and unknown. A courageous first lady like Eleanor Roosevelt, with a solid commitment to human rights, surely must stand in the respected circle of heroes.

You might conclude essay topics differently depending on your subject and approach. In a persuasive essay, you might suggest action, list the reasons why a particular approach would be beneficial, or ask thought-provoking questions. The next chapter will give you many options for writing a conclusion.

## REVISE THE ESSAY

### Step 4: FIX

The next step requires you to reread the essay carefully, keeping in mind certain requirements. To ensure a painless revision process, you should be very familiar with these lists.

## Big-Picture Considerations

- Does your essay accurately respond to the writing prompt?
- Is your thesis present in the introduction, and is it specific and strong?
- Do the parts of your essay follow the plan mapped out in your thesis?

## Paragraph Considerations

- Do you have one central idea in each paragraph?
- Are the parts of your essay logically connected with transitions?
- Are your words appropriate for the audience and purpose?
- Did you remove slang and clichés?
- Can you remove unnecessary sentences without changing the focus of your essay?
- Do you have any repeated words that you should either remove or substitute?
- Are there throwaway phrases or clauses, like *in terms of* or *In this paper, I will discuss,* that you should get rid of? Remember, you can cross out words and sentences as long as your paper looks neat and is readable.

Read this paragraph from a student paper about a place the student didn't like. The writing task specifies that the student should use "concrete sensory details for sights, sounds, and smells of a scene. The writer should use specific actions, movements, gestures, and feelings of the characters..."

The sentences are numbered in this example although they would not be in an actual essay. Look for sentences that need revision.

## ROUGH DRAFT

(1) There was a big window I could look out of and see the planes taxiing to and from the runway. (2) At first, I watched them as if the window were a big-screen TV. (3) After the second hour, though, the scene got pretty boring. (4) Then I started to watch my fellow passengers-to-be. (5) There were a lot of people waiting. (6) Some of them looked really cool. (7) A well-dressed woman quietly read a newspaper, ignoring the fussing of a two-year-old seated across from her. (8) The stressed parents of the child had clearly run out of ways to keep her amused, and we still didn't know when we would be boarding the

plane. (9) A large man sat down next to me and opened a fast-food box, suddenly filling the air with the fragrance of hot pizza. (10) I sat there with my stomach growling angrily, and I was hungry. (11) The bottom line was that I wondered when we would board the plane. (12) At least I'd probably be given pretzels and a soft drink.

Let's analyze some of the the individual sentences. Look at the revisions.

**(1) There was a big window I could look out of and see the planes taxiing to and from the runway.**

This sentence is wordy. It also needs more details.

**(1) A huge, ceiling-to-floor window gave me a clear view of the planes taxiing to and from the runway.**

**(5) There were a lot of people waiting.**

This is an extraneous sentence that does not add anything to the paragraph. It can be crossed out.

**(6) Some of them looked really cool.**

This sentence should be crossed out. It uses inappropriate slang and adds nothing to the description.

**(9) A large man sat down next to me and opened a fast-food box, suddenly filling the air with the fragrance of hot pizza.**

This would be a good place to use more sensory details. Also, *fragrance* is not the best word to use in this instance.

**(9) A large man sat down next to me and opened a square, fast-food box, suddenly filling the air with the aroma of hot pepperoni-and-sausage pizza.**

**(11) The bottom line was that I wondered when we would board the plane.**

*The bottom line* is a cliché. It should be crossed out.

**(11) I wondered when we would board the plane.**

## Editing Your Essay

When you revise, you consider focus and flow. You look at the main idea and the paragraphs and sentences and decide if they express your idea in the best way.

**Editing** means checking spelling, grammar, and punctuation. This is the time to proofread your paper carefully. You can begin with the first paragraph. It is absolutely vital that your introduction contain no errors. You want the reader to know that you, as a writer, are in control of your writing conventions. Again, you should be familiar with the checklist so that you know what to look for automatically. If you have problems editing, try starting at the end of your essay, reading each sentence separately and even backward! It's a good way to catch sentence fragments, misspellings, and other serious errors that you might otherwise miss.

## Editing Checklist

- ☐ Do you have any sentence fragments?
- ☐ Do you have any run-on sentences?
- ☐ Are there any comma splices?
- ☐ Did you use verbs in the correct tense and form?
- ☐ Do all your verbs agree with the subject?
- ☐ Do all your pronouns match what they refer to (antecedents)?
- ☐ Are your adjectives and adverbs in the correct form?
- ☐ Do you have any misplaced or dangling modifiers?
- ☐ Did you use parallel structure appropriately?
- ☐ Did you use commas with coordinating conjunctions between two independent clauses?
- ☐ Are your commas correctly used with introductory clauses or phrases?

☐ Did you place commas correctly with names and dates?

☐ Are your apostrophes used correctly with contractions or to indicate noun possession?

☐ Did you make sure apostrophes are NOT used when a noun is in plural form?

☐ Are your quotations punctuated correctly with commas and quotation marks?

☐ Did you capitalize proper nouns and the first word in each sentence?

## SUMMARY

You have learned several important points in this chapter. Let's review Kaplan's 4-Step Method for Writing.

**Step 1:** Think.

- The writing task must be read several times for complete understanding.
- It is essential to think about the task and get ideas before writing. Do not be overly critical at this point. Write down every idea you can think of that relates to the writing task.

**Step 2:** Organize.

- Decide on the purpose of your essay and arrange ideas accordingly. Will you explain, describe, inform, or persuade?
- Organize those ideas that most effectively address the writing task BEFORE beginning to write.

**Step 3:** Write.

- Make sure that the introduction contains a thesis that explains what you will discuss in the paper.
- In the introduction, be sure to attract the reader's attention.
- Each body paragraph should include a topic sentence to state the main topic and include supporting details.
- The final paragraph should be a satisfactory conclusion to the essay.

**Step 4:** Fix.

- Make sure you have completely answered the writing task.
- Cross out any extraneous or repetitious sentences.
- Add detail words and transitions where appropriate.
- Check each sentence and correct fragments, run-ons, and comma splices.
- Check sentences for subject-verb and pronoun agreement.
- Make sure that commas are used correctly with introductory phrases and clauses and with coordinating conjunctions that separate two independent clauses.
- Check for correct use of apostrophes and quotation marks.
- Check for correct capitalization.

Chapter 7

# Parts of an Essay

In the previous chapter, you learned about the different types of possible writing tasks you might be given. You learned how to follow steps to write a basic well-organized and easy-to-read essay. In this section, you'll learn more about how to add details (razzle-dazzle) and examples (flair) to make your writing come alive or have significance for the reader. You'll also learn about how to target your writing to a specific audience to get a higher score.

## WRITING GENRES AND THEIR CHARACTERISTICS

If you're asked to write a biographic narrative of a famous person, you should list milestone events in that person's life and how these events are important. You will want your writing to highlight scenes and incidents that occurred in that person's life that have meaning for you and for the reader. Good writing may include all the action of an event, all the sounds and smells of a place, or all the feelings that someone famous may have experienced. Your essay should make history come to life and show how a famous person's life may not be so different from what you've experienced in your lifetime.

If you're presented with a literary passage, you will want to show that you understand the piece. You can do this by pulling out important ideas and opinions from the author's work. You can also draw comparisons between this piece of writing and another text that you have read. An important part of writing a response to literature is showing what you know about the author's literary devices and how they strengthens the writing. You will also want to keep an eye out for details that hint at something larger or more complex that isn't immediately clear from the surface of the story.

The CAHSEE may present you with a scientific or analytical topic and ask you to draw a thesis and conclusion about it. You will have to present evidence from different viewpoints. You may have to use more than one source to support your writing. In many ways, your essay will be an argument for or against the topic based on logical thinking and reasoning.

Persuasive essays are typically among the easiest types of writing prompts to write because they're based on what you think and believe. All you're doing is telling your audience what you feel and why they should feel exactly the same way. To make a strong persuasive essay, you will need to have a well-organized outline with the points that you want to drive home to the reader. To make these points crystal clear, you will use time-honored devices such as a personal anecdote or an appeal to the reader's emotions. Your writing may be based strictly on your opinion, but you will need to defend your opinion by supporting your argument with facts, expert opinions, or other commonly held public opinions.

Like most people, you probably find that writing about what you believe is easy. On the other hand, you may find writing something like a business letter very challenging and difficult to achieve. In many cases, however, business letters are often written because of something that you want to accomplish or achieve. In this way, they aren't so different from a persuasive essay. Chances are, at some point in your life, you'll need to know how to write a business letter, especially if you want to get an interview or a job.

Business letters, however, might be much more formal than you might be used to writing. In a business letter, you will want to address your audience in an appropriate businesslike tone. You will want to cover key points and ideas effectively and efficiently. Business letters are not meant to be long-winded or rambling! You will also want to follow a conventional business letter style and you will want to present a clean, clear, easy-to-understand document that will impress the reader and get you what you want or need quickly and easily.

## WRITING TO AN ESSAY PROMPT

Suppose you were given this writing prompt.

For the moment, assume that you have already listed and organized your ideas. Now it is time to begin writing the essay.

---

### Writing Task

Every year, millions of people in the United States take vacations. They travel to the mountains, the seashore, different cities, state parks, and other destinations. Think about a popular vacation choice.

Write an essay in which you discuss this choice. Explain why this is a popular destination. Use details and examples to support your ideas.

---

## CRAFTING AN INTRODUCTION

The introductory paragraph is very important in an essay. It is the reader's first impression of your work, and it should be a positive impression. A successful introduction will indicate that the writer fully understands the writing task and is able to express ideas competently. It will make the reader want to continue reading.

### Elements of a Good Introduction

A good introduction should accomplish two things:

1. grab the reader's attention

2. express the main idea of the essay in a satisfactory thesis

The introduction must indicate that all parts of the writing task will be addressed. Often, the introduction seems as if it is the hardest part to write. It can become easier if the writer answers a few questions before beginning.

What is the writing task?

What information might the reader need to understand the task?

What type of introduction fits best with this task?

## Types of Introductions

A writer has a choice of several methods of introduction, some of which depend on the type of writing task. It is wise to be familiar with the types of introductions so that you can avoid sitting at your desk or table with a blank piece of paper in front of you wondering how to begin. Use Kaplan's 4-Step Method for Writing an Introduction.

## Kaplan's 4-Step Method for Writing an Introduction

**Step 1:** Use a statement and explanation.
**Step 2:** Write an anecdote.
**Step 3:** Use a quotation.
**Step 4:** Ask a question.

### Step 1: Use a Statement and Explanation of the Subject

This common type of introduction states the general subject and then clarifies and narrows the subject to arrive at the writer's thesis. It addresses all parts of the writing task. An introduction written to the "vacation" writing task might look like this:

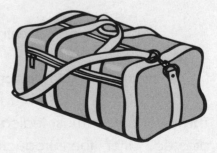

Americans are a traveling people. Each year, millions of dollars are spent on airline tickets, rental automobiles, and hotel and motel rooms. Much of this travel is the result of business, but most travel is done for pleasure. What is the most exciting part of this "pleasure travel"? For many, it is a trip to a theme park. These parks serve a definite need for Americans. Here, they can escape the everyday routine, experience "safe" terror, and pretend, at least for a little while, that the world is a magical place.

## Step 2: Write an Anecdote

People love stories. A simple but *related* anecdote will get the reader's interest. Using an anecdote might look like this:

When I was eight years old, my parents told me we were going on a very special vacation. They wouldn't tell me where, so my imagination went wild all summer. On Mondays, I knew we were going to the North Pole. By the time Wednesdays arrived, I was packing for a trip to Africa. On Fridays, I would take my cowboy hat and boots from the closet because I was certain we would be traveling to the Wild West. Actually, we went to a theme park, and I thought it was better than any other place in the world. My parents and I escaped our daily routine, had fun being terrified on some rides, and pretended, at least for a little while, that the world was a magic place.

## Step 3: Use a Quotation

An appropriate quotation can be a good way to begin a research paper. A student can find a quotation on the general topic and use it as a "jumping off place" to start an essay. A quotation could, in fact, be an old saying, or perhaps something a relative once said or something you heard on television.

The reporter pushed the microphone up close to the Olympic gold medal winner in gymnastics and asked, "What are you going to do now?" The answer was simple: "I'm going to visit a theme park!" Her reasons for going were exactly the same as everyone else's. She could escape from her daily routine, enjoy "safe" terror, and pretend, at least for a little while, that the world is a magical place.

## Step 4: Ask a Question

An essay can begin with a question that is answered either in the first paragraph or in the body of the essay itself.

Do we, as a nation, play too much? Each year, millions of dollars are spent on airline tickets, rental automobiles, and hotel and motel rooms. Much of this travel is the result of business, but most travel is done for pleasure. What destinations are the most appealing? For many, it is a theme park. Is this popularity just another example of "playing too much"? No. Theme parks fill a definite need. Here, people can escape the everyday routine, experience "safe" terror, and pretend, at least for a little while, that the world is a magical place.

**Remember:** A good introduction should:

- grab the reader's attention and interest
- contain the thesis sentence

A good introduction should NEVER:

- apologize for the ignorance of the writer or lack of knowledge about the subject matter. This will make the reader doubt your ability to complete the writing task effectively.
- contain a series of vague sentences or repetitious generalizations. You want your essay to intrigue your reader, not to put him or her to sleep.
- be only one sentence that may or may not be a thesis. Even if it were a long sentence, this is not a good way to begin an essay. The introduction needs to create a good impression on the reader. It should not be a curt nod in the reader's direction.
- be wordy or announce the topic (In this essay, I will discuss. . . , The purpose of this essay is to...). These are considered "padding." Your essay should be to the point without being abrupt or weighted with pointless words.
- contain grammatical or spelling errors—which signal to your reader that you are not a competent writer.

## THE THESIS STATEMENT

The thesis is an important part of the introduction for both the writer and reader. The writer must focus on the task, and the reader must understand both the task and the writer's position. The thesis must be explicit. That is, it cannot be a general statement such as "There are many interesting things to do in a city." The thesis serves as the center, or hub, of the essay. Everything in the essay relates to—and supports—the thesis.

The thesis is generally written in one sentence. It is only a PART of the introduction. The thesis should be a positive statement that reflects the writing task. The thesis is the basis of your paper, and the points it mentions must be covered in the essay. A thesis should never be too broad or too narrow. Either way, you will have problems writing. If you consider your thesis as a mini-outline that you will follow throughout the essay, you will find the essay easier to write.

Look again at the writing task.

---

## Writing Task

**Every year, millions of people in the United States take vacations. They travel to the mountains, the seashore, different cities, state parks, and other destinations. Think about a popular vacation choice.**

**Write an essay in which you discuss this choice. Explain why this is a popular destination. Use details and examples to support your ideas.**

---

First, *think about* a place people like to go on vacations. Next, *explain* why people want to go to this place. The explanation is accomplished in the body paragraphs.

## BODY PARAGRAPHS

Writing body paragraphs can sometimes be difficult. You can make the task easier by using Kaplan's 4-Step Method for Writing Paragraphs.

### KAPLAN'S 4-STEP METHOD FOR WRITING PARAGRAPHS

**Step 1:** List your essay points

**Step 2:** Turn the points into sentences

**Step 3:** Write quick details

**Step 4:** Decide on your conclusion

## Step 1: List Your Essay Points

Decide how many points you want to cover in your paragraph. Make a list or outline of these points. Your paragraph should be strong enough for you to get across two or three points.

## Step 2: Turn the Points into Sentences

Write a brief sentence for each point. Writing a completely defined and clear sentence is not necessarily required, but doing so will guide you in the right direction when you start to flesh out the paragraph.

## Step 3: Write Quick Details

Underneath each point, write two to four words for each sentence.

## Step 4: Decide on Your Conclusion

In your concluding sentence, you want an idea that will sum up or summarize the ideas in your paragraph. At this point, you don't have to write the entire conclusion, but you want to have an idea of how you will finish your paragraph.

## Key Points

Let's assume that the introduction will use a simple statement or explanation of the subject. This is what is written so far. (Note that the thesis is underlined in this example. It would not be underlined in the essay.)

Americans are a traveling people. Each year, millions of dollars are spent on airline tickets, rental automobiles, and hotel and motel rooms. Much of this travel is the result of business, but most travel is done for pleasure. What is the most exciting part of this "pleasure travel"? For many, it is a trip to a theme park. These amusement parks, centered around a particular concept or idea, provide a delightful vacation for many Americans. Here, they can escape the everyday routine, experience "safe" terror, and pretend, at least for a little while, that the world is a magical place.

What are the key points that will be discussed in the essay?

- escape
- "safe" terror
- magical place

The thesis is a kind of contract between the writer and the reader. The writer promises to construct the essay based on the thesis. Therefore, the points must be discussed in the same order as they are stated in the thesis.

## Topic Sentences

Each body paragraph should have an explicit topic sentence telling what the paragraph is about. Imagine that a topic sentence is like a mini-thesis. Instead of telling what the entire essay is about, it focuses on a specific paragraph. Usually, it is easier if a writer makes the topic sentence the first or second sentence in a paragraph. This helps guide the writer in constructing the paragraph, and it helps guide the reader in understanding the paragraph.

What might be an appropriate topic sentence for the first paragraph of this essay?

Look at these possibilities:

1. There are a lot of reasons why people need to get away.

2. A person's routine consists of a group of repetitive activities that must be completed every day.

3. Everybody needs to escape sometime.

4. People who go to work in an office get tired and need a vacation.

5. Theme parks provide a complete escape from daily routine.

Which of these topic sentences would really work?

1. There are a lot of reasons why people need to get away.

This sentence is too vague. It does not relate closely to the topic. Furthermore, it is wordy. Using *there is* (*are, was, were*) in a sentence is not good writing. It puts the real subject at the end of the sentence. It can also easily cause an inattentive writer to create a subject-verb agreement error, which must be avoided in the essay.

2. *A person's routine consists of a group of repetitive activities that must be completed every day.*

If the writer were going to define "daily routine" and make that definition the basis of the paragraph, this is an acceptable topic sentence.

3. *Everybody needs to escape sometime.*

This sentence is very vague. Why does *everybody* need to escape? Escape from what? To where? Many questions are raised but not answered in this sentence.

4. *People who go to work in an office get tired and need a vacation.*

This sentence is somewhat imprecise. People who don't work in an office can still become tired and need vacations. Furthermore, this sentence does not closely relate to the main topic of the essay.

5. *Theme parks provide a complete escape from daily routine.*

If the writer were going to discuss the sort of escape provided by a theme park, this would be an acceptable topic sentence.

## Support for Key Points

The key point of each paragraph is stated in the topic sentence. The body of the paragraph must have specific, related support for the idea expressed in the topic sentence. Prewriting helps identify this support so that it can be used in the essay.

A writer has several options in terms of specific support.

## SPECIFIC INFORMATION

Using examples or specific information is probably the most common way to support an idea. This is particularly appropriate for writing tasks that ask for a response to literature or an expository or persuasive essay or letter.

Be sure that the information actually supports the main idea of the essay as well as the main idea of the paragraph. Next, be certain that the examples or information are, in fact, specific. Ask questions to test the specificity.

Look at these sentences written to support the key point *escape*.

1. People should get away from their work activities.

2. Individuals need to try new things, or they will get bored.

3. Going to work or school every day is very routine.

4. It is bad to do the same thing every day.

5. At a theme park, you will experience something different.

Are these examples of specific support? Consider them one by one and ask questions.

1. People should get away from their work activities.

What activities? Who needs to get away? Why?

2. Individuals need to try new things, or they will get bored.

What kinds of new things? Does this mean new activities, new products, or even new technology?

3. Going to work or school every day is very routine.

This sentence simply states an obvious fact. It does not provide specific support. Ideally, specific support would follow this sentence.

 4. It is bad to do the same thing every day.

Why is it bad? Don't we have to repeat some things every day, like eating and sleeping? This sentence is far too general.

 5. At a theme park, you will experience something different.

Different from what? This sentence is both vague and general.

It is always best to think about and evaluate examples before using them.

Do they answer one or all of the reporter's questions with specificity?

| Question | Bad Example | Good Example |
|----------|-------------|--------------|
| Who? | individuals, people, someone | hardworking sales personnel, factory workers and those bound by repetitious work, teachers with predictable schedules |
| What? | activities, things they do | fighting traffic on the way to work, getting up at 5 A.M. and eating the same cereal, eating a pasta casserole and watching a rerun of a sitcom |
| When? | sometime, every day | 9 A.M., at the 10:30 A.M. coffee break, 11 P.M. |
| Where? | some place | at the cluttered desk in a cubicle, behind the wheel of a five-year-old station wagon |
| Why? | busy, bored | working more than eight hours a day, watching the same television shows every night, shopping at the same grocery store every week |

Facts are another type of support. If you can state specific, pertinent facts in your paragraph, you will be able to develop it well.

For example, the writer might point out that at some theme parks centered around water, a visitor can watch exotic fish, see performing animals, and ride exciting water roller coasters. It is important to remember the difference between fact and opinion. A fact can be verified. An opinion is what someone believes about something. It cannot be verified or checked. The statement, "The killer whales are really beautiful," is an opinion because one person's concept of beauty is very different from someone else's.

## ANECDOTE OR NARRATION

As was pointed out in the section on introductions, readers like a good story. This strategy would be appropriate when writing a biographical narrative.

For our sample writing task, a narrative about an average person's experience of *safe terror* on thrill rides would be appropriate. The story could describe what it is like to get into a high-speed roller coaster and accelerate at intense speeds. The organizational strategy for this type of narrative would be chronological or would follow a time sequence. In other words, the story would begin as "Henry" stood in line at the ride, continue as he climbs into the car, the ride starts, and the coaster ascends a steep incline. The narrative could describe how Henry felt as the ride progressed.

## SENSORY DESCRIPTIVE DETAILS

This type of support would be appropriate in a narrative when describing a scene. By using images from as many senses as possible, the writer creates a description that is both concrete and vivid.

## DEFINITIONS

A **definition** explains the meanings of technical terms, notations, or the characteristics of a particular concept. In our sample essay, the term *safe terror* would be defined because it seems to be an oxymoron. How can terror be safe? Definitions are appropriate in expository or analytical essays as well as persuasive compositions and business letters.

## ANALYSIS

Developing a paragraph by using analysis means breaking the subject into parts and then carefully considering each part. This is an appropriate development for a response to a literature paragraph. For example, if you are analyzing a poem to determine the speaker's views on a city, you might want to consider each stanza of the poem separately.

## COMPARISON OR CONTRAST

To support a key point, a writer could compare what is being discussed to something with which the reader is familiar. Alternatively, the writer could contrast two ideas or situations.

## Persuasive-Specific Support

If you are writing a persuasive essay, you may use many of the same types of support. You also have additional options.

## STATISTICS

If you can remember any statistics about your topic, even generally, this can provide good support. Remember, this is a writing test. Your memory, or knowledge of history or any particular subject, is not being tested.

## PERSONAL OBSERVATION

This type of support is very appropriate for persuasive essays and personal narratives. The key, once again, is specificity.

## EXPERT TESTIMONY

Can you remember what an expert said about your topic? This can be powerful support, especially in a persuasive essay. Remember, the expert does not have to be someone famous. If Uncle Louie is a successful fisherman, then his statements about how to catch a fish would be considered expert testimony.

## THE CONCLUSION

The last paragraph of an essay should be the conclusion. Just as there are many options for beginning an essay, there are also many ways to close it.

- Summarize. This means exactly what it says: Sum up what you have written. Carefully restate your main points in clear language. This type of conclusion works well for any type of writing task.
- Restate the main idea or thesis. Be careful NOT to simply rewrite

the introduction in other words. Because you provided so much additional information in your essay, you should be able to expand upon your thesis. This technique works well for most essays and is excellent for persuasive essays or business letters.

- Create a memorable impression or image. This approach is particularly successful with biographical narratives.

- Use a quotation. This is much like the use of a quotation in the introduction. You might restate that quotation and apply it more directly to your main idea. You might use a different but applicable quotation to add power to your ideas. Again, this type of conclusion can work well for most writing tasks.

- Explain the implications—hopefully or with despair. This is very effective with a persuasive essay. If your suggestions are accepted, you can imply that something good will happen. Show the benefits of accepting your ideas. If your suggestions are not followed, you can suggest that something dire will occur (this must, of course, be based upon ideas in your essay).

- Suggest that the reader do something. If you are writing a business letter or a persuasive essay, you might call for action. You might remind the reader of what needs to be done or suggest ways to solve a problem.

Remember the following important tips for creating a powerful conclusion. A good conclusion should provide a satisfactory and logical ending to the essay.

A conclusion should NOT:

- simply restate the introduction in other words. This will detract from the essay. Remember, your conclusion is the last part of your essay the reader will evaluate, and you want to leave a lasting impression.

- introduce a new idea or subject. This is NOT the time to tack on an idea you thought of halfway through the writing process.

- assume more than is supported by the evidence in the essay. This is not where you want to add a really strong point that popped into your mind when you finished the body of the essay. If you did not support the idea in your essay, forget it.

- apologize. Remember, this is the last impression a reader has of your work. Don't imply or suggest outright that you don't know what you're doing. The reader will regard your work with great suspicion if you do so.

- contain a series of vague sentences or repetitious generalizations.

- contain only one sentence. It is best to have several sentences in a conclusion. If, however, you are running out of time, it would be better to leave the conclusion as one sentence and go back quickly to proofread your paper.

- be wordy or pointless (In this conclusion, I will. . . , I nearly forgot that. . . , And this is all I have to say about it. . . , etc.).

- contain grammatical or spelling errors. Again, remember that this is the last impression a reader will have of your work.

## SUMMARY

You learned a lot in this chapter. Let's review the most important points:

- An introduction answers the writing task, engages the reader, and states the thesis sentence.
- Body paragraphs begin with a topic sentence.
- You must provide specific support in each paragraph for the main ideas.
- Paragraphs are joined to each other by some sort of transition.
- A concluding paragraph provides a logical ending to the essay.

# Chapter 8

# Writing Applications

You've probably written a lot of essays by now. You most likely have a good idea of how essays are scored by your teacher's comments and feedback on your essays at school. The way your writing will be scored on the CAHSEE will be slightly different than how your teacher scores your writing, but you will find many similarities between the scoring processes. In this chapter, you will be given several writing tasks and sample essays to show you how to write strong CAHSEE essays that will score points. At the end of this chapter, you will have an opportunity to practice your writing responses with writing prompts that are similar to what you might see on the CAHSEE.

## RESPONSE TO LITERATURE ESSAY

You will be asked to read a poem or story on the CAHSEE. Then you will be given a writing prompt.

First, read the poem on the following page.

This is a poem by Emily Dickinson. She often did not label her poems, but they were collected and assembled into a poetry collection after her death and published in 1924.

Will there really be a morning?
Is there such a thing as day?
Could I see it from the mountains
If I were as tall as they?

Has it feet like water-lilies?
Has it feathers like a bird?
Is it brought from famous countries?
Of which I have never heard?

Oh, some scholar! Oh, some sailor!
Oh, some wise man from the skies!
Please to tell a little pilgrim
Where the place called morning lies!

Now read the writing prompt.

## Writing Task

In this poem, Emily Dickinson writes of a curiosity about what really defines morning. Through descriptive language and questions, the poet challenges us to think about morning and what really makes it distinct.

Write an essay in which you explain the poet's perception of morning. Is there a definitive answer to explain what morning is like? What descriptions does the poet include that could possibly define morning? Use details and examples from the poem to support your ideas.

## Kaplan's 4-Step Method for Writing a Response to Literature Essay

**Step 1:** Think.

**Step 2:** Organize.

**Step 3:** Write.

**Step 4:** Fix.

Remember Kaplan's 4-Step Method for Writing? If not, try this tip. Write down the first four letters: T, O, W, and F. Now when you need to recall the steps to organizing an essay, use this acronym, TOWF. When you remember the steps, it will be easy for you to attack the writing prompt. Now let's consider the steps for the "morning" writing prompt.

### STEP 1: THINK

The first step is to *think* about what you are asked to do. Ask yourself some questions. What is the poet saying? What is the poem about? Does the poet answer the question posed in the first line? What descriptions included in the poem might actually answer the question? Finally, consider how the poet tries to discover a definition for morning. What technique does she use?

Think about the complexities of the poem. Is there any irony? Are any words used that might have several meanings? What kind of figurative language is used? Is there any symbolism? These are things you must always consider if you want to achieve an excellent score on the essay.

### STEP 2: ORGANIZE

Next, **organize** your ideas. Do not simply paraphrase the poem. If the writing prompt is based on a story, do not simply retell the story. Think about how to answer the questions posed in the writing prompt. Make a rough outline or chart listing your ideas and the specific support for those ideas. Remember, you must use specific and detailed support from the text. This means that you will need to quote parts of the poem (or a story). Make sure you remember how to punctuate quotations correctly.

**Remember:** There is no right or wrong answer. Simply state your ideas and give ample, specific support.

Look at the checklist suggestions included with the writing prompt.

# Writing Checklist

**The following checklist will help you write your best. Make sure you do the following:**

☐ **Carefully read the poem and the description of the task.**

☐ **Organize your writing with a strong introduction, body, and conclusion.**

☐ **Use specific details and examples from the passage to demonstrate your understanding of the main ideas and the author's purpose.**

☐ **Use precise language that is appropriate for your audience and purpose.**

☐ **Vary your sentences to make your writing interesting to read.**

☐ **Check for mistakes in grammar, spelling, punctuation, capitalization, and sentence formation.**

Accomplish the first three steps as you are considering what ideas you will express in the essay.

## STEP 3: WRITE

**Write** your essay using precise and appropriate language and vary your sentence structure.

## STEP 4: FIX

Reread your essay carefully, and **fix** any mistakes you find in sentence structure, spelling, grammar, punctuation, capitalization, and sentence formation.

When Julio read the writing task, the first thing he did was reread the prompt. Then he reread the poem and made a few quick notes. Finally, he numbered the ideas so he knew how he would organize his essay.

Read Julio's response.

## Julio's Response

In Emily Dickinson's poem, the poet uses descriptive language and questions to make the reader think about something most of us have probably always taken for granted: the arrival of morning. The poet tries to discover what defines morning by asking questions and using descriptive language. The last stanza concludes with a request for some wiser, more experienced person to answer the question rather than providing a definitive answer.

The poet basically asks two questions. In stanza 1, the poet asks if morning is ever going to arrive. This suggests that the poem is written at night and, because the question is asked, implies that it is a very long night for the speaker in the poem. The second question, posed in lines 3 and 4, is simply, what is morning like? Is it something that we can see, if we were tall enough?

In the second stanza, the poet suggests possible visual descriptions that might explain what morning looks like. Dickinson uses personification in the first line: "Has it feet like water-lilies?" Feet suggest walking, which can be a slow process. Morning is in fact slow to arrive based on the questions in stanza 1. The next sentence is more hopeful. If morning has feathers, perhaps it could fly into the speaker's existence much faster. The next question might suggest an exotic source for morning ". . . famous countries? / Of which I have never heard?" The suggestion here of an uneducated, simple speaker is picked up again in the final stanza.

In the last stanza, the speaker makes an appeal to people who might know more about morning. She lists a scholar, a sailor, or "some wise man from the skies!" Scholars, of course, study many things and are knowledgeable. Sailors, because of their lives at sea, are fully aware of the arrival of morning. The reference to the wise man is confusing. To whom is she referring? God? An alien? Or just somebody she can't identify who is "out there" and might know the answer? She describes herself as a "little pilgrim" wanting to understand where morning comes from. A pilgrim is a traveler, journeying to foreign, possibly unknown lands or sacred religious sites.

Does she answer her own questions? No. Dickinson simply poses the questions for the reader to answer.

Now consider the rubric or scoring requirements for a response to a literature essay.

## Response to Literary/Expository Passages

4: The response—

- provides an insightful, thorough grasp of the passage.
- precisely and logically provides specific passage details and examples to back up the argument and main topics.
- shows an excellent understanding of the ambiguities, tones, and difficulties of the passage.
- offers a mix of sentence types and incorporates exact, evocative language.
- includes few, if any, errors in standard English, which are considered first-draft mistakes.

3: The response—

- provides a thorough grasp of the passage.
- correctly and coherently provides general passage details and examples to back up the argument and main topics.
- shows a general understanding of the ambiguities, tones, and difficulties of the passage.
- offers a mix of sentence types and incorporates some exact language.
- includes some errors in standard English, but they do not hinder the reader's comprehension.

2: The response—

- provides an imperfect grasp of the passage.
- offers few, if any, passage details and examples to back up the argument and main topics.
- shows incomplete or no comprehension of the ambiguities, tones, and difficulties of the passage.
- offers little, if any, variety of sentence types and incorporates conventional, bland language.

- includes many errors in standard English, which may disrupt the reader's comprehension.

## 1: The response—

- provides little grasp of the passage.
- offers no passage details or examples to back up the argument and main topics.
- shows no comprehension of the ambiguities, tones, and difficulties of the passage.
- offers no sentence mix and uses simple language.
- includes egregious errors in standard English, which hinder the reader's comprehension.

Now read the commentary on Julio's essay.

## Commentary

In this response, the writer addresses all parts of the writing task. In the first paragraph, the writer sets up the essay by stating that the poem describes how morning is truly distinct, yet is something we rarely spend time wondering about, and he summarizes the poem.

Next, the writer analyzes the questions asked in the poem. The questions define the poem's structure.

The third paragraph analyzes the figurative language of the second stanza, identifying the implications. Reference is made to the personification in the first line of stanza 2 and to the tone of hope in the second line.

In the fourth paragraph, the writer explains Dickinson's attitude and feeling of ignorance. The writer explores the reasons the individuals mentioned and appealed to in the poem might be considered knowledgeable about the topic and refers to the multiple connotations of the word *pilgrim*. The use of precise language and a variety of sentence types help make the essay successful. The essay is precise and specific and shows some sophisticated use of vocabulary. Overall, this is a sample of a 4-point response.

## EXPOSITORY ESSAY

> # Writing Task
>
> **By the time students enter high school, they have learned about many amazing, trailblazing discoveries made by scientists.**
>
> **Write a composition in which you discuss an important scientific discovery. Explain its importance in today's world, and show how it has improved people's lives. Be sure to support the description of the discovery with details and examples.**

In an expository essay, you are asked to explain something. Look at the writing prompt. What does the writing task ask you?

1. You must discuss a scientific discovery.
2. You must explain its importance today.
3. You must show how it has improved people's lives.
4. You must use specific details and examples.

Remember the acronym TOWF? The first step is to **think** about possible topics. Before you can begin writing, you have to choose a scientific discovery. Remember, the prompt is asking you to write about a *scientific* discovery, not for a *technological* discovery, so you could not write about computers, navigational systems, or microchips.

Okay, you've selected your topic. Now, **think** about why this scientific discovery is important. What problem has it solved? What new areas of research might have begun because of this scientific discovery? How has this scientific discovery benefited people? How has this scientific discovery improved their lives? You must keep your focus on a *scientific discovery*. It would be all too easy to begin discussing an invention or a piece of technology. Always refocus on the topic.

**Organize** your ideas in a logical order. Considering the topic, you might choose chronological order, cause and effect, or deductive reasoning. Quickly list your ideas and your supporting details.

**Write** your essay, keeping in mind the need for sentence variety, specific details, and precise language.

Reread your essay, and **fix** any mistakes in spelling, punctuation, and grammar.

When Brittany read the writing task, she immediately remembered studying Alexander Fleming in class. He discovered penicillin. Brittany knew his discovery fit the requirements of the writing prompt. She made a few quick notes about what she remembered. Then she chose the examples that answered the question in the prompt.

Read Brittany's essay.

## Brittany's Response

The goal of science is to learn more about the world around us so that we can hopefully improve human lives. One of the most significant medical discoveries was the discovery of penicillin by the Scottish scientist Alexander Fleming. Scientific discoveries in the field of medicine are some of the most significant because they improve the health, and extend the lives, of people.

One interesting thing about Fleming's discovery was that it was an accident. He was working in a lab and saw that a slide was contaminated with some mold and that the mold kept the bacteria on the slide from growing. This mold turned out to be penicillin.

At first, it was hard for scientists to figure out how to get the dosages of penicillin strong enough to work on people, but then they figured it out just in time. Our troops had penicillin for World War II, and it saved the lives of up to 15% of casualties. Penicillin kills bacteria that can cause infections, saving countless lives and limbs that were previously lost to illnesses like gangrene. Today, penicillin treats infections like strep throat, which, in the olden days, could lead to scarlet fever or even death. Penicillin has helped save many lives.

I've learned about lots of amazing scientific discoveries in high school, but the ones that make our lives better are especially important if they help us live longer, better lives. Even though the discovery of penicillin was an accident, it is still an amazing scientific discovery. We still use penicillin today to fight infections that people get and it's amazing to think all those lives can be saved from a simple mold!

Now read the commentary by a scorer of the essay.

## Commentary

In this essay, the writer tackles all areas of the writing task. The writer begins the first paragraph with an insightful thesis that presents the idea that scientific discoveries in the area of medicine are especially significant because they can often impact the health and lifespan of people so directly. Then the author presents the discovery of penicillin, including the detail of the name of its discoverer, in order to let the reader know what the essay's main focus will be.

In the second paragraph, the author describes how amazing the discovery of penicillin was, especially because it was accidental. The third paragraph explains how important penicillin's discovery was in a specific way, namely the lives it saved in World War II. It also explains how penicillin works to kill infection-causing bacteria.

The final paragraph of the essay is meant to sum up the main points of the essay, which it does in a clear and direct manner. It reiterates the idea that medical discoveries are especially significant scientific discoveries because they make our lives better, and the writer adds that we still use penicillin today to fight infections. The essay is clear, and the author shows a varied and sophisticated vocabulary. There are only a few errors in the conventions of the English language within this response, but they are generally first draft in nature. Overall, this essay is a sample of a 4-point response.

## PERSUASIVE ESSAY

### Writing Task

Some students at your school are concerned that there are not enough opportunities for students to socialize outside of the classroom, and they worry that very few students at your school are involved in extracurricular activities.

Write a persuasive essay for your school paper in which you convince the readers of the importance of getting involved in after-school extracurricular activities. Convince your readers using specific reasons and examples.

Persuasive essays require careful thinking and organization.

First, make a quick chart. The prompt tells you what needs to be considered: *Write a persuasive essay for your school paper in which you convince the readers of the importance of getting involved in after-school extracurricular activities.* **Think** about some reasons. List as many reasons as you can in a quick chart.

Then in the next column of the chart, state specific examples to support your ideas. Stop a minute and look at your chart. Remember, you must address the reader's concerns and biases, and you must do so with authority. **Organize** by ordering your ideas. You might want to put the most important idea first. **Write** your essay, and then **fix** grammar, punctuation, and spelling errors.

When Kevin read the writing prompt, he stopped and reread the prompt. He quickly realized that he needed to think about different after-school extracurricular activities and consider what they have in common. Then he had to think about why these activities were fun and worthy of student participation. The next challenge was to persuade the reader. Kevin remembered that a positive tone was the first step in reader appeal. The next was to get the reader involved in the topic by the end of the first paragraph. He wanted to put his most persuasive idea first in the essay. He also wanted to include some persuasive support.

Read Kevin's essay. Notice how he attracts the reader's attention in the introduction and how he uses transitions to move smoothly from one idea to the next.

## Kevin's Response

Do you feel like you are a part of your high school community? Do you think you have friends from high school who you will still be close to once you have graduated? Do you know as many people at our school as you want to? If you answered any of these questions with a "no," then you need to get involved in after-school extracurricular activities!

Just going to classes every day doesn't always help you meet people or make lasting friendships. The primary purpose of school is to learn, so classes are focused on that. Even though you get to work with classmates on group projects, you aren't really getting to know them. When you are doing an extracurricular activity, you are getting to spend time with your classmates, and the focus is not necessarily on individual work but on group projects or team activities. You will make a lot of friends when you participate in these activities.

Another reason you should join these activities is that you will get to know more people who share your interests. In school, you may hate math class and your classmates might like it, but you all have to be there because it is a required course. Because extracurricular activities aren't required, the people who join them are really interested in the topic. You will get to meet people who like the same things as you do if you join a group you like, and you can make more friends. And you will learn more about something that really interests you. Are you doing anything after school that is better than that?

Having more students in after-school activities is also good for the whole school. We will all get to know each other more if we're in clubs and groups, and we'll have more school spirit because of that. Colleges look for students who aren't just getting good grades but who are also involved in their schools and their communities. The college recruiter who spoke to seniors last week said that it was important to be a well-balanced person. More of us will get into college if we're involved in extracurricular activities, and the ranking of our school could go up.

If you want to get the most out of your high school experience, you want to enjoy school both academically AND socially. By joining after-school extracurricular activities, you get to learn more about something you're interested in, and meet other people who share those interests. You get to talk to people outside of class and make more friends, and those friendships are likely to continue even after you graduate. Finally, getting involved in after-school activities is better for the whole school because we'll have more school spirit and more of us will get into college.

Now read the scoring guide for a persuasive essay.

## Response to Writing Prompt Scoring Guide

**4: The essay—**
- provides a thoughtful argument that responds appropriately to the writing prompt.
- completely supports the argument and main topics with exact details and examples.
- shows a strong tone and focus and demonstrates a firm grasp of organization.
- has an excellent sense of audience.
- supplies a strong mix of sentence types and uses exact, evocative language.
- includes few, if any, errors in standard English, which are considered first-draft mistakes.

**3: The essay—**
- provides a decent argument that responds to the writing prompt.
- supports the argument and main topics with good details and examples.
- shows a good tone and focus and demonstrates a grasp of organization.
- has a good sense of audience.
- supplies a mix of sentence types and uses exact language.
- includes some errors in standard English, which do not hinder the reader's comprehension.

**2: The essay—**

- provides an inexact argument that responds to the writing prompt.
- supports the argument and main topics with a few details and examples.
- shows some tone and focus and demonstrates some grasp of organization.
- has an unclear sense of audience.
- supplies less of a mix of sentence types and uses conventional language.
- includes many errors in standard English, which may disrupt the reader's comprehension.

**1: The essay—**

- provides a weak argument that doesn't respond to the writing prompt.
- supports the argument and main topics with little or no details and examples.
- shows little tone and focus, and demonstrates hardly any grasp of organization.
- has no sense of audience.
- supplies no mix of sentence types and uses very basic language.
- includes egregious errors in standard English, which hinder the reader's comprehension.

This guide describes the attributes of student writing at each score level. Each paper receives the score that best fits the overall evidence provided by the student in response to the prompt. However, papers that do not meet the standard for conventions at a 4 or a 3 score point receive a score that is at most one point lower.

Now read the scorer's commentary on Kevin's essay.

## Commentary

This essay provides straightforward reasons that would appeal to students and encourage them to get involved in after-school extracurricular activities. The introductory paragraph begins with some attention-grabbing questions for readers, making the essay pertinent to their personal experiences and desire for friends, an important appeal for adolescents.

The second paragraph explores how after-school activities differ from classroom time, and the third paragraph expands on this idea and explains how students who do extracurricular activities make more friends who share their interests.

The fourth paragraph broadens the discussion to show students the long-term advantages of being involved in after-school activities and uses two main arguments: that it improves school spirit overall and that it will help more students get into colleges, possibly improving the school's ranking. The conclusion succinctly sums up the argument.

The essay is not as nuanced as it could be and sometimes makes statements that are not backed up by any analysis, such as, *We will all get to know each other more if we're in clubs and groups and we'll have more school spirit because of that.* The essay also has a few minor syntax errors and awkward sentences, but overall it is well written and well structured, earning it a score of 4.

## BUSINESS LETTERS

### Writing Task

**You are trying to sell a new service that you have created to a business. Write a formal business letter that explains clearly and concisely what your new service is and what it can offer the business. Remember that the letter must be informative and to the point.**

When you look at a business letter writing task, realize that you must first decide on your purpose. **Think**: Is it to inform? Persuade? Complain? Are you offering suggestions for change? Are you congratulating someone? Or is it a combination of these?

Read the prompt and ask yourself what it wants you to do. In this case, you must explain the service that you offer and tell the business how it will help. **Organize** your ideas so that they flow logically.

It is vital to think of your audience with this sort of prompt. The person you are addressing in the salutation is the reader. Make sure your letter is clear and concise and does not wander.

When you **write** your letter, remember to begin with a salutation and sign your name at the bottom.

You want to come across as a professional, and any mistakes you make in writing conventions reflect poorly on you, and also your service. Be very careful to **fix** your grammar, punctuation, and spelling.

With this particular prompt, you must first imagine a product or service. When Nick read the writing task, he knew at once what service he wanted to sell to the reader. He also knew that he had to persuade the reader to purchase the service.

Read Nick's response to the writing task.

## Nick's Response

Dear Mr. Jones:

My company's new service, "Multi-Delivery in Minutes," can make your business more effective and save you time and money. We are so confident that you will love our service, in fact, that recipients of this letter can try "Multi-Delivery in Minutes" free for one week!

How many times have you had to drive all over town buying supplies or run out of the middle of a meeting to pick up food for an event? Wouldn't your time (and your company's money) be so much better spent having you in the office? With "Multi-Delivery in Minutes," you can be! This new service allows you to have unlimited errands run for your company for the low monthly subscription price of $400.

This service is not only affordable, but also versatile. We will do ANY errand for your company at any time. Picking up a guest speaker from the airport? No problem, even if it's at 11 P.M.! Need flowers for a client from a particular florist across town? We have it covered! Our services are also fully confidential, and our errand-running workers are given background checks and extensive training to ensure that you will love "Multi-Delivery in Minutes."

I hope that you will try out the "Multi-Delivery in Minutes" system free for one week. Find out firsthand how much better it feels to never miss a meeting or a deadline because you were running an errand that we could take care of for you!

Sincerely,
Nick Smith
Executive Director, Delivery Unlimited

Now read the scorer's commentary on Nick's letter.

## Commentary

In this response, the writer addresses all parts of the writing task. The letter is informative and to the point. It begins by stating in the first sentence that "Multi-Delivery in Minutes" can save the company time and money. This acts as a hook, resulting in the reader wanting to know more. The second sentence makes reading the rest of the letter appealing by giving the reader a free offer, and making him want to know what the free services entail.

The second paragraph, makes "Multi-Delivery in Minutes" seem appealing by trying to get the reader to identify what problems he may have because of annoying work errands. Because businesses are always concerned with saving money and increasing productivity, the paragraph ends by explaining how much cheaper it is to have "Multi-Delivery in Minutes" do the errands.

The third paragraph in the letter stresses another key benefit of the service, its versatility. The author uses specific examples to show the service's real-life usefulness. The paragraph ends by saying that the service is also confidential and that the employees are safe and well trained. Because it is thoroughly detailed, and well organized, this essay scores a 4.

## SUMMARY

You learned a lot in this chapter. Let's review some of the most important points.

- Memorizing the acronym TOWF will help you remember the very important steps to answering the writing task effectively (think, organize, write, fix).
- Read the prompt carefully.
- Think about what the prompt is asking you to do.
- Make quick notes about the subject.
- Be certain that the notes will help you answer the prompt requirements.
- Write the essay or letter carefully, following your notes.
- Make certain that the introduction addresses the prompt and gets the reader's attention.
- Include all the major points in the body of your essay.
- Write a satisfactory conclusion to your essay.
- Check for correct sentence structure.
- Check for grammar, spelling, and punctuation errors.

# Chapter 8
# Writing Applications Quiz

# The Tiger
## by William Blake

Tiger, tiger, burning bright
In the forests of the night,
What immortal hand or eye
Could frame thy fearful symmetry?

In what distant deeps or skies
Burnt the fire of thine eyes?
On what wings dare he aspire?
What the hand dare seize the fire?

And what shoulder and what art
Could twist the sinews of thy heart?
And, when thy heart began to beat,
What dread hand and what dread feet?

What the hammer? what the chain?
In what furnace was thy brain?
What the anvil? what dread grasp
Dare its deadly terrors clasp?

When the stars threw down their spears,
And watered heaven with their tears,
Did He smile His work to see?
Did He who made the lamb make thee?

Tiger, tiger, burning bright
In the forests of the night,
What immortal hand or eye
Dare frame thy fearful symmetry?

## REMINDER

✓ Write a response to the writing prompt shown.

✓ You may title your passage if you like, but it is not required.

✓ Dictionaries are NOT allowed. If cannot spell a word, try sounding the word out. Then write the word in the best way you can.

✓ You may write in either print or cursive

✓ Make sure you write clearly! Any erasures or strike-outs should be as neat as possible.

---

## Writing Task 1: Write Responses to Literature and Poetry

In the poem "The Tiger" by William Blake, the narrator of the poem addresses a question to the tiger about an unseen creator. Write an essay in which you describe your understanding of the narrator's question. What does the tiger symbolize in the poem? How did the narrator feel about this unseen creator and his creation? Use details and examples from the poem to support your ideas.

---

# Writing Checklist

This writing list will help you make your writing better. Make sure you check the following:

☐ Read the description of the prompt carefully.

☐ Organize your essay with a strong introduction, body, and conclusion.

☐ Support your ideas with specific, detailed examples.

☐ Use precise language that is appropriate for your audience and purpose.

☐ Use words that your audience can understand and that fit the purpose of the writing task.

☐ Check for errors in grammar, spelling, punctuation, capitalization, and sentence formation.

# REMINDER

✓ Write a response to the writing prompt shown.

✓ You may title your passage if you like, but it is not required.

✓ Dictionaries are NOT allowed. If cannot spell a word, try sounding the word out. Then write the word in the best way you can.

✓ You may write in either print or cursive

✓ Make sure you write clearly! Any erasures or strike-outs should be as neat as possible.

## Writing Task 2: Write Expository Compositions

In high school, students learn a lot about our history and what life was like in the past. Historic events are interconnected. They don't happen without a reason; on the contrary, they often occur as a direct result of the state of the world around them at that time.

Write a composition in which you discuss a historical event and explain what life was like at that time. Explain how the current events and/or social issues of that time shaped the major historical event you choose to focus on. Be sure to support the connection between the event and the time period with details and examples.

# Writing Checklist

This writing list will help you make your writing better. Make sure you check the following:

☐ Read the description of the prompt carefully.

☐ Organize your essay with a strong introduction, body, and conclusion.

☐ Support your ideas with specific, detailed examples.

☐ Use precise language that is appropriate for your audience and purpose.

☐ Use words that your audience can understand and that fit the purpose of the writing task.

☐ Check for errors in grammar, spelling, punctuation, capitalization, and sentence formation.

# REMINDER

✓ Write a response to the writing prompt shown.

✓ You may title your passage if you like, but it is not required.

✓ Dictionaries are NOT allowed. If cannot spell a word, try sounding the word out. Then write the word in the best way you can.

✓ You may write in either print or cursive

✓ Make sure you write clearly! Any erasures or strike-outs should be as neat as possible.

## Writing Task 3: Write Persuasive Compositions

Some students at your school feel uncomfortable because they don't have the "right" clothes and can't afford to get the latest styles. This makes them worried that they are being judged by what they wear and that they won't be able to fit in because of it. They think that having mandatory school uniforms would make school less about clothes and more about education.

Write a persuasive essay for your school paper in which you convince the readers of the importance of creating a new dress code at your school that requires uniforms. Convince your readers using specific reasons and examples.

# Writing Checklist

This writing list will help you make your writing better. Make sure you check the following:

☐ Read the description of the prompt carefully.

☐ Organize your essay with a strong introduction, body, and conclusion.

☐ Support your ideas with specific, detailed examples.

☐ Use precise language that is appropriate for your audience and purpose.

☐ Use words that your audience can understand and that fit the purpose of the writing task.

☐ Check for errors in grammar, spelling, punctuation, capitalization, and sentence formation.

# REMINDER

✓ Write a response to the writing prompt shown.

✓ You may title your passage if you like, but it is not required.

✓ Dictionaries are NOT allowed. If cannot spell a word, try sounding the word out. Then write the word in the best way you can.

✓ You may write in either print or cursive

✓ Make sure you write clearly! Any erasures or strike-outs should be as neat as possible.

## Writing Task 4: Write Business Letters

Imagine that you are trying to solicit donations from companies for a charity event that you are organizing. Write a business letter to a company asking for its donations. Be sure to explain what type of donations you will need, why the charity is important, and explain what the event is. Try to make the letter as convincing as you can, but also be sure that it is specific and to the point.

# Writing Checklist

This writing list will help you make your writing better. Make sure you check the following:

☐ Read the description of the prompt carefully.

☐ Organize your essay with a strong introduction, body, and conclusion.

☐ Support your ideas with specific, detailed examples.

☐ Use precise language that is appropriate for your audience and purpose.

☐ Use words that your audience can understand and that fit the purpose of the writing task.

☐ Check for errors in grammar, spelling, punctuation, capitalization, and sentence formation.

# Sample Essays and Scoring Explanations

## Writing Task 1: Score Point 4

### STUDENT RESPONSE

The speaker begins by asking the majestic, but fierce tiger, "What immortal hand or eye / Could frame they fearful symmetry?" The speaker compares the job of crafting the tiger to the fiery work of a blacksmith. The questions continue in each stanza, but all the stanzas frame the original question, "Who made you? And in making the tiger, how did your creator manage to face the fiery eyes of this ferocious creature? What reserves of courage did the creator call on to make your cruel heart and vicious claws?" Referring to an unseen creator, Blake asks if he was happy with the result, "Did He smile?"

The poem is carefully arranged. The six stanzas of rhymed couplets have a regular and rhythmic meter, which imitate the pounding of a blacksmith's hammer. The poem is also carefully composed in overall appearance. Each line and stanza is similar in length, and most of the lines are questions that reference the original central idea, "How is it possible that someone could have made you so beautiful and perfect, yet so terrible?"

While Blake compares the tiger's creation to a blacksmith's art, he is asking a question of deeper moral meaning. He is impressed by the tiger's splendor, but he is also repulsed by the tiger's nature. Blake implies that the tiger is a reflection of the creator's own cruel internal nature. The tiger becomes Blake's metaphor for the existence of evil in the world. The poem is a rebuke, even though the narrator never outright accuses the creator of wrongdoing. By bringing the image of a lamb into the poem, Blake contrasts the faith and innocence he once had with the sorrowful knowledge he possesses at the end.

## COMMENTARY

In the first paragraph of this essay, the author frames the main questions around which the poem revolves. The author does this by referencing lines from the poem. The author also explains the poem's metaphors, which helps the reader understand the central images.

In the second paragraph, the author addresses the organization and design of the poem. The author notes how the questions asked in each line direct the reader to the poem's larger question.

In the third paragraph, the author reveals the poem's message and how the narrator felt about both the tiger and the unseen creator. The author draws conclusions about the poem and accurately presents them to the reader.

This essay gives a thoughtful analysis of the poem and answers the main questions of the essay prompt in a clear and organized series of paragraphs. The writer uses a variety of vocabulary and details from the poem. Therefore, even though a few sentences are somewhat unclear, this is a 4-point response.

## Writing Task 2: Score Point 4

### STUDENT RESPONSE

Sometimes it may seem like each major event in history is its own separate event because, when we are tested on them, we have to remember each event separately to do well. However, in order to truly understand the events that stand out in the pages of history textbooks, we also have to remember all of the social issues that were happening at that time, and think about how they made that historical event possible. One event in history that always stands out in my mind is the "I Have a Dream" speech that Dr. Martin Luther King Jr. gave in 1963 during the March on Washington for Jobs and Freedom. By analyzing what the world was like for Dr. King at that time, we can better understand what led to that famous historic speech being given.

In looking at the "I Have a Dream" speech, we have to remember that it was part of the whole Civil Rights movement that was happening at that time in which King played a key role. Since Rosa Parks refused to move to the back of the bus in 1955, all over America, people began fighting for racial equality and the Civil Rights movement grew quickly. King's arrest during his leadership of the Montgomery Bus Boycott eventually led to the Supreme Court desegregating public transportation, even before the "I Have a Dream" speech. This shows that exciting, major events were happening that helped lead to this speech. Also, the notoriety he achieved for the Supreme Court decision made him more famous and got more people to listen to his speech.

Another major issue at the time was the Vietnam War. Dr. King spoke out against the war in 1965, and as did many other activists. The peace movement had many connections to the Civil Rights movement, because both were interested in the idea of nonviolent protest. If people weren't already upset with the government regarding racial inequalities at that time, their Issues with the war could also get them interested in nonviolent protest.

The "I Have a Dream" speech that Dr. Martin Luther King Jr. gave in 1963 is a very important event in American history, but it couldn't have happened if it weren't for all the other important issues happening in America at that time. The strength of the Civil Rights movement before that, King's other activities prior to the speech, the social issues for women and workers, and the creation of the peace movement in objection to America's war with Vietnam all played a part in how influential Dr. King's speech was. Because of these issues, the idea of nonviolent protest was popular and people were able to make real changes in the world.

## COMMENTARY

This essay chooses Dr. Martin Luther King Jr.'s "I Have a Dream" speech as the main historical event and does a good job of looking broadly at other events happening socially at that time. The first paragraph gives a strong introduction, restating the essay question's idea that history doesn't exist in a vacuum, but is interconnected.

The second paragraph looks at how Dr. King's work was influenced by the Civil Rights movement and how he had done other important work even before the speech. That work, the author says, helped make him more famous and made his speech more influential.

Likewise, the author's third paragraph talks about the antiwar movement and how it strengthened the Civil Rights movement through a shared belief in nonviolent protest.

This essay gives many specific examples about what was happening at the time in history that Dr. King made his famous speech, and the writer gives us some ideas about how these events helped the speech be as influential as it was. The paragraphs are fairly well organized, and the author uses varied language choices, earning a 4-point score for the response.

## Writing Task 3: Score Point 4

### STUDENT RESPONSE

We all want to feel normal in high school; we don't want to stand out as weird or feel like people look at us differently. We all like to wear clothes that make us feel good and make us feel like we look good and look normal, but sometimes people put too much emphasis on having expensive clothes in order to be considered cool. Creating a dress code where we all wear school uniforms could make school more fun and less stressful for everyone.

Just because you are wearing a school uniform doesn't mean you are no longer an individual. You can wear your hair how you want, wear the shoes you want, and have your own accessories. Also, remember that we are all different because we are all unique and therefore are going to look one-of-a-kind no matter what. People will have to take the time to get to know each other more as people and less by appearances, which is a better, deeper way of knowing someone.

Spending less money on clothes also means you would have more money to spend on other things that are more fun, like games or music. For people who don't have the money for expensive clothes, school will be more enjoyable for them because they don't have to be worried about being unpopular based on their style.

Without the distraction of worrying about clothes, we can be more productive in school. We will not have each other's clothes to distract us and can concentrate more on what we are trying to learn in class. Even though the social aspect of school is important, if things like clothes are making it harder for us to learn, it is better for all of us in the long run to try to solve that problem.

I hope that you agree that our school should institute a dress code that requires school uniforms. This plan would benefit all of the school's students both socially and academically, helping us get to know one another as people and not for superficial reasons.

## COMMENTARY

This essay writer does an excellent job of outlining three major reasons why the school should adopt a dress code policy, pulling ideas from the essay prompt and elaborating on them as well as coming up with his or her own unique arguments. The first paragraph tells the reader how all students essentially want the same thing: to feel like they are normal participants in their school's social and academic experience. This sets good groundwork for the three major points the author is going to make in favor of instituting a dress code.

The author's first point is that having a dress code doesn't erase someone's individuality, but actually forces people to look beyond the clothes at the real person. The second point the author makes is that school uniforms are cheaper, so students can save money on clothes and spend it on other, more fun things; the author also states that people who can't afford expensive clothes won't have to worry about it causing them to be unpopular. The last point the author makes in favor of a dress code is that it will make school less distracting and return the focus to academics.

The essay is clearly organized and speaks directly to the needs of its intended audience. It covers all of the issues raised in the essay prompt and has multiple specific examples of why a dress code would be useful. The essay also uses a variety of sentence types and precise, descriptive language. Overall, this essay is a sample of a 4-point response.

## Writing Task 4: Score Point 4
STUDENT RESPONSE

May 22, 20___

Dear Ms. ____:

People often say that teenagers don't do enough to help out in the community, but we at Students for Students want to prove them wrong, and we hope that you will help us. By donating to Students for Students, you are empowering teenagers to help one another and giving them valuable, life-long leadership skills.

Students for Students is a group of high school students whose mission is to help disadvantaged middle school students through organizing and leading activities with them. We believe that, as students who are a bit older but who can still remember what it's like to be their age, we can give them the support they need through their early teen years and relate to them as mentors. We are planning activities like after-school study groups, a touch-football league, museum trips, and other outings that give them things to do outside of school that are both fun and educational.

Because we are still teenagers ourselves, we need your help with raising funds for these activities. We are looking for donations from local businesses and restaurants for a picnic fund-raiser we are hosting. We are hoping to get food to sell donated from area restaurants and to sell raffle tickets for items from local shops that we can raffle off. Please contact me if you are able to help, and I've enclosed our monthly newsletter, which contains updates on our organization's activities.

Sincerely,

Kristen Makawe

President, Students for Students

## COMMENTARY

This business letter successfully meets the main requirements of the writing prompt, which is asking for a business letter to solicit donations for a cause that the writer has to create. The letter must be convincing and concise.

The first paragraph gives a direct argument to the reader, saying that *people often say that teenagers don't do enough to help out in the community, but we at Students for Students want to prove them wrong, and we hope that you will help us.* Then the author states why it is important to help the organization by donating.  Paragraph 2 does the work of explaining what Students for Students' mission is in greater detail and why the author thinks the group is important.  The final paragraph explains exactly why they need the donations:  for the fund-raising picnic event they are planning, and because they are teenagers and don't have full-time jobs. This paragraph also ends by suggesting that the businessperson read the monthly newsletter, which is smart, because even if she chooses not to donate at this time, maybe the newsletter will change her mind.

The letter is well structured and divided clearly into three paragraphs, each functioning to convince the reader to donate. The errors in the essay are minor, those of a first draft, so it earns a 4-point score.

Full-Length Practice Test 1
Answer Sheet

# Section 3
# Full-Length Practice Tests

# Full-Length Practice Test 1
# Answer Sheet

**Remove or photocopy this answer sheet and use it to complete the practice test.**

1. Ⓐ Ⓑ Ⓒ Ⓓ    5. Ⓐ Ⓑ Ⓒ Ⓓ    9. Ⓐ Ⓑ Ⓒ Ⓓ    13. Ⓐ Ⓑ Ⓒ Ⓓ    17. Ⓐ Ⓑ Ⓒ Ⓓ
2. Ⓐ Ⓑ Ⓒ Ⓓ    6. Ⓐ Ⓑ Ⓒ Ⓓ    10. Ⓐ Ⓑ Ⓒ Ⓓ    14. Ⓐ Ⓑ Ⓒ Ⓓ    18. Ⓐ Ⓑ Ⓒ Ⓓ
3. Ⓐ Ⓑ Ⓒ Ⓓ    7. Ⓐ Ⓑ Ⓒ Ⓓ    11. Ⓐ Ⓑ Ⓒ Ⓓ    15. Ⓐ Ⓑ Ⓒ Ⓓ    19. Ⓐ Ⓑ Ⓒ Ⓓ
4. Ⓐ Ⓑ Ⓒ Ⓓ    8. Ⓐ Ⓑ Ⓒ Ⓓ    12. Ⓐ Ⓑ Ⓒ Ⓓ    16. Ⓐ Ⓑ Ⓒ Ⓓ    20. Ⓐ Ⓑ Ⓒ Ⓓ

21. Ⓐ Ⓑ Ⓒ Ⓓ    25. Ⓐ Ⓑ Ⓒ Ⓓ    29. Ⓐ Ⓑ Ⓒ Ⓓ    33. Ⓐ Ⓑ Ⓒ Ⓓ    37. Ⓐ Ⓑ Ⓒ Ⓓ
22. Ⓐ Ⓑ Ⓒ Ⓓ    26. Ⓐ Ⓑ Ⓒ Ⓓ    30. Ⓐ Ⓑ Ⓒ Ⓓ    34. Ⓐ Ⓑ Ⓒ Ⓓ    38. Ⓐ Ⓑ Ⓒ Ⓓ
23. Ⓐ Ⓑ Ⓒ Ⓓ    27. Ⓐ Ⓑ Ⓒ Ⓓ    31. Ⓐ Ⓑ Ⓒ Ⓓ    35. Ⓐ Ⓑ Ⓒ Ⓓ    39. Ⓐ Ⓑ Ⓒ Ⓓ
24. Ⓐ Ⓑ Ⓒ Ⓓ    28. Ⓐ Ⓑ Ⓒ Ⓓ    32. Ⓐ Ⓑ Ⓒ Ⓓ    36. Ⓐ Ⓑ Ⓒ Ⓓ    40. Ⓐ Ⓑ Ⓒ Ⓓ

41. Ⓐ Ⓑ Ⓒ Ⓓ    45. Ⓐ Ⓑ Ⓒ Ⓓ    49. Ⓐ Ⓑ Ⓒ Ⓓ    53. Ⓐ Ⓑ Ⓒ Ⓓ    57. Ⓐ Ⓑ Ⓒ Ⓓ
42. Ⓐ Ⓑ Ⓒ Ⓓ    46. Ⓐ Ⓑ Ⓒ Ⓓ    50. Ⓐ Ⓑ Ⓒ Ⓓ    54. Ⓐ Ⓑ Ⓒ Ⓓ    58. Ⓐ Ⓑ Ⓒ Ⓓ
43. Ⓐ Ⓑ Ⓒ Ⓓ    47. Ⓐ Ⓑ Ⓒ Ⓓ    51. Ⓐ Ⓑ Ⓒ Ⓓ    55. Ⓐ Ⓑ Ⓒ Ⓓ    59. Ⓐ Ⓑ Ⓒ Ⓓ
44. Ⓐ Ⓑ Ⓒ Ⓓ    48. Ⓐ Ⓑ Ⓒ Ⓓ    52. Ⓐ Ⓑ Ⓒ Ⓓ    56. Ⓐ Ⓑ Ⓒ Ⓓ    60. Ⓐ Ⓑ Ⓒ Ⓓ

61. Ⓐ Ⓑ Ⓒ Ⓓ    65. Ⓐ Ⓑ Ⓒ Ⓓ    69. Ⓐ Ⓑ Ⓒ Ⓓ
62. Ⓐ Ⓑ Ⓒ Ⓓ    66. Ⓐ Ⓑ Ⓒ Ⓓ    70. Ⓐ Ⓑ Ⓒ Ⓓ
63. Ⓐ Ⓑ Ⓒ Ⓓ    67. Ⓐ Ⓑ Ⓒ Ⓓ    71. Ⓐ Ⓑ Ⓒ Ⓓ
64. Ⓐ Ⓑ Ⓒ Ⓓ    68. Ⓐ Ⓑ Ⓒ Ⓓ    72. Ⓐ Ⓑ Ⓒ Ⓓ

# Full-Length Practice Test 1

This full-length practice test for the CAHSEE has 72 multiple-choice questions and one writing prompt.

The section you are about to start is the Reading portion of the CAHSEE. This part of the test is composed of reading passages followed by multiple-choice questions.

There is no time limit on the CAHSEE, but make sure you pace yourself on the questions. When you have completed your practice exam, turn to page 331 for the answers and explanations.

Read the following passage and answer questions 1 through 5.

# Learning that Sticks

1   There are many components of effective language arts instruction. Wise teachers will make sure they include all five aspects as they make their overall lesson plans because, of course, the purpose of teaching is to create effective student learning.

2   The first component of effective instruction is to make sure that the teaching that takes place invokes the students' background knowledge. Students must connect what is being taught to things they already know. This is called positive transfer. If a person already knows the area code for the city in which his friend lives, it is much easier for him to memorize the remaining seven digits of the friend's phone number than to memorize a full ten-digit phone number. If a person knows someone who lives near the person being called, the caller may already know the first three digits, as well. Thus, a ten-digit phone number becomes a seven-digit phone number and, finally, a four-digit phone number. It is much easier to memorize four digits than ten.

3   Another component is to help students use the higher-order thinking skills. These include analysis, thought synthesis, and evaluation. While many of these concepts are taught and tested at the lower levels of knowledge, comprehension, and application, it is at the higher levels of thinking skills where students internalize the information so that it can be useful in other areas of their lives.

4   A third component is to use repetition, but with variety. This means to present the ideas more than once, but using diverse strategies. For instance, a teacher might present the information first in lecture form, then in activity form, and finally through allowing the students to discuss a book on the same concept.

5   A fourth component involves teaching the students not only the information, but also the strategies they can use for learning the information. A teacher may help the students come up with an acronym to remember a list (such as HOMES to remember the Great Lakes of **H**uron, **O**ntario, **M**ichigan, **E**rie, and **S**uperior).

6   The final component involves teaching students things that will be useful to them. Students will learn best those things that make sense to them and that they know they can put to immediate use.

7 Let's consider how some concepts could be taught using some of the aforementioned components of effective language arts instruction. For instance, children in elementary schools often learn the colors of the spectrum using the mnemonic device, ROY G. BIV. The first letter of each word stands for one of the colors of the spectrum. **R** stands for red, **O** stands for orange, **Y** stands for yellow, **G** stands for green, **B** stands for blue, **I** stands for indigo, and **V** stands for violet.

8 A mnemonic device, such as the two given in this passage, allows people to do something called positive transfer. Positive transfer occurs when a person retrieves some information that has been stored in his long-term memory and places new information into that stored file. It might be hard to name the planets just by memorizing them. However, if a teacher has the students learn about the various planets, and then use a mnemonic device, chances are that they can both retrieve the names of the planets, in order, and then tell some information about each. It is not enough to just teach a mnemonic device. It has to be used with something one already has familiarity with (i.e., the word HOMES). In addition, the new information has to make sense and have meaning.

1. **What is the main idea of this passage?**

A Students have the ability to learn difficult concepts.

B Following an effective instruction plan helps students learn.

C Mnemonic devices can help students learn.

D There are seven colors in the spectrum and five Great Lakes.

2. **This passage would most likely be found in—**

A a science textbook.

B a teacher's edition of a biology textbook.

C an introduction to a third-grade literature book.

D a textbook on teaching strategies.

3. **According to paragraph 8, which of the following would NOT be part of the positive transfer process?**

A Information is stored in the short-term memory.

B Information is retrieved from the long-term memory.

C New information is added to current information in the long-term memory.

D A person considers how the information in the long-term memory and the new information are related.

4. **Which of the following statements can be inferred from the passage?**

A   Mnemonic devices are crutches that should not be used once information has been mastered.

B   Teachers should use a single method to teach a concept so as not to confuse students.

C   Mnemonic devices are useful only if the student can connect them to some previous knowledge.

D   Some mnemonic devices are useful, but others are detrimental to positive transfer.

5. **According to the passage, all of the following are examples of good instruction in language arts EXCEPT—**

A   connecting information to background knowledge.

B   repetition.

C   emphasis on knowledge and comprehension.

D   usage of higher-order thinking skills.

**Read the poem that follows and answer questions 6 through 9.**

> The following poem was a part of a collection of short stories by Rudyard Kipling entitled *Rewards and Fairies*. Originally published in 1910, it has been often republished in many anthologies since.

# If

### by Rudyard Kipling

1    If you can keep your head when all about you
    Are losing theirs and blaming it on you,
    If you can trust yourself when all men doubt you
    But make allowance for their doubting too,
5    If you can wait and not be tired by waiting,
    Or being lied about, don't deal in lies,
    Or being hated, don't give way to hating,
    And yet don't look too good, nor talk too wise:

    If you can dream—and not make dreams your master,
10   If you can think—and not make thoughts your aim;
    If you can meet with Triumph and Disaster
    And treat those two impostors just the same;
    If you can bear to hear the truth you've spoken
    Twisted by knaves to make a trap for fools,
15   Or watch the things you gave your life to, broken,
    And stoop and build 'em up with worn-out tools:

    If you can make one heap of all your winnings
    And risk it all on one turn of pitch-and-toss,
    And lose, and start again at your beginnings
20   And never breathe a word about your loss;
    If you can force your heart and nerve and sinew
    To serve your turn long after they are gone,
    And so hold on when there is nothing in you
    Except the Will which says to them: "Hold on!"

25   If you can talk with crowds and keep your virtue,
    Or walk with kings—nor lose the common touch,
    If neither foes nor loving friends can hurt you;
    If all men count with you, but none too much,

If you can fill the unforgiving minute
30  With sixty seconds' worth of distance run,
Yours is the Earth and everything that's in it,
And—which is more—you'll be a Man, my
son!

**6. What is the main theme of the poem?**

A    being a good son

B    acting honorably in life's difficult
     situations

C    becoming a person who takes gambles
     in life

D    being a leader

**7. In line 26, what does the author mean
    by the phrase *nor lose the common
    touch*?**

A    being a friend

B    losing one of the five senses

C    acting better than others

D    staying grounded

**8. In the beginning of the second stanza,
    what does the author infer about
    dreams?**

A    A man should never have a dream.

B    A man who dreams should not take it
     seriously.

C    A man can have a dream, but not be
     consumed by accomplishing it.

D    Dreams should be accomplished at all
     costs.

**9. What is the relationship of the author
    to the person to whom he is writing the
    poem?**

A    He is his son.

B    He is an older person instructing a
     younger person.

C    He is his brother.

D    It cannot be determined from the
     passage.

Read the following science passage and answer questions 10 through 12.

# The Brain's Internal Features

The brain contains two thermometers that take the temperature for a person's body—the thalamus and the hypothalamus. These two parts of the brain act like an indoor and outdoor thermometer.

The thalamus, which is directly connected to a person's sensory organs, takes the temperature of the environment surrounding a person. It determines if there is danger in the environment and helps the person recognize information that may be beneficial to him or her and other information that may be harmful. The sensory organs report to the thalamus, and this part of the brain decides whether the environment has something in it to which the organism needs to respond.

The hypothalamus also takes temperature, but it is more concerned with the inside of the body. In addition to taking a person's actual body temperature, it also checks to see if other internal aspects are as they should be.

The hypothalamus checks to see if the skin is still enclosing the body and has not been punctured. It checks to see if there are good

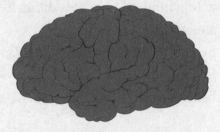

things (i.e., nutrients) in the body or if there are bad things (i.e., viruses or infective agents) in the body. If things are as they are supposed to be, it does nothing. If, however, things are awry, it immediately notifies the organism to take action.

10. **It can be inferred from the passage that—**

A    a person needs both the thalamus and the hypothalamus to be working correctly in order to function well.

B    the thalamus is much more important than the hypothalamus in terms of informing people about their health.

C    the hypothalamus is directly related to the sensory organs and relies on their input.

D    the sensory organs cannot function if the hypothalamus is not functioning.

11. **According to the passage, the actual internal body temperature is—**

A    mainly monitored by the thalamus, with help from the hypothalamus.

B    checked by the hypothalamus.

C    processed in the thalamus.

D    determined by the sensory organs.

12. **The primary purpose of the passage is to—**

A    show how the hypothalamus is more important than the thalamus.

B    identify the brain's two thermometers.

C    show that the brain has many different parts with many different functions.

D    create a map for understanding the brain.

Read the following science passage and answer questions 13 through 16.

# Understanding Friction

Friction is the resistance encountered when one body is moved in contact with another. In other words, it is the tendency of two surfaces to stick together. This occurs because the raised portion of one surface becomes trapped in the valley portion of another surface (in the same way a zipper works), or because the atoms that make up each surface are attracted to one another. The ability of a surface to stick to another is called its coefficient of friction. There are two types of coefficients. One is the coefficient of static friction, meaning how much force it takes to move an object that is not in motion, and the coefficient of kinetic friction, the amount of force needed to move an already moving object. The kinetic coefficient is always lower.

To increase friction, the coefficient must be raised. For this reason, gymnasts cover their hands with rosin, a powdered form of sticky resins from wood, before performing. The rosin makes their normally slick hands stick to the normally slick wood of the parallel bars or plastic of the athletic rings.

Although, as in the gymnast example, sometimes one would want to increase friction, more often people seek to decrease friction. In engines, parts are greased so that they will slide easily, and with less force, across one

another. Silicon, a substance that decreases a surface's coefficient of friction, is sprayed on household window tracks to make the windows move up and down more easily. Water, a substance with a low coefficient, is often run between two sticky surfaces to decrease the friction. Petroleum products, which are made up of long chains of molecules that slide easily past one another, have been found to be superior to water because petroleum products do not cause rust or corrosion.

13. **What is the primary purpose of the passage?**

A   to show how friction can be increased and decreased

B   to introduce and discuss the concept of friction

C   to identify ways petroleum products affect friction

D   to endorse the use of friction in sports

14. **What two mechanisms listed in the passage explain how friction works?**

A   the coefficient of static friction and coefficient of kinetic friction

B   the decrease of the coefficient of kinetic friction and increase of the coefficient of static friction

C   the insertion of higher and lower parts of a surface into the opposite parts on another surface or atom attraction

D   rosins and resins

15. **Which of the following would be TRUE based on the information given about the two types of coefficients?**

A   It takes more force to get a stationary boulder moving than it does to push a boulder that is already moving.

B   Pushing a car that is stuck in the mud is easier if the car is standing still than if it is already moving.

C   The force of an elephant pulling a tree stump out of the ground is greater than the force of a tow truck pulling a car.

D   A balloon will stick to a wall if it has first been rubbed against a person's hair.

16. **Which of the following is NOT a correct rewording of the following sentence?**

> The ability of a surface to stick to another is called its coefficient of friction.

A   If one surface sticks to another but not to a different one, that is its coefficient of friction.

B   A surface's ability to stick to another surface is called its coefficient of friction.

C   The coefficient of friction is one surface's ability to stick to another.

D   A surface's coefficient of friction is its ability to stick to another surface.

Read the following selection and answer questions 17 through 20.

# Protecting Internet Rights

1   The Electronic Frontier Foundation is a non-profit organization established to protect the rights of people who publish works on the Internet. Its members believe that the Internet should be a place where a person can create and publish what is called a blog—a work anonymously on any subject. In that way, it is not different from other media. On its website, it lists a "bill of rights," including one that states a person has the right to blog anonymously, keep one's sources confidential, write about elections, and even discuss one's workplace in a blog without retribution.

2   The Foundation further employs lawyers and researchers to help people make fair use of intellectual property. They believe that a blogger also has the right to allow readers to post comments without fear that he or she will be held responsible for these comments and responses. Responsibility lies with the comment writer.

3   Another purpose of the Foundation is to educate bloggers about their right to public information and their ability to attend and have access to public events as a media representative. The Foundation also reminds bloggers that they have the right to protect their server from government seizure in the same way that other media representatives protect their media products.

4   The Foundation has created several guides for bloggers, including a legal guide. Another discusses the importance of safety in blogging.

5   A related topic to blogs is the idea that information can be placed on a website in such a way that anyone can come in and edit it at any time. This idea, called a "wiki" by techies, is the basis for the online encyclopedia entitled Wikipedia. To add an entry to Wikipedia, one simply has to register a working email address. A person can then go in and write entries and edit other people's entries. Although anyone off the street can add, delete, or change an entry, a recent study by *Nature* magazine found that the number of errors in Wikipedia was approximately the same as the number of errors found in a traditional encyclopedia.

6   It is yet to be seen how the Electronic Frontier Foundation and Wikipedia, as well as other aspects of the Internet, will impact the world. But one thing is for certain: Change is inevitable.

**17.** An assumption on which this passage is based is that—

A   Internet media is inferior to print media.

B   freedom of speech is a freedom that applies mainly to magazines and newspapers.

C   the Internet is simply another form of media.

D   blogging is considered mainstream media.

**18.** What is the author's attitude toward the Internet?

A   The author thinks the Internet is a valuable tool.

B   The author thinks the Internet cannot compete with the electronic or print media.

C   The author thinks the Internet has many invalid sites from which children need protection.

D   The author does not offer an opinion about the Internet.

**19.** According to paragraph 2, if a reader posts a response on a blogger's site, who is responsible for the information?

A   the blogger

B   a lawyer

C   the Electronic Frontier Foundation

D   the reader who posted the response

**20.** Which of the following statements, if true, would weaken the information put forth in this passage?

A   Bloggers are always given press passes.

B   The website for the Foundation has links to its guides, including the legal guide.

C   The bill of rights on the Foundation's website includes links to articles demonstrating court cases that have been won.

D   Bloggers are never given press passes even if they file complaints.

Read the following story and answer questions 21 through 24.

# Mongolian Warrior Strategy

Although history has referred to Genghis Khan and the Mongolian army as Mongolian hordes, Mongolian superiority was most likely not a result of their overwhelming numbers. The quality, not the quantity, of the Mongolian warrior was the key to Mongolian military victories. Each Mongolian warrior was extremely well trained, disciplined, and prepared. The Mongolian army was tightly organized according to a decimal system. The largest unit of fighters was a tjumen, which consisted of 10,000 soldiers. A large army would be made up of three tjumens: one of infantry troops who would perform close combat and two others whose job was to encircle the opponent. Each tjumen consisted of ten regiments. Each of these 1,000-strong regiments, or mingghans, was further broken down into squadrons of 100 men. The 100-men jaghun was then broken down further into groups of ten. Each group of ten, known as an arban, elected its commander by a majority vote. Khan was personally appointed by the leaders of the tjumens, based on ability, rather than age or social status.

On the battlefield, each unit was expected to participate in a major coordinated effort and, at the same time, be able to act independently. Therefore, warriors carried an extensive collection of equipment, including a battle-axe, a curved sword, a lance, and two Mongolian bows. One bow was designed for rapid use on horseback. The other was heavier and more useful from a long-range ground position. Each rider also carried a sharpening stone for his metal arms, a knife, an awl, and a needle and thread in case he needed to repair his equipment in the field.

The warrior's dress was extremely important military equipment, too. Because the winter temperatures in Siberia and Mongolia fell well below zero, warm clothing was essential. Mongolians wore felt socks and heavy leather boots. They would typically don a coat of fur or sheepskin, under which they wore several layers of wool. Even a Mongolian warrior's underclothes were designed for military use. They preferred Chinese silk for this purpose. Not only was it warm, but heavy silk could also prevent an arrow from piercing human skin. If an arrow did penetrate into a warrior's arm or chest, it could be drawn out by pulling the silk thread around it. If the arrow were poisoned, this technique might also keep the poison from entering the bloodstream.

21. The author's attitude toward the Mongolian army is one of—

A   fear.

B   respect.

C   disbelief.

D   awe.

22. The smallest unit of the Mongolian army was—

A   a jaghun.

B   a tjumen.

C   a mingghan.

D   an arban.

23. This passage is mostly about—

A   Mongolian battle equipment.

B   Genghis Khan's victories in China.

C   the organization of the Mongolian army.

D   reasons for Mongolian military success.

24. According to the passage, Mongolian warriors were expected to be—

A   excellent farmers and horsemen.

B   well dressed and fashionable.

C   independent yet cooperative.

D   competitive and mistrustful.

Read the following passage and answer the questions 25 to 28.

# Universally Speaking

The English language is the closest thing the planet Earth has to a universal language. It is the first language, or at the very least the second language (and often the official language, meaning it is used for governmental purposes), for most of the countries throughout the world that were once a part of the British Empire. Because it was said that "the sun never set on the British Empire," the British not only governed in all parts of the world, but also spread their language to all parts. The United States, Canada, Australia, and New Zealand all use English as their first language. Likewise, English is the primary second language for most of Eastern Africa and the southern countries of Africa, India, and numerous islands around the world.

In India, employees who have learned English throughout their elementary and secondary years of schooling take further classes to enable them to adopt and American accent. Once mastered, this skill allows an Indian national to work for an American company in an answer center. Many large U.S. corporations have their customer service calls diverted to answer centers, which they boast are available 24 hours a day. Companies have found that American consumers complain, or are sometimes un-

cooperative, when the service representative appears to have a different accent. Therefore, the Indian people who want to work in what are considered high-paying jobs by Indian standards spend much of their time speaking "American English" even on their time off.

**25. What would be the BEST title for the passage?**

A   People in India Learn English

B   The British Empire

C   Commonalities of Americans and Indians

D   The Almost-Universal Language

**26. Which of the following would NOT be a logical inference one could derive from reading this passage?**

A   People in India converse only in English.

B   In order to work for an American company, a person in India will need to have mastered English.

C   American consumers prefer to talk to an American-sounding voice when calling with a consumer concern.

D   Not only can a different language be learned, but inflections of accents can also be learned.

**27. The organization of the passage is which of the following?**

A   There are two equal paragraphs, each introducing a unique idea.

B   The second paragraph expresses the broader idea that was introduced in the first paragraph with a more specific example.

C   The first paragraph introduces a broad idea; the second introduces a subtopic within that broad topic.

D   An argument is presented and then refuted.

**28. What does the phrase *the sun never set on the British Empire* mean in the passage?**

A   The British were constantly taking over countries throughout the world.

B   The British stay up all night.

C   The British ruled countries in the Arctic Circle, where there are times during the year when the sun never goes down.

D   Britain ruled countries all over the world, so it was always daylight in at least one of its countries.

# College Funding

As she put on her makeup, she looked in the mirror. The woman staring back had a few wrinkles, and a touch of gray in her hair but she looked young. She was still the same woman who had carried the boxes, clothes, and desk accessories up the three flights of stairs to the tiny dorm room that would be her daughter's first real home away from home that hot August day several years before. She found herself tearing up as she tried to apply the mascara, just as she had those several years before as she and her husband drove away, watching the campus get smaller in the rearview mirror. She wondered if she'd be able to hold the tears back this time.

As she walked hand in hand with her husband across the football field (covered with rows and rows of folding chairs set out to allow for the crowd that could not be accommodated by the 10,000-seat stadium), the woman thought what a beautiful day it was. Her only daughter was graduating from college. While others in the extended family had tried college, her daughter was the first to actually complete it. But, it had been a long, hard fight. Money had always been an issue. She and her husband had provided as many funds as they could, but sometimes,

it wasn't enough. Their daughter had worked part-time jobs throughout, and had even had to sit out a semester when the college raised tuition and she could not afford the increased amount. An unnecessary impediment had been her father's obstinate attitude that the daughter not take out a loan, even a low-interest student loan, to gain her degree. However, as she and her husband sat there in the sun, she had to think that both their daughter and her father felt a great satisfaction in the fact that not only had she obtained a degree, but that she was graduating debt-free.

29. **What would be the best title for this passage?**

   A   Money Woes for the College Student
   B   A Mother's Reflection
   C   Student Loans Aren't For Everyone
   D   Father Knows Best

30. **In the passage, the author used the word *obstinate*. If the author decided to replace that word with a different word, which of the following would WEAKEN the argument?**

   A   stubborn
   B   steadfast
   C   strong
   D   wavering

31. **It can be inferred from the passage that the author—**

   A   had always been thankful her daughter had chosen not to take out a student loan.
   B   did not agree with her husband's requirement that their daughter remain debt-free while in college.
   C   felt that student loans were traps that ensnared unwitting students.
   D   regrets that her daughter is graduating later than she should have.

32. **Which sentence from the passage is an example of foreshadowing?**

   A   As she put on her makeup, she looked in the mirror.
   B   She wondered if she'd be able to hold the tears back this time.
   C   Money had always been an issue.
   D   An unnecessary impediment had been her father's obstinate attitude that the daughter not take out a loan, even a low-interest student loan, to gain her degree.

This passage is about the term *googol* and the company Google. Read the passage and answer questions 33 through 37.

# Metaphor for Success

As science has expanded through the years, scientists have found the need to use very large numbers. Most people are familiar with millions and billions, and, even trillions. However, fewer people know about the concept of the googol.

The term *googol* was invented by the American mathematician Edward Kasner in the 1930s. It is a unit equal to a 1 followed by 100 zeros. Kasner reported at the time that when he asked his young nephew, Milton, what name he would give to a really large number, the child answered, "Googol." Later, Kasner would expand on his original moniker by coining the term *googolplex*, which means a 1 followed by a googol of zeros.

Interestingly, in 1998, a search engine company named Google Inc. was created. The company's name was a derivation of the mathematical term. In the spirit of fun, the company's executives named the company's headquarters the Googleplex. Today, throughout the world, the search engine has become so popular that the term *google* has become a verb, as in, "She googled the company to prepare for her job interview." And, of course, when one googles a name of a company, the Google response does indeed render a very large number of websites full of information about that company. Thus, Milton was right: Googol is a good name for a really big number.

33. **Which of the following is accurate according to the passage?**

A   Milton named both the googol and the Googleplex.

B   Kasner started the company Google Inc.

C   Milton and Kasner were both mathematicians.

D   Milton coined the term *googol*, but others coined the term *google*.

34. **Which of the following phenomena is demonstrated in the passage?**

A   the creative nature of language

B   the confusion of complex mathematical concepts

C   the explanation of scientific notation

D   the naming of scientific concepts after the person who discovers them

35. **Which of the following, if true, would WEAKEN the argument of the passage?**

A   Google Inc. was created by relatives of Kasner.

B   Google Inc. grew out of a research company started, and named, in the 1920s.

C   Kasner sued Google Inc. for misusing his term.

D   In the early days, sometimes Google Inc. executives misspelled Google as Googol.

36. **What is the basic mood of the passage?**

A   formal

B   casual

C   expository text written with a friendly tone

D   lecturelike

37. **The terms *googolplex* and *Googleplex* in the passage represent—**

A   a very large number and a building.

B   information and a search engine.

C   synonyms with only slightly different spellings.

D   the number 1 followed by 100 zeros.

**Read the following passage and answer questions 38 through 41.**

# Office Politics
THE PETER PRINCIPLE: Show your incompetence and get promoted!

One of the unfortunate business practices that businesspeople sometimes encounter is called the Peter Principle. It states that people who are incompetent in their jobs are often promoted. This seems counterintuitive, but it is indeed the method often used to take unproductive people and move them out of the way. Because most of the work is done at the lower levels of an organization, the promotion of a person at that level to a level of middle management is often a way to open up a position at the lower level for a more productive worker. Because most decisions are made in upper management, and most work is done at the lower levels, a person in middle management can sometimes be completely ineffective and not actually affect the output of the organization.

Another current principle of business is the concept that brainstorming is a successful way to find solutions to problems. Obviously, in order for brainstorming to occur, two factors must be in place. One is the idea that collaboration is encouraged. The other is that there is perceived safety that allows the employees not only to share their ideas, but also *think outside the box*. Brainstorming will not work if the participants are afraid they will be ridiculed or, worse, sanctioned for nontraditional thinking.

However, at brainstorming meetings, one often sees the Peter Principle at work. Incompetent people often don't even attend the meetings, or if they do, they show little engagement. At those meetings, high-level effective workers throw out broad goals so that lower-level workers can help them turn those goals into practical, workable processes. Out of those meetings, the higher-level workers may actually give a middle-level "Peter" an assignment to collect reports from the "actual" workers and compile them into a combined report. However, a good upper-level leader always asks that the lower-level leaders have duplicates of those same reports sent directly to the upper-level office, as they put it, for accounting purposes. The reality is, whether the middle-level Peter Principled nonworker turns in a combined report or not, the lower-level employees will ensure the work is completed, and the upper-level workers will have documentation indicating the effectiveness of it.

**38. Which of the following would be an example of the Peter Principle in practice?**

A  A CEO of a company loses his job and is replaced by a less-expensive worker.

B  A teacher becomes a lead teacher because she is extremely effective.

C  A college professor who often cancels classes and is seldom prepared for class is promoted to a supervisory position.

D  An administrator is demoted because he does not meet deadlines.

**39. Which of the following statements is supported by the material in the passage?**

A  Middle management is more important than either lower-level workers or higher-level workers.

B  Middle management is less important than either lower-level workers or higher-level workers.

C  All levels of management are equal in stature.

D  The work is done at the high-management levels, and the decisions are made at the lower levels.

**40. Which of the following phrases could BEST replace the italicized phrase in the passage without changing its meaning?**

A  get to work immediately

B  come up with creative ideas

C  show you're worthy of being promoted to middle management

D  show your intelligence

**41. What is the main idea of the passage?**

A  an explanation of current business principles

B  the organization of organizations

C  middle management and competence

D  the lack of good workers in the workplace

Read the following biographical passage and answers questions 42 through 45.

# Pavlov's Discovery

Ivan Pavlov, a physiologist, psychologist, and physician, is famous for work discovering the concept of classical conditioning. On his way to the discovery of that concept, and his creation of the theory, he demonstrated that a dog would naturally salivate when he knew he was going to be fed and could be made to salivate when an association between some nonconnected stimuli had been correct. Ultimately, the association he created was between the ringing of a bell and the presentation of food. For this work, he was awarded the Nobel Prize in 1904.

Pavlov was born in the mid-1800s, in a small town in Russia. From the beginning, he was not only a good student, but he was also very inquisitive about all kinds of things. The natural curiosity of all small children continued throughout his entire life. Thus, by the time he was old enough to go to college, he decided to study in a seminary, believing that religious studies would provide overarching answers to his questions about virtually everything. However, he found seminary studies stifling, and realized that religion was not the area that attracted his attention the most. Instead, it was science. He then transferred to the University of St. Petersburg to study the natural sciences. He received his Ph.D.

in 1879, and he immediately began working as a researcher. While studying the gastric digestive systems in dogs, he noticed that the dogs tended to salivate before the food had actually reached their mouths. He termed this a psychic secretion, and at that point, he changed the direction of his research because he felt he had found his niche.

Working throughout the 1890s, he termed his original work on the phenomenon as the basic laws of the establishment and extinction of conditional reflexes. While most people know of the association Pavlov created between the ringing of a bell and the salivation of the dogs, few people know that he originally worked to create an association between a canine's food and a tuning fork. Before hitting upon the idea of using a bell, he used a number of objects. In all cases, given enough repetition, an association would occur between the unrelated stimulus (food) and the conditioned stimulus. Thus, ultimately, the point of his work was that no matter what the neutral stimulus was, either a tuning fork, a bell, or any other object that did not have a natural relationship to the digestion of food, the dog would salivate when the conditioned stimulus was connected to the unconditioned stimulus, and both resulted in the same response.

| food (unconditioned stimulus) | bell (conditioned stimulus) |
|---|---|
| leads to salivation (unconditioned response) | leads to salivation (conditioned response) |

The whole point of an unconditioned stimulus is that nothing is done to cause the emotional or physiological response. For instance, in a classroom, no one has to make a student feel good about getting a gold star on the board. Recognition, the unconditioned stimulus in this case, simply feels good. That good feeling is the unconditioned response. If a teacher promises the class an ice cream party once they have collectively read 100 books, no one has to make the unconditioned stimulus/response pairing happen. Having an ice cream party feels good. It is unconditioned. By pairing the two stimuli (the reading of the books with the ice cream party), the students will perform the conditioned stimulus so they can get the unconditioned response, which is feeling good.

Interestingly, Pavlov was a very disciplined researcher. He was known for being in his laboratory early in the morning at exactly the same time each day, for having lunch at exactly noon, and for going to bed at exactly the same time each evening. Some scholars, when analyzing Pavlov's work, believe that he used his research to associate disciplined work (his conditioned stimulus) with the fact that the creation of a product, theory, etc. (an unconditioned stimulus) felt good (its unconditioned response). Thus, his being organized and disciplined (which led to publishable research) felt good.

| creation of a product (unconditioned stimulus) | being disciplined and organized (conditioned stimulus) |
|---|---|
| leads to feeling good (unconditioned response) | leads to feeling good (conditioned response) |

It is thus apparent that Pavlov not only discovered the unconditioned stimulus/response connection (i.e., something naturally feels a certain way) and created the theory, but also walked the walk.

42. **In the passage, which of the following is the conditioned stimulus?**

A   the ice cream party

B   the good feeling that occurs when one reads

C   the good feeling that occurs when one has an ice cream party

D   the reading of the books

43. **Based on the passage, in classical conditioning, the—**

A   unconditioned stimulus is always the same as the conditioned stimulus.

B   conditioned stimulus is always the same as the unconditioned response.

C   conditioned response occurs naturally.

D   unconditioned response is the same as the conditioned response.

44. **Which of the following strategies does the author use the MOST frequently to describe the concept of classical conditioning?**

A   descriptive quotes

B   statistics

C   real-life examples

D   similes and metaphors

45. **The final phrase in the passage is . . . *but also walked the walk.* In the context of the passage, what does that mean?**

A   Pavlov enjoyed physical exercise

B   Pavlov showed he believed his theory by behaving in a way consistent to it

C   Pavlov often had to receive punishment for his work, so he simply decided that was part of the profession

D   Pavlov could talk about not only the subject but also other closely related subjects

The section you are about to start is the Writing portion of the CAHSEE. This part of the test is composed of multiple-choice questions followed by a writing task.

The following is a rough draft of an essay discussing a psychological concept. It may contain errors in grammar, punctuation, sentence structure, and capitalization. Some of the questions may refer to underlined or numbered sentences or phrases within the text. Read the essay and answer questions 46 through 50.

## The Meaning of Color

(1) Colors have meaning. (2) That is for sure. (3) Today, we say, "Real men wear pink." (4) However, inherent in that statement is the fact that pink has a meaning.

(5) Yellow has two meanings. (6) It can be sunny and bright. (7) It can also mean cowardice. (8) Somehow, we accept both of them as true. (9) We paint our kitchens yellow so they will be appetizing and fresh. (10) But, we call a person "yellow" when he slumps away from his chance to show bravery.

(11) Blue means loyal. (12) Green means fertile, and increasingly, means the ability to make money. (13) Red means fierce and strong. (14) Orange means flamboyant. (15) White means pure. (16) Black means solid. (17) Gray means boring. (18) Purple means regal.

(19) Is it any coincidence the U.S. flag is red, white, and blue? Strong. Pure. Loyal.

46. **Which of the following sets of words that appear in the passage are antonyms?**

A   sunny, appetizing

B   meaning, coincidence

C   regal, flamboyant

D   cowardice, bravery

47. **Which of the following describes how the passage is organized?**

A   It is formal in nature and contains only facts.

B   It is an expository essay containing factual information.

C   It is a persuasive piece including the author's opinion.

D   It is a short story containing factual elements.

48. **Which of the following would MOST improve the first paragraph?**

A   Combine sentences 1 and 2.

B   Delete sentence 2.

C   Combine sentences 2 and 3.

D   Delete sentence 3.

49. **In sentence 14, the word *flamboyant* could BEST be replaced with which of the following while changing the meaning the least?**

A   showy

B   floating

C   fiery

D   format

50. **Which of the following ideas is supported by details or evidence in the essay?**

A   There is some general agreement among the population that colors do have meanings.

B   Colors and their meanings do not have general consensus.

C   Real men do not wear pink.

D   All colors have multiple meanings.

The following is a rough draft of an essay. It may contain errors in grammar, punctuation, sentence structure, and capitalization. Some of the questions may refer to underlined or numbered sentences or phrases within the text. Read the essay and answer questions 51 through 55.

## Sometimes You Wonder

(1) Sometimes life is ironic. (2) <u>Once upon a time</u> when athletic shoes were called "tennis shoes." (3) Tennis shoes were casual shoes worn to play tennis. (4) They were made of canvas and were significantly cheaper than the leather shoes worn for non-tennis playing everyday wear. (15) Tennis shoes were the shoes that one didn't mind getting muddy because they were one's cheaper shoes. (16) Some tennis shoes have Velcro fasteners rather than laces. (17) Then, "tennis shoes" became "athletic shoes" as a whole industry changed. (18) Today, athletic shoes cost far more than their dress shoe counterparts. (19) And, interestingly, many people who spend large amounts of money for athletic shoes would never set foot on a tennis court. (20) That's irony at its best.

**51. Which is the MOST effective substitution for the underlined part of sentence 2?**

A There was once a time

B From time immemorial

C Time was

D As time passed

**52. Which of the following sentences does NOT fit the paragraph well?**

A They were made of canvas and were significantly cheaper than the leather shoes worn for non-tennis playing everyday wear. (sentence 14)

B Tennis shoes were the shoes that one didn't mind getting muddy because they were one's cheaper shoes. (sentence 15)

C Some tennis shoes have Velcro fasteners rather than laces. (sentence 16)

D Then, "tennis shoes" became "athletic shoes" as a whole industry changed. (sentence 17)

**53. What is the BEST way to write sentence 20?**

A Therein lies the ironical conclusion.

B That is not only ironic but also laughable.

C Some people would think that showed ironic leanings.

D Leave as is.

**54. In sentence 15, the word *cheaper* could be replaced with which of the following to make the passage more clearly written?**

A more cheaper

B somewhat more cheap

C less expensive

D least cheap

**55. Which of the following ideas is supported by details or evidence in the passage?**

A Athletic shoes evolved from the original tennis shoes.

B Tennis shoes evolved from athletic shoes.

C Tennis shoes are very different from athletic shoes.

D Most people who buy a pair of tennis shoes also buy a pair of dress shoes at the same time.

The following is a rough draft of an essay. It may contain errors in grammar, punctuation, sentence structure, and capitalization. Some of the questions may refer to underlined or numbered sentences or phrases within the text. Read the essay and answer questions 56 through 60.

## The History of Common Words

(1) Fry had based his work on word frequency counts and early research done by a researcher named Thorndike, and later, a man named Carroll who created a five-million-word list. (2) Carroll recorded every word, or word form, found in textbooks, magazines, newspapers, and other printed text. (3) He then collapsed the variant forms into the most common form of the word to create his common word list.

(4) Common words are words that appear, or whose forms appear, most frequently in text. (5) They are divided into 100-word lists, with the most commonly used words in the first list, the second hundred in the second list, etc. (6) Principals often give their teachers the common word lists and request that they make sure the students know the lists corresponding to their grade levels before promoting them to the next grade level. (7) What were known as sight words in the American education system of the 1950s through the 1970s fell out of favor with educators in the 1980s and 1990s. (8) However, those same lists have returned now to the classroom. (9) They are now called high-frequency words. (10) Students begin learning high-frequency words as early as kindergarten.

(11) The ten lists created by Fry combine to form the 1,000 most common words used in the language. (12) They have been the basis for foreign language textbooks. (13) In fact, native English speakers who decide to take up a foreign language will often begin with a primer that contains the 1,000 most common words found in the language they're attempting to learn.

**56. Which of the following sentences would be the MOST effective one to begin the first paragraph?**

A   The origins of language are based on common word lists.

B   Lists of common words came about as the result of the work of Edward Fry.

C   Some people believe sight words are a crutch.

D   Fry, Thorndike, and Carroll were important teachers.

**57. Which of the following titles would best replace the current title?**

A   Variant Forms of Words

B   From Common Words to High-Frequency Words

C   Fry and Carroll's Work

D   Usage of Common Word Lists

**58. Which of the following does NOT describe the relationship of the researchers listed in the passage?**

A   Thorndike preceded both Fry and Carroll.

B   Carroll based his work on Thorndike's and Fry based his work on Carroll's.

C   They were all collaborators.

D   Carroll used Thorndike's work as did Fry later.

**59. Which of the following would be the best way to combine sentences 8 and 9 into a single sentence?**

A   However, those same lists have returned now to the classroom, and they are now called high-frequency words.

B   Thus, now those same lists have returned to the classroom now as high-frequency words.

C   However, those same lists have now returned to the classroom as high-frequency words.

D   Fry's lists are now called high-frequency word walls.

**60. Which of the following could be a logical first sentence for a concluding paragraph?**

A   While the 1,000-word lists apply mostly to English, other English-language learners can benefit from them.

B   The teachers of the lower grades teach more common words than do teachers of higher grades.

C   All 1,000 common words should be learned by the end of third grade by most students.

D   Thus, we can conclude that virtually every language has a list of approximately 1,000 common words.

For questions 61 through 66, choose the answer that is the most effective substitute for each underlined part of the sentence. If no substitution is necessary, choose "Leave as is."

61. My current teacher, <u>who attended school with my mother seems</u> much younger than my parents.

   A   attended school, with my mother, seemed
   B   attended school with my mother, seems
   C   attended school, with my mother seems
   D   Leave as is.

62. A marinated steak cooks more quickly and more thoroughly <u>as a nonmarinated one because</u> the marinade starts the breaking-down process.

   A   than a nonmarinated one so
   B   as a nonmarinated one because
   C   than a nonmarinated one because
   D   Leave as is.

63. <u>Having finished mopping the floor, the floor</u> appeared shiny and clean.

   A   The floor was mopped; it
   B   Once the floor completed mopping, it
   C   After the floor had been mopped, it
   D   Leave as is.

64. <u>By inserting the corrections in the first chapter changes</u> the page numbers of the entire thesis.

   A   The insertion of the corrections in the first chapter changes
   B   Inserting the corrections in the first chapter change
   C   The insertion of the corrections in the first chapter change
   D   Leave as is.

65. <u>If I would have known how much</u> the sight of the destroyed school would bring me to tears, I would not have driven by it.

   A   When I found out how much
   B   If I knew how much
   C   Had I known how much
   D   Leave as is.

66. The concessionaire required that the suppliers <u>provide there products</u> in unopened packages and within at least two weeks of the invoice date.

   A   supply products of theirs
   B   provide they're products
   C   provide their products
   D   Leave as is.

For questions 67 through 72, choose the word or phrase that best completes the sentence.

67. A seasoned singer is able to recover more quickly from laryngitis _____ _____ the singer's vocal cords are regularly exercised.

A   as the average person, partly because
B   than the average person; because
C   than the average person, partly so
D   because, unlike the average person,

68. _____, the flag was raised to its permanent position above the scoreboard.

A   Having saluted the flag
B   After the sailors saluted the flag
C   Once he saluted
D   Having been saluted

69. I will give the reward _____ shows up first with the correct answer.

A   to whoever
B   whomever
C   to what person
D   to whomever

70. Because the sushi was almost _____ _____ took it off the menu.

A   gone so the chef
B   gone; so the chef
C   gone, the chef
D   nearly gone so the chef

71. While many people are attempting to eat healthy, some young women are eating _____ to grow into maturity.

A   too little as to what they need
B   less than what they need
C   less than what she needs
D   less as to what they need

72. The maître d' _____ 50 customers at a time, all the while taking reservations for later seating times.

A   has the capability of handling
B   handles
C   can handle
D   was capable and handles

# REMINDER

✓ Write a response to the writing prompt shown.

✓ You may title your passage if you like, but it is not required.

✓ Dictionaries are NOT allowed. If you cannot spell a word, try sounding the word out. Then write the word in the best way you can.

✓ You may write in either print or cursive.

✓ Make sure you write clearly! Any erasures or strike-outs should be as neat as possible.

## 73. Writing Task

Some schools have dress codes for their students. Other schools believe that dress codes are unnecessary. The administration at your school has been considering the option, and it is being widely debated among the stakeholders (i.e., students, teachers, administrators, parents, school board).

Decide whether you are for or against dress codes, and write an opinion column that will be published in your local school newspaper. Remember to include reasons to back up your belief.

# Writing Checklist

This writing list will help you make your writing better. Make sure you check the following:

☐ Read the description of the prompt carefully.

☐ Organize your essay with a strong introduction, body, and conclusion.

☐ Support your ideas with specific, detailed examples.

☐ Use words that your audience can understand and that fit the purpose of the writing task.

☐ Use different types of sentences to make your writing interesting.

☐ Check for errors in grammar, spelling, punctuation, capitalization, and sentence formation.

# Answers and Explanations

**1. B**

Although choice A is an accurate statement, it is not the main idea of the passage. Mnemonic devices are described as one strategy in a portion of the text, but they are not the overall theme of the entire passage. Therefore, choice C is incorrect. Choice D simply describes two examples given in the passage for which mnemonic devices can be used. Thus, only choice B fully describes the main idea of the passage and can be applied to every paragraph.

**2. D**

Choices A and B are both incorrect because the textbooks mentioned would cover information about other fields, not language arts. Choice C is not correct because the target audience for the information in the passage is not third-grade children. Because the passage's intended audience is language arts teachers, the correct answer is D.

**3. A**

This question asks for the answer that is NOT a part of the process. Therefore, choice A is the correct answer—positive transfer deals with long-term memory, not short-term memory. The final paragraph of the passage discusses the concept of positive transfer. Choices B, C, and D describe (in order) exactly how positive transfer occurs—it stores information in your long-term memory and then adds other relevant information to it later on.

**4. C**

The final paragraph states that mnemonic devices work only if a student can use the words or letters in the device to remember previous concepts. Therefore, choice C is the correct answer. The passage promotes the use of mnemonic devices, so choice A is incorrect. The passage gives a five-step method to teaching, not a one-step method, so choice B is incorrect. Finally, the passage does not mention anything about detrimental mnemonic devices, so choice D is incorrect.

**5. C**

This is a specific detail question. If you go back into the passage and read the topic sentences of paragraphs 2 through 6, you will find the five effective components of language arts. Choices A, B, and D are among those listed. Choice C, on the other hand, is the opposite of using the higher-order thinking skills because knowledge and comprehension are the lower-level thinking skills.

**6. B**

Throughout the poem, the author offers advice for how a person can act correctly even when life is hard. Choice A is not accurate because, although in the last line, he mentions *my son*, the main theme is about one's actions toward others. One portion of the poem in the third stanza deals with a person taking a gamble, but it is not the main idea, so choice C is not correct. The same is true for choice D, because the poem is about many aspects of life, not just leadership.

**7. D**

The author is not talking about the literal sense of touch (choice B). Also, while being a friend might be a good answer (and might or might not come from staying grounded), it is not the best one. The best answer is choice D because it is talking about how a man can be successful (walking with kings) but remain down-to-earth in his attitude. Choice C is an opposite—not losing the common touch means not acting better than others.

**8. C**

When the author says, *If you can dream—and not make dreams your master,* he is saying that a man can have a dream, but that he should not let it control his life. Choice C best reflects this statement. Kipling says man should dream, so choice A is incorrect. Even if one should not be consumed by his dreams, that doesn't mean he should not take them seriously (choice B). Choice D says that man should make dreams his master—the opposite of what Kipling is saying.

**9. B**

Although in the last line, the author refers to the reader as *my son,* it does not indicate whether the person is his actual son or simply someone younger than the poet to whom the poet is giving advice. Choice A is not correct because it reverses the relationship. Choice C is not correct because brothers are more equal in stature. Choice D is not correct because, indeed, the final line suggests it is an older person instructing someone younger.

**10. A**

The passage describes how both the thalamus and the hypothalamus protect and alert the body, so choice A is the best answer. Choice B is incorrect because the passage says nothing about how one *thermometer* is more important than the other—both perform vital functions. Choices C and D are incorrect because the passage states that the thalamus, not the hypothalamus, relates to the sensory organs.

**11. B**

Choice B is correct—sentence 1 of the third paragraph clearly states that the hypothalamus takes the inside temperature. Choices A and C refer to the thalamus, which is incorrect. Choice D refers to the sensory organs, which respond to information from the thalamus, not the hypothalamus.

**12. B**

The passage really details information about the two thermometers of the body—the thalamus and the hypothalamus. The passage does not say that one part of the brain is more important than the other, so choice A is incorrect. Choice B is the correct answer. Choices C and D are too broad—the passage doesn't talk about the brain as a whole or its many parts, just two components.

## 13. B

This passage both introduces and discusses the concept of friction, so choice B is the best answer. Choices A, C, and D are specific details mentioned in the passage, but they are not the primary purpose.

## 14. C

The third sentence of the passage clearly indicates that friction occurs by the insertion of higher parts of one surface into lower parts of another or through atom attraction—choice C is correct. Choice A describes types of friction, choice B describes how objects are set in motion due to friction, and choice D lists specific elements a gymnast uses to reduce friction.

## 15. A

The first paragraph of the passage discusses static friction (meaning from a position of standing still) and kinetic friction (from something already moving). The passage states that an object already in motion takes less effort to move, so choice A is the correct answer. Choice B says the opposite of this, so it is incorrect. In choice C, you don't know whether or not the car is stationary or moving, so you have no way of inferring the correct answer. Finally, the passage's information about the two coefficients of friction has to do with movement, not attraction, as in choice D.

## 16. A

Choices B, C, and D are all correct ways to reword the sentence. Choice A, however, includes the word *if*, indicating that two surfaces might or might not have a coefficient. All surfaces would have one; it's simply the level that would change.

## 17. C

An assumption is a thought authors have before they write a passage. They don't necessarily state it, but their statements indicate it is part of their belief system. In this passage, the author repeatedly indicates that the same rights that apply to other types of media should apply to the Internet. Choice C best reflects this stance. Choices A and B are opposites of the correct answer—the author feels the Internet is an equivalent form of media. Choice D is incorrect because the author feels blogging should be mainstream, not that it already is mainstream.

**18. D**

Throughout the passage, the author simply discusses issues related to the Internet. He does not give his opinion about its validity, so none of the other answer choices can be the best answer.

**19. D**

This is a specific detail question. The last two sentences in paragraph 2 indicate that the writer of the response is the one who is responsible for the content. The people in the other three choices are therefore not responsible.

**20. A**

This is a question in which there are three answer choices that support the passage, and the correct answer is one that does not. Choices B and C offer more information about the Electronic Frontier Foundation that would fit well in the passage. Choice D would support the section that states that bloggers should be treated like other journalists and should receive press passes. Choice A would weaken the argument because the passage indicates that the Foundation believes that bloggers are not treated like the traditional media and are not supplied with press passes. If all bloggers were supplied, this would seriously weaken the Foundation's mission.

**21. B**

This is an inference question. Although the author does not state a specific attitude about the Mongolian army directly, there are many clues in the passage that allow us to reach a logical conclusion. The first paragraph alone uses the adjectives *superior, well trained, disciplined*, and *prepared*. The author obviously respects the Mongolian army, but does not fear it. Also, despite this respect, the author is not in awe of the army.

## 22. D

This is a detail question. The exact answer is found directly in the passage. You should not have memorized the definitions of each of these foreign words or spent too much time on them as you read. Instead, you should have circled or underlined them so that you could find them more easily. Remember to research detail questions by locating the information you need using your topic sentences, and then rereading it before you answer the question.

## 23. D

This is a main idea question. Choices A, B, and C take details from the passage (although victories in China are not discussed). Only choice D is the main idea of the entire passage.

## 24. C

This is a detail question. Use your topic sentences to help you locate the answer to this question in paragraph 2. The correct answer is a rephrasing of sentence 1 from paragraph 2, which states, *On the battlefield, each unit was expected to participate in a major coordinated effort and, at the same time, be able to act independently.* Notice that the incorrect answer choices are either not mentioned at all in the passage (*farmers* or *mistrustful*), or are taken out of context (*well dressed*). Only choice C works for this question.

## 25. D

Choices A, B, and C all deal with smaller aspects of the passage, but only choice D addresses the whole passage, which talks about English as a main language around the world.

## 26. A

This is a negative question. Therefore, you are looking for the three answers that are inferred in the passage. The one answer choice that is not inferred is the correct answer. Choice A is the only answer that is not inferred from the passage—people in India don't converse only in English. Some learn English early on in their schooling and continue to study the language and its inflections in order to work for American companies. Choices B, C, and D are all points addressed in the second paragraph.

**27. C**

The introductory paragraph of the passage deals with the fact that English is spoken all over the world—a broad introduction. Then, the second paragraph gives a more specific example of that topic—people in India who learn English early on and perfect it in order to work for American companies. Therefore, the paragraphs are not equal, as stated in choice A. Choice B is the opposite of the correct answer. Choice D is incorrect, because the main idea is never refuted.

**28. D**

Although choices A and C are true statements, they are not the direct meaning of the phrase used in this context. Choice D is the correct answer because, indeed, after taking over the countries and colonizing them, it was always daytime in at least one of Britain's countries around the world. Choice B is a generalization and a false statement.

**29. B**

The whole tone of the passage relates to the mother reflecting on her daughter's college years and graduation. Choice A is one main theme of the passage, but not the tone of the passage as a whole. Choices C and D are also minor points mentioned, that might be inferred, but are not reflective of the passage as a whole.

**30. D**

This is a question written in the negative—you're looking for the one word that does NOT strengthen the passage. Therefore, you are looking for three synonyms for *obstinate*, which are choices A, B, and C. The one word that is not its synonym is *wavering*, choice D.

**31. B**

The words *unnecessary impediment* indicate that the mother did not agree with the father's insistence that their daughter not take out loans. Choices A and C are opposite sentiments to the correct answer. The mother never expresses any regret toward *when* her daughter is graduating, so choice D is incorrect.

**32. B**

Foreshadowing gives the reader a hint about something that is going to happen. Choice B clues the reader in that an important event is going to happen (for which the mother was going to try to hold back the tears), but it does not tell the reader what that event is just yet. Choice A is simply a descriptive statement that does not foreshadow anything to come. Choices C and D are factual statements about the family's situation, but they do not give clues about future events.

**33. D**

Choice A is not correct because Milton is the eight-year-old who came up with the term *googol* to name a really big number. Choice B is incorrect because Kasner (with the help of his nephew) was the mathematician who named the large number *googol*, but he had nothing to do with the company Google Inc. Choice C is not correct because Milton was eight years old and definitely not a mathematician. Thus, choice D is the correct statement, which can be backed up with the information provided in the passage.

**34. A**

What began as a name from a child's imagination became a mathematical term, which then became a search engine company name. This definitely shows the creativity of our language, making choice A correct. Choices B, C, and D are not topics covered in the passage.

**35. B**

If, indeed, the company had been named in the 1920s prior to the mathematician naming the large number *googol* in the 1930s, that would weaken the author's argument in passage. Choices A and C, even if true, would not weaken the argument at all. Choice D might even strengthen the argument that *Google* derived from the word *googol*.

**36. C**

From the beginning, you can eliminate choices A and D—the tone of the passage is not formal or lecturelike, but rather easy to read and casual. You are looking for the best answer here. Because the passage does include expository text (which describes a concept in detail), choice C is the best answer.

### 37. A

As directly stated in the passage, the lowercase *googolplex* represents a 1 followed by a googol of zeros. The uppercase *Googleplex* represents the building that houses the company Google Inc. Choice A is the only answer choice that correctly defines the terms.

### 38. C

Choice A is not accurate because it does not deal with the CEO being ineffective nor does it deal with him being promoted. Choice B is not accurate because the teacher was promoted for being effective. To exemplify the principle, she would have had to be ineffective but still promoted. Choice D includes a person being demoted instead of promoted. That leaves choice C as the correct answer.

### 39. B

The final sentence of paragraph 1 clearly states that the important decisions are made at the upper levels and the most work is done at the lower levels. Therefore, middle management is not very important, according to the passage. Choice B directly states this. Choices A, C, and D describe opposite and incorrect theories.

### 40. B

While getting to work is important, a brainstorming session is about thinking of creative ideas, not about beginning the actual work. Therefore, choice A can't be the correct answer. In the context of the passage, being promoted to middle management (as in choice C) would occur not from thinking outside the box, but from not doing one's work well. Choice D is the second-best answer, but choice B is the best answer because it is creativity that is related to the phrase *think outside the box*.

### 41. A

Choice A indicates that the passage is about current business principles, which is correct—reading it, you learn about brainstorming and the Peter Principle. Choices B, C, and D are tangential in nature and mentioned in the passage, but definitely not the main idea of the passage.

**42. D**

In choice A, the ice cream party is the unconditioned stimulus because it naturally makes one feel good. Choice C is the unconditioned response for the same reason. Choice D is the conditioned stimulus because the teacher has associated it with the ice cream party. Choice B is the conditioned response because it is hoped that the more the children read to earn the ice cream party, the more they will associate it with feeling good.

**43. D**

This exact statement is found in the last sentence of the third paragraph. Choices A and B are incorrect because the unconditioned response is the same, not the stimulus. Choice C is incorrect because the unconditioned response occurs naturally, not the conditioned response.

**44. C**

Throughout the passage, the author discusses real-life examples. Choices A, B, and D are not mentioned in the passage to illustrate concepts.

**45. B**

The final sentence indicates that Pavlov not only developed the theory, but also used it to condition himself to do the work. Choice A is a literal, and incorrect, interpretation of *walk the walk*. Choices C and D are incorrect statements that have nothing to do with the information presented in the passage.

**46. D**

Antonyms are opposites. *Cowardice* and *bravery* are used as opposites in this passage. The sets of words in the other answer choices have no direct relationship to one another.

**47. C**

This passage is not factual, so choices A, B, and D are ruled out. That leaves choice C, where the author is trying to persuade the reader to see her point of view.

**48. B**

Sentence 2 does not really serve a purpose in the text. If it were removed, the first paragraph would sound more professional. Choices A and C are incorrect, because the paragraph would be better served without sentence 2. Choice D is incorrect because sentence 3 adds to the author's purpose and argument.

**49. A**

This question is asking for a synonym for *flamboyant*. Choice A, *showy*, is an exact synonym. The other answer choices are unrelated to the word. You may have mistaken choice D, fiery, because orange is the color of fire. However, flamboyant and fiery are not synonyms.

**50. A**

There is indeed some agreement about the fact that certain colors have meanings. Choice B is not correct because there is consensus about some of the meanings. Choice C is an opinion, and while it is mentioned, it is not necessarily supported by the passage. The passage also does not support the statement in choice D, that all colors have multiple meanings.

**51. A**

Choice B won't work because tennis shoes are a relatively new invention, and certainly not from time immemorial. Choice C is slang. Choice D implies that time passed after the first sentence. Therefore, only choice A makes sense.

**52. C**

The *Velcro* information has really nothing to do with the content of the paragraph. The other sentences are all relevant and add to the paragraph's overall statement.

**53. D**

As it is written, the sentence is straightforward. Thus, it should be left alone, so answer choice D is correct. Choice B does not make sense in the context of the paragraph. Choices A and C make the sentence longer and more confusing than it needs to be.

**54. C**

The words *less expensive* match the tone of the passage better than *cheaper*. Choice A is improper grammar. Choice B is unnecessarily wordy. Choice D is the opposite of *cheap*.

**55. A**

Only choice A is supported by the passage. Choice B is the reverse of the truth. Because athletic shoes did evolve from tennis shoes, choice C is not correct. Choice D is not relevant at all to the passage.

**56. B**

The first paragraph is about Fry, so choice B is the natural first sentence. The other choices, if used, are better placed later on in the paragraph.

**57. B**

Choice B is the best and most accurate replacement for the current title. The other three possibilities touch on aspects of the passage, but do not cover all the parts of the passage.

**58. C**

The correct order is Thorndike, then Carroll, then Fry. However, nothing in the passage indicates that the three collaborated (worked together) on any project.

**59. C**

The word *however* is needed to show a change of direction, so choices B and D are not correct. Choice A is too wordy (including the word *now* twice), so choice C is the best answer.

**60. D**

Because the last paragraph that is written is about other languages, it makes sense that the concluding sentence would be choice D. Choice A is already essentially stated in the last paragraph. Choices B and C would be better placed in the preceding paragraph.

**61. B**

The phrase *who attended school with my mother* is an appositive and should be set off by commas. Choices A and C divide the appositive into two thoughts instead of the one that is needed to make the sentence sensible.

**62. C**

The word *than* is needed, ruling out choices B and D. Of the remaining two, choice C is better because it shows the relationship between the two parts of the sentence using the word *because*.

**63. C**

Although choice A could be grammatically correct, it is awkward. Both choices B and D indicate that the floor is doing the mopping. Thus, choice C is the best answer.

**64. A**

Choice A is the only answer that has a correct subject-verb agreement.

**65. C**

This is a circumstance of using the most straightforward wording. The other answer choices all make the sentence awkward.

**66. C**

The only appropriate spelling, *their* (showing possession), is used in choice C.

**67. D**

For each of the distracters, there is a problem. Choice A uses *as* instead of *than*. Choice B misuses a semicolon. Choice C has the incorrect word choice of *partly so*. Thus, choice D, when inserted in the passage, is the only one that makes sense.

**68. B**

This is a case of a misplaced modifier. Because the flag is the subject following the blank, choices A and C both make it sound like the flag was doing the saluting. Choice D features awkward wording. Therefore, the subordinating clause in choice B fully indicates that the sailors saluted the flag.

**69. D**

This is a subjective/objective question as well as a sentence needing a prepositional phrase. *Whom* (or *whomever*) is the objective case and should be used as an objective of the preposition (*to*). Therefore, choice D is the correct answer.

**70. C**

Choices A and B cannot be correct because the combination of the words *because* and *so* are redundant. Choice D shows redundancy with *nearly* and *almost*. Therefore, only choice C is grammatically correct.

**71. B**

Choice C is ruled out because the pronoun *she* does not match the plural antecedent *girls*. Choice A is too wordy, and choice D is awkward. Therefore, choice B is the correct answer.

**72. C**

Choice A is not correct because it is too wordy. Choice B is not accurate because it implies that he is always handling 50 customers at a time, rather than that he is able to handle that many. Choice D won't work because it has two tenses in it. Thus, the simple answer, choice B, *handles*, is the best answer.

## 73. WRITING TASK

### A sample answer that received a 4:

Years ago, when my parents were attending school, dress codes were not only very stringent, but also strictly enforced. Skirts had to go to the top of a girl's knee. Boys' shirts had to have button-down collars and the shirt itself had to be tucked in. Over the years, the dress codes have been relaxed and, in some cases, completely done away with. However, here at Stanley High School, the issue has been revived in an even stricter manner, as it considers requiring that all students wear school uniforms. I personally believe that requiring school uniforms at Stanley High School is a good idea. There are three reasons I am in favor of this new dress code.

The first reason I am in favor of a dress code is that requiring students to dress professionally will prepare them for life. The whole purpose of education is for students to learn the things they need to know to become productive members of society. However, if a person learns the academic things she needs to know, but can't present herself professionally by dressing appropriately for job interviews or a job, her knowledge and skills will do her little good.

Another reason I believe that a dress code would be appropriate at Stanley High is that some students put so much emphasis on wearing the latest trends that it puts a burden on their parents to provide them with constantly stylish clothes. In fact, sometimes students actually take on jobs themselves to buy the latest fashions. This can be detrimental to their learning because they are spending their evenings working rather than working on their studies.

A final reason that I believe school uniforms would be a good idea is because it would give the students who go to school there a sense of pride. The athletic teams wear uniforms. The cheerleaders wear uniforms. I don't know why our students couldn't wear uniforms and show as much pride for our academics.

In conclusion, I do believe that school uniforms are a good idea. It would prepare us for dressing professionally, save our parents money, and give us a chance to show pride in our schools. Besides, it would make it much easier to decide what to wear every morning.

## A sample answer that received a 3:

Our school is considering having students begin to wear uniforms. They will be mandatory. I am against that because I believe the school years are when we get to develop our identity, when we can be creative, and when we can learn to express ourselves.

First, I believe that clothes make the person. Therefore, through the clothes we wear, we develop our sense of fashion. That helps us more fully develop our identities. If we all wear the same clothes, meaning a uniform, we will not have the chance to develop that part of our identity when we go to school each day.

Secondly, fashion allows us to be creative. A person can dress up a pair of jeans, or dress them down. He can simply wear nice clothing to school, or he can be more casual in what he wears. On one day, a person might want to wear something to represent a cause (like a pink shirt to support research for breast cancer), while on another day, a person simply might want to wear a shirt with a favorite slogan on it.

Thirdly, we can learn to express ourselves through our clothing. With everyone wearing the same uniform, that will be eliminated. Whether it is to wear a shirt and tie, or an oversized pair of jeans, one is making a statement with his/her clothing. It is an expression of one's self.

So, there are at least three good reasons that we should not have a school uniform. Creativity, development of identity, and self expression are three examples. There are probably many others.

## A sample answer that received a 2:

The uniform question that has been debated at the school is coming to a conclusion. Soon, they will be making a decision. I hope the decision is for us to have uniforms.

I don't like how some kids can afford better clothes than others. Therefore, school clothes that all look alike make sense to me. Sometimes, I see students leaving private schools in their uniforms and I think they look nicely. Sometimes, I have thought about wearing a uniform. I think it is a good idea.

A good reason for wearing a uniform is to make it simply as to what to wear to school on any given day. Another good reason is to show school pride. When I see someone wearing a uniform (like a cop, et. al.), I have respect for them.

A final good reason would be to save money. Uniforms could be useful for all of us because we could buy one set for a whole week and then just wash them on them on the weekend.

In conclusion, I'm in favor of our school adopting uniforms. How about you?

## A sample answer that received a 1:

Some schools require uniforms. We have uniforms here at our school. However, you have to join a group to wear one. The sports teams wear uniforms. The cheerleaders wear uniforms. The band wears uniforms. Therefore, I think that our school should not have more uniforms. We have enough already.

So, my opinion is because too much of anything is not good. We don't need more uniforms.

# Full-Length Practice Test 2
# Answer Sheet

**Remove or photocopy this answer sheet and use it to complete the practice test.**

1. Ⓐ Ⓑ Ⓒ Ⓓ    5. Ⓐ Ⓑ Ⓒ Ⓓ    9. Ⓐ Ⓑ Ⓒ Ⓓ    13. Ⓐ Ⓑ Ⓒ Ⓓ    17. Ⓐ Ⓑ Ⓒ Ⓓ
2. Ⓐ Ⓑ Ⓒ Ⓓ    6. Ⓐ Ⓑ Ⓒ Ⓓ    10. Ⓐ Ⓑ Ⓒ Ⓓ    14. Ⓐ Ⓑ Ⓒ Ⓓ    18. Ⓐ Ⓑ Ⓒ Ⓓ
3. Ⓐ Ⓑ Ⓒ Ⓓ    7. Ⓐ Ⓑ Ⓒ Ⓓ    11. Ⓐ Ⓑ Ⓒ Ⓓ    15. Ⓐ Ⓑ Ⓒ Ⓓ    19. Ⓐ Ⓑ Ⓒ Ⓓ
4. Ⓐ Ⓑ Ⓒ Ⓓ    8. Ⓐ Ⓑ Ⓒ Ⓓ    12. Ⓐ Ⓑ Ⓒ Ⓓ    16. Ⓐ Ⓑ Ⓒ Ⓓ    20. Ⓐ Ⓑ Ⓒ Ⓓ

21. Ⓐ Ⓑ Ⓒ Ⓓ    25. Ⓐ Ⓑ Ⓒ Ⓓ    29. Ⓐ Ⓑ Ⓒ Ⓓ    33. Ⓐ Ⓑ Ⓒ Ⓓ    37. Ⓐ Ⓑ Ⓒ Ⓓ
22. Ⓐ Ⓑ Ⓒ Ⓓ    26. Ⓐ Ⓑ Ⓒ Ⓓ    30. Ⓐ Ⓑ Ⓒ Ⓓ    34. Ⓐ Ⓑ Ⓒ Ⓓ    38. Ⓐ Ⓑ Ⓒ Ⓓ
23. Ⓐ Ⓑ Ⓒ Ⓓ    27. Ⓐ Ⓑ Ⓒ Ⓓ    31. Ⓐ Ⓑ Ⓒ Ⓓ    35. Ⓐ Ⓑ Ⓒ Ⓓ    39. Ⓐ Ⓑ Ⓒ Ⓓ
24. Ⓐ Ⓑ Ⓒ Ⓓ    28. Ⓐ Ⓑ Ⓒ Ⓓ    32. Ⓐ Ⓑ Ⓒ Ⓓ    36. Ⓐ Ⓑ Ⓒ Ⓓ    40. Ⓐ Ⓑ Ⓒ Ⓓ

41. Ⓐ Ⓑ Ⓒ Ⓓ    45. Ⓐ Ⓑ Ⓒ Ⓓ    49. Ⓐ Ⓑ Ⓒ Ⓓ    53. Ⓐ Ⓑ Ⓒ Ⓓ    57. Ⓐ Ⓑ Ⓒ Ⓓ
42. Ⓐ Ⓑ Ⓒ Ⓓ    46. Ⓐ Ⓑ Ⓒ Ⓓ    50. Ⓐ Ⓑ Ⓒ Ⓓ    54. Ⓐ Ⓑ Ⓒ Ⓓ    58. Ⓐ Ⓑ Ⓒ Ⓓ
43. Ⓐ Ⓑ Ⓒ Ⓓ    47. Ⓐ Ⓑ Ⓒ Ⓓ    51. Ⓐ Ⓑ Ⓒ Ⓓ    55. Ⓐ Ⓑ Ⓒ Ⓓ    59. Ⓐ Ⓑ Ⓒ Ⓓ
44. Ⓐ Ⓑ Ⓒ Ⓓ    48. Ⓐ Ⓑ Ⓒ Ⓓ    52. Ⓐ Ⓑ Ⓒ Ⓓ    56. Ⓐ Ⓑ Ⓒ Ⓓ    60. Ⓐ Ⓑ Ⓒ Ⓓ

61. Ⓐ Ⓑ Ⓒ Ⓓ    65. Ⓐ Ⓑ Ⓒ Ⓓ    69. Ⓐ Ⓑ Ⓒ Ⓓ
62. Ⓐ Ⓑ Ⓒ Ⓓ    66. Ⓐ Ⓑ Ⓒ Ⓓ    70. Ⓐ Ⓑ Ⓒ Ⓓ
63. Ⓐ Ⓑ Ⓒ Ⓓ    67. Ⓐ Ⓑ Ⓒ Ⓓ    71. Ⓐ Ⓑ Ⓒ Ⓓ
64. Ⓐ Ⓑ Ⓒ Ⓓ    68. Ⓐ Ⓑ Ⓒ Ⓓ    72. Ⓐ Ⓑ Ⓒ Ⓓ

# Full-Length Practice Test 2

This full-length practice test for the CAHSEE has 72 multiple-choice questions and one writing prompt.

The section you are about to start is the Reading portion of the CAHSEE. This part of the test is composed of reading passages followed by multiple-choice questions.

There is no time limit on the CAHSEE, but make sure you pace yourself on the questions. When you have completed your practice exam, turn to page 387 for the answers and explanations.

Read the following passage and answer questions 1 through 5.

# America's Christmas Songwriter

Israel Isadore Baline, Izzy, a Jewish young man, was born in Russia as the son of a rabbi. His family immigrated to America when Izzy was five years old. In America, the only job his father could find was working as a man who could certify kosher meat. When Izzy's father died three years later, Izzy suddenly needed to help the family survive. As an eight-year-old, he sold newspapers and did odd jobs. This would have a lasting effect on him throughout his lifetime.

While working as a singing waiter in New York, he was asked to sing an original song for the tavern in which he worked as its theme song. He did that, and when it was published, it listed his name as I. Berlin instead of I. Baline.

Although he did not know how to write musical notation, he became noted composer Irving Berlin, one of America's most prolific and influential songwriters. He was considered a Tin Pan Alley songwriter, and he was one of the few who wrote both music and lyrics. Although he never learned much about actually writing musical notation beyond the <u>rudimentary</u> concepts, he ended up writing, or shall we say composing, more than 3,000 songs throughout his lifetime. Many were first performed on Broadway or in movies,

and he quickly became a household name in the 1930s. Ultimately, he wrote the entire scores for dozens of movies and Broadway shows.

On the Monday after he wrote the song "White Christmas," he told his musical secretary that he had not only written the best song *he* had ever written, but the best song *anyone* had ever written. "It's a song that seems to have always been around," states a singer who has a current rendition of the song out. It is generally believed that Berlin penned the song while working as a musical director on a movie in Hollywood over a Christmas season some years earlier. However, he came across it again in the fall of 1940 when he was looking through his papers for inspiration. It was then that he polished the song over a weekend, and sent it out for publication.

Bing Crosby then recorded the now-infamous version for that Christmas season, but it was not immediately a big hit. Berlin offered the American public another version of it in the movie *Holiday Inn* in the following year. Still, it was not a big hit. However, later that year, shortly after the bombing of Pearl Harbor, the year-old recording began playing regularly on Armed Services Radio on service bases around the world, and Berlin's self-aggrandizement became true. In fact, it became an anthem for people everywhere away from home on Christmas. Although Berlin also wrote "God Bless America" and "You're a Grand Ole Flag," the song most music and culture experts consider the most patriotic song he ever wrote never mentions the word *America*.

1. **According to the passage, what does the author believe is Berlin's most patriotic song?**

   A   "God Bless America"

   B   "White Christmas"

   C   a tie between "God Bless America" and "You're a Grand Ole Flag"

   D   *Holiday Inn*

2. **What can one conclude from the passage?**

   A   The author is not a fan of Irving Berlin.

   B   The author does not believe that a man from Russia can write American songs that are truly patriotic.

   C   The author thought Berlin was a braggart who couldn't really deliver.

   D   The author thinks Berlin's own feelings about his music were deserved.

3. **What would be the BEST title for this passage?**

   A   Russian Writer Makes Good in America

   B   Composer Writes Christmas Song

   C   Irving Berlin and His "White Christmas"

   D   Broadway Songwriters

4. The passage provides the LEAST information on which of the following?

   A   his childhood

   B   his mother's life

   C   his father's life

   D   his songwriting

5. Which of the following words or phrases could replace the underlined word in the third paragraph and maintain the author's meaning in that sentence?

   A   very basic

   B   rooting on

   C   unpleasant toward

   D   skillful

Read the following poem excerpt and answer questions 6 through 9.

# Bill and Joe

### by Oliver Wendell Holmes

COME, dear old comrade, you and I
Will steal an hour from days gone by,
The shining days when life was new,
And all was bright with morning dew,
The lusty days of long ago,
When you were Bill and I was Joe.

Your name may flaunt a titled trail
Proud as a cockerel's rainbow tail,
And mine as brief appendix wear
As Tam O'Shanter's luckless mare;
To-day, old friend, remember still
That I am Joe and you are Bill.

You've won the great world's envied prize,
And grand you look in people's eyes,
With H O N. and L L. D.
In big brave letters, fair to see,—
Your fist, old fellow! off they go!—
How are you, Bill? How are you, Joe?

You've worn the judge's ermined robe;
You've taught your name to half the globe;
You've sung mankind a deathless strain;
You've made the dead past live again:
The world may call you what it will,
But you and I are Joe and Bill.

6. Which of the following would be a way to reword the following line and NOT change the meaning?

> Will steal an hour from days gone by

A   will reminisce

B   will brag and laugh

C   will show our friends

D   will become friends again

7. According to the poem, which of the following can be inferred?

A   Joe and Bill have remained in close contact through the years.

B   Bill kept in touch with Joe, but Joe didn't keep in touch with Bill.

C   They were friends when they were younger but hadn't maintained contact through the years.

D   They used to be friends, but now dislike one another.

8. According to the poem, which of the following ideas is accurate?

A   Bill has had more public success than Joe.

B   Joe has had more public success than Bill.

C   Both men have had great success in their lives.

D   Neither man has had success in life.

9. What is the theme of the poem?

A   Some people have all the luck; others don't.

B   Politicians get rich off the working-class people.

C   The rich and famous don't mix with average folks.

D   Old friends can rekindle the friendship even if their lives have taken different paths.

Read the following passage and answer questions 10 through 12.

# Curriculum Teaching

*Teaching across the curriculum* is a current trend. In the past, classroom subjects were taught individually. A student would begin the day with a spelling class. The words might all be words with *-ing* endings, or they might all be compound words. It would be structure that they had in common, not meaning. Students would then put away their spelling books and get out their history books. They would have a history lesson. After recess, math would be taught, followed by a period of reading from a basal reader. After lunch, the students would work on grammar exercises. Sometimes, those grammar exercises were related to the story they had read in their basals, sometimes not.

Now, however, students are often taught material in a particular discipline in the context of another classroom subject. This particular strategy embodies the concept that true learning involves making connections and invoking positive transfer. Positive transfer involves having a student remember prior knowledge and then attaching the new concepts being taught to the previously learned concepts. For example, if the students are learning about trees in science, their multiplication tables might include word problems concerning leaves on the trees or cords of firewood cut

from the trees. The story in the basal reader might be about a boy climbing a tree, and the history class might involve the Oklahoma Land Rush when settlers called Sooners rushed across the border into Oklahoma to clear the trees, build themselves houses, and apply for a deed to the land.

In real life, individuals invoke positive transfer all the time. If a man's car begins making a noise, and he takes it to a mechanic who tells him that one of the belts has come loose, later, when it makes a similar noise, he might look to see if one of the other belts on the engine is becoming worn or is no longer properly attached. If a woman buys fruit from a particular market and it spoils very quickly, she may choose to bypass that market the next time and purchase her fruit at a different grocery store.

Because one of the purposes of education is to teach students to function well in adulthood, it makes sense that they should also be taught to use positive transfer. This is done by using the strategy of teaching across the curriculum.

10. Which of the following would exemplify a *teaching across the curriculum* experience in a classroom?

   A   having the students create graphic organizers laying out the important characters in a story

   B   having the students place important history dates on a timeline and then figure out the number of years between the various dates

   C   using cooperative learning where the students are divided into homogeneous ability groups for brainstorming about how to create a mural

   D   organizing the students into two groups and having one group finish the spelling sentences while the other does math problems

11. Which of the following pairs of words are synonyms as they are used in the passage?

   A   bypass, buy
   B   purchase, bypass
   C   spoils, bypass
   D   buy, purchase

12. According to the passage, we can infer that the author believes—

   A   positive transfer should not occur in school.
   B   children who aren't taught to use positive transfer are missing out.
   C   children are simply little adults.
   D   teachers should teach only the subject area in which they are trained.

Read the following science passage and answer questions 13 through 16.

# Do Nanos Affect the Environment?

The production of nanoparticles has drastically increased in the last several years. This is mostly because of their potential medical applications, but they may also be used in environmental cleanup and remediation. However, the impact of releasing these extremely small particles into the environment, either as byproducts, medical waste, or intentionally as environmental tools, needs to be investigated. Of particular interest is the impact on aquatic organisms as waste moves into freshwater systems. This is especially relevant in the Great Lakes region where many large cities, such as Chicago and Milwaukee and their accompanying sewage systems, sit on the banks of these large waterways.

Small, planktonic crustaceans, such as *Daphnia*, are easily affected by waste contamination and are therefore a good study specimen. *Daphnia* are also a vital connection in the food chain between the primary producers that they consume and the ecologically and economically important fish that consume them. In other words, *Daphnia* are small aquatic fleas. They feed on microorganisms smaller than themselves. They feed by filtering particles to obtain algae for food, and in this process, they can select against

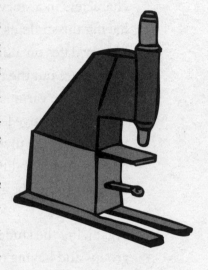

certain elements (and thereby, not take them in), but may also take in other materials inadvertently. These accidental particles may interfere with the physiology or feeding ability of the animal. Therefore, in this study, we will expose *Daphnia* to three sizes of nanoparticles to determine if particle size affects these biological processes. We will examine the effects of the nanoparticles using Environmental Protection Agency (EPA) standard acute and chronic toxicity assays. The effects of individual particle types on *Daphnia* growth and mortality rates will be compared. The expectation is that this project will influence future environmental policy pertaining to nanoparticle management.

13. In what type of document is this passage most likely to have appeared?

A    an elementary science textbook
B    a biology survey
C    a college guidebook
D    a thesis proposal

14. Which of the following questions will the described study answer?

A    What are nanoparticles?
B    What is the effect of nanoparticles on *Daphnia*?
C    What is the effect of nanoparticles on a lake's environment?
D    Who should be worried about nanoparticles?

15. According to the passage, *Daphnia* are—

A    aquatic environments.
B    tiny creatures that live in water.
C    microscope parts.
D    environmental pollutants.

16. What is the ultimate reason the experiment is being planned?

A    to help *Daphnia* become a stronger organism
B    to guide entrepreneurs who are interested in growing *Daphnia* for profit
C    to determine the safety, or lack of safety, of nanoparticle usage
D    to determine the feasibility of breeding nanoparticles commercially

Read the following passage and answer questions 17 through 20.

# Fictionalizing History

Historical fiction is a genre of literature that can be tricky. This is because good historical fiction must be both true and made-up at the same time.

The historical fiction writer must tell a good story, but place it in a true historical setting. To be a good story, the author must include an interesting plot, believable characters, and engaging action. However, the restraints are in the setting. The setting must be accurate to the history of the time.

The advantage of historical fiction is that a student can learn about the everyday details of a time period while enjoying a story and learning some history. Most students find it much more interesting to hear a story about George Washington's neighbor who was swindled out of a horse rather than to read expository text about George Washington's life and times.

Historical fiction is often told from one of three viewpoints. It can be written as a fictionalized memoir. In this viewpoint, authors take an event that they lived through and fictionalize the story. However, they remain true to the setting and the historical events that actually happened. An example would be a cowboy returning home and writing a story about his

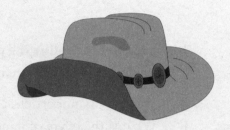

experience on the frontier. He could fictionalize the story and make himself a hero, but the outcome of the story must include an actual outcome that took place. Another viewpoint that can be used is the family story viewpoint. In this, authors take events in their families and tell the stories in fictionalized form. For instance, a woman growing up in the 1960s can use actual events that took place as the setting for a story about her family. However, for it to be fiction, she can't just chronicle the mundane events. Instead, she has to craft a good story using these characters. A third viewpoint, and the most common type, involves authors choosing a time frame, researching it, and writing a story in that setting.

Students enjoy good historical fiction. The key is to make sure that the stories that the teacher chooses contain a good story as well as accurate history.

**17.** What would be the best title for this passage?

A  Historical Fiction—It's Not for Everyone

B  Lies and Fact, All Rolled Up in One

C  A Good Story and Good History— That's the Key

D  History Taught in Story Form—It Can't Be Done

**18.** Which of the following is NOT one of the viewpoints from which historical fiction can be written?

A  the fictionalized memoir viewpoint

B  the family story viewpoint

C  the omniscient factual viewpoint

D  the research-based setting viewpoint

**19.** With which of the following statements would the author MOST likely agree?

A  In historical fiction, the most important aspect is the story.

B  In historical fiction, the most important aspect is the accuracy of the history.

C  Some people like historical fiction and some people don't.

D  Both a well-crafted story and history that is true are important in the historical fiction genre.

**20.** What is the structure of the passage?

A  A controversial topic is introduced and then strongly defended.

B  A topic is presented, details about the topic are given, and a conclusion repeats the introductory thesis statement.

C  Two topics are presented and one is shown to be more important than the other.

D  A question is asked, possible answers are given, and resolution is achieved.

Read this story about an ice-skater and answer questions 21 through 24.

# Pursuing Greater Things

1  The girl's father did not want her to ride the roller coaster because she was in training for the regional ice-skating finals. Already, she had given up breakfast with the family because she was on the ice practicing from 5–7:30 each morning. She often missed dinner with them as well because she was working with her choreographer or having fittings with the tailor who constantly had to readjust the elaborate array of costumes needed for competition to her ever-growing body. Even if she were at dinner with her family, she could eat only the salad, a bite or two of meat, and the vegetables. She never got to enjoy the bread or the desserts. Now, not riding the roller coaster reminded her once again of another thing she couldn't do with her family.

2  Her only friend seemed to be her journal. She wrote in it on breaks, while waiting for other skaters to clear the ice, or while the Zamboni machine erased the marks and indentures made by all the skaters. Once every few hours, depending on the usage of the rink, the machine would come out, and with six horizontal passes and four vertical ones, always in that order, the Zamboni man (she thought she'd heard him called Bud) would erase her hard work of the day—<u>the per-</u><u>fect figure eights,</u> <u>the straight lines</u> <u>of her flying ara-</u><u>besque, the tiny</u> <u>holes drilled into</u> <u>the floor from her</u> <u>dizzying spins</u>. Maybe Bud was her friend because he always waved at her. She tried to befriend a couple of the other skaters, especially the one who seemed to always be alone on the ice when she arrived early on Saturdays, but it never seemed to happen. Maybe the competition was too cutthroat for that.

3  She knew her father loved her, and of course, her family always told her that she was the one who pushed them to let her begin skating when she was only six. The truth was, a neighbor girl, Tammy, was taking lessons and Brianna simply wanted to join her. When it turned out that Brianna had talent, and brought home the beginner's trophy at the end of the season, she and her parents were hooked.

4  But now she was here at the amusement park with her family (on the single day off she'd had during that entire month), and she was being told she could not participate with her family again. Would it ever stop? Would she ever feel normal? What was normal?

The sign on the roller coaster said, "Live life without regrets—ride the WAVE!" But she could not.

5 "Oh, well," she sighed as she went to sit on the park bench and wait for her family to finish riding the wave. She wished she had her journal with her.

**21. Who is the main character in the passage?**

A   the girl's father
B   Brianna
C   Tammy
D   an ice-skater whose name is not given

**22. For what purpose did the author most likely insert the underlined phrases in paragraph 2?**

A   to show how the girl was lazy
B   to indicate she was a beginning skater
C   to add visual imagery
D   to lend support to the topic sentence of the paragraph

**23. The tone of the passage is one of—**

A   regret.
B   a change of heart.
C   practicality.
D   pragmatism.

**24. One can infer from the passage that the ice-skater is—**

A   unwilling to follow her father's advice concerning the roller coaster.
B   a rebellious teenager.
C   a young girl incapable of making appropriate choices.
D   a young girl living with family members.

Read the following passage about the very common stimulant, caffeine. Then, answer questions 25 through 28.

# Caffeine—Friend or Foe?

Caffeine is a stimulant that occurs naturally in approximately 60 plants. These are plants that are found throughout the world in great abundance. However, converting the caffeine in the plant into a form that is usable by humans is not an easy task. Some plants are conducive to this transformation, while others are not. The most common one is, of course, the coffee bean. It is used as a morning drink in many countries. The stimulant effect from that first cup of coffee in the morning is what wakes up many people around the world.

Caffeine has the effect of heightening physiological alertness. Thus, mental alertness and physical endurance have been associated with its usage. People who consume caffeine from the coffee bean find they have an immediate jolt in brain activity and the generalized feeling of being awake. Caffeine is also found in the kola nut, but when it is extracted from it, much less of the stimulant is available for usage. That is why drinking three or four cans of soda is approximately equal to drinking a single cup of coffee in terms of their stimulant power. However, reports indicate that many people who drink cola drinks often do consume more of their beverage than the coffee drinkers consume of theirs.

Stress causes the body to release cortisol in large amounts. Both cortisol and caffeine do the same thing to the brain, which is to block the relaxing effects of adenosine. Thus, people who have high-stress jobs and consume caffeine end up getting double the effect. This is why some people get a jittery feeling as the day wears on and the amount of caffeine consumed increases. In the long run, this can cause negative health effects on the body's ability to function and the brain's ability to process information.

25. This passage is primarily concerned with—

A  adenosine's relationship with caffeine.
B  caffeine and its positive effects on the body.
C  caffeine and cortisol and their effects on the body.
D  cortisol's relationship with adenosine.

26. Two of the chemicals listed in the passage have a direct effect on another chemical. Which describes this relationship accurately?

A  Cortisol and adenosine affect caffeine.
B  Adenosine and caffeine affect cortisol.
C  Cortisol and caffeine affect adenosine.
D  Caffeine affects cortisol and adenosine.

27. We can assume that the author of the passage would agree with which of the following statements?

A  Children should be given caffeine at an early age because they experience stress, too.
B  Children should not be given caffeine, especially if they are experiencing stress.
C  High-level corporate executives should drink coffee throughout the day.
D  Drinking coffee to wake up in the morning is good for people in high-stress jobs.

28. Which is accurate about the facts and opinions in the passage?

A  All the statements in the passage are stated as facts.
B  All the statements in the passage are stated as opinions.
C  The statements about the chemicals are facts; their effects are opinions.
D  There are no facts stated in the passage.

Read the following passage and answer questions 29 through 32.

# Is It Really Ethnocentrism?

The concept of *ethnocentrism* involves the tendency of a person to view the way his or her own culture, family, or gender does things as the right way or, if one allows for diversity, as the best way. Some sociologists believe that this is a natural tendency. However, the 1994 studies by David and Myra Sadker have baffled such sociologists. In those studies, the Sadkers found that most elementary teachers are more likely to call on males rather than females and are more likely to give positive reinforcement to males rather than to females. Because the vast majority of elementary teachers are female, this seems to be in conflict with the idea of ethnocentrism.

One sociologist, a female, concludes that the studies are not baffling at all. She states that those teachers were raised in male-dominated societies. Thus, though they are females, their belief system, even on a subconscious level, involves the notion that males are superior and thus should receive more attention. Further, she states, the teachers may actually believe the male way of thinking presented by their male students is the superior one, which supports their giving them positive reinforcement. In addition, the test scores of the males, especially in the hard sciences,

seem to prove that maybe the male way of doing things does lead to more success than the female way of doing things.

When studies were done on male teachers, the conclusion was the same. They also gave more attention to the males than the females. This would seem to bear out the sociologist's view because those males were exposed to those same belief systems in the society.

29. **Which of the following questions does the passage answer?**

A   How does ethnocentrism compare to gender bias?

B   What is one possible reason for teachers giving more attention to males than to females?

C   Are females more ethnocentric than males?

D   What is one possible reason for female teachers being ethnocentric?

30. **From the passage, we can determine that which of the following statements is TRUE?**

A   Most teachers give more attention to female students than to male students.

B   Male teachers give more attention to male students and female teachers give more attention to female students.

C   Both female and male teachers give more attention to female students.

D   Both female and male teachers give more attention to male students.

31. **On which of the following assumptions is the passage based?**

A   The female sociologist identified in the second paragraph is a feminist.

B   The female sociologist is a close friend of the Sadkers.

C   The female sociologist has read and scrutinized the Sadkers' research.

D   The Sadkers have been sociologists longer than the female sociologist identified in the second paragraph.

32. **Which of the following examples would NOT exemplify the concept of ethnocentrism?**

A   A couple allow their children to only associate with their ethnic group.

B   A teenager dresses like most of the other teenagers as his school.

C   Corporate officers hire people of the same gender as themselves.

D   A child chooses a school where he or she will be a minority.

Read the following fictional piece from the lesser-known classic *Eight Cousins* by Louisa May Alcott and answer questions 33 through 37.

# from *Eight Cousins*

1   Rose had no mother and father, only her great-aunts. She had been with them only a week, and, though the dear old ladies had tried their best to make her happy, they had not succeeded.

2   They had given her the freedom of the house, and for a day or two she had amused herself roaming all over it, for it was a capital old mansion, and was full of all manner of odd nooks, charming rooms, and mysterious passages. <u>Windows broke out in unexpected places</u>, little balconies overhung the garden most romantically, and there was a long upper hall full of curiosities from all parts of the world; for the Campbells had been sea captains for generations.

3   Aunt Plenty had even allowed Rose to rummage in her great china closet, a spicy retreat, rich in all the "goodies" that children love; but Rose seemed to care little for these toothsome temptations. Gentle Aunt Peace had tried all sorts of pretty needlework, and planned a doll's wardrobe that would have won the heart of even an older child. But Rose took little interest in pink satin hats and tiny hose, though she sewed dutifully till her aunt caught her wiping tears away with the train of a wedding-dress, and that discovery put an end to the sewing society.

4   Then both old ladies put their heads together and picked out the model child of the neighborhood to come and play with their niece. But Ariadne Blish was the worst failure of all, for Rose could not bear the sight of her, and said she was so like a wax doll she longed to give her a pinch and see if she would squeak. So prim little Ariadne was sent home, and the exhausted aunties left Rose to her own devices for a day or two.

5   Seeing this, the poor aunties racked their brains for a new amusement and determined to venture a bold stroke, though not very hopeful of its success. They said nothing to Rose about their plan for this Saturday afternoon, but let her alone till the time came for the grand surprise, little dreaming that the odd child would find pleasure for herself in a most unexpected quarter.

**33. The mood of the passage could best be described as—**

A    starting out sad and moving to glad.

B    starting out glad and moving to sad.

C    melancholy throughout.

D    happy and lively, especially toward the end.

**34. In paragraph 2, the underlined portion means—**

A    the house is old and has many broken windows.

B    there are various sizes of windows throughout the house.

C    the windows make breaks in the walls in unusual places.

D    some windows are missing while others are fully closed with shutters.

**35. Which of the following can we conclude from the passage?**

A    The aunts did not care about the child.

B    The aunts wanted to help the child overcome her grief.

C    The girl did not like her aunts.

D    Rose simply cannot be consoled.

**36. What is the primary setting of this passage?**

A    outside in a garden of a small cottage

B    an aviary where birds are kept

C    a large country home

D    a village square with lots of activity

**37. The organization of this passage is—**

A    a theme presented and then explained.

B    a narrative used to establish a moral.

C    chronological.

D    primarily a discussion between characters.

Reading the following biographical passage and answer questions 38 through 41.

# The Great Buffett

1   James William Buffett was born on Christmas Day in Pascagoula, Mississippi, and grew up to be one of the most prolific songwriters of the late 20th century. His songs are often about escaping to the islands, particularly the Caribbean islands, and his laid-back lifestyle is reflected in his songs. In addition to writing songs, he is also a singer and a film producer.

2   Jimmy Buffett grew up on the Eastern Shore of Mobile Bay in Mississippi, graduated from high school there, and began college at Auburn University. It was in college that he began playing the guitar and found his life's calling. He later transferred to the University of Southern Mississippi and received his bachelor's degree, with a major in history. After graduation, he went to work for *Billboard* magazine, covering the Nashville country music scene. He also continued to develop his own musical career as a country artist in Nashville. He released his first album, called *Down to Earth*, in 1970. Most people dubbed it folk rock.

3   To promote interest in his music, Jimmy was often seen <u>busking</u>, playing in public for tips or donations from passersby, in Nashville and later in New Orleans and Key West. Finally, he established his home in Key West and further developed his persona as a representative of the laid-back style of island life. When he released his 1977 *Changes in Latitudes* album, with the number-one-selling crossover hit "Margaritaville," he became known throughout the country as a serious artist. Throughout the rest of the 20th century and into the 21st, he continued to release albums to his very loyal fans, who became known as "Parrotheads" because they tended to show up at his concerts wearing floral shirts (often with parrots on them). Some show up with pirate hats, and die-hard fans wear stuffed parrots on their shoulders.

4   Interestingly, although Jimmy sings of the quiet island life, spending time on the beach, living with few things away from the rat race, he is actually one of the hardest working artists of his time. In addition to continuing to produce recordings and going on regular live tours, he has produced some musicals and films, and has opened two restaurant chains.

The first is called *Cheeseburgers in Paradise* and the other is called *Margaritaville Cafes*. He is not only a co-owner of each of these chains, but he also actively participates in their functioning. He has also produced and recorded a Christmas album as well as a children's album of his songs, with lyrics that are more appropriate for young children with simpler melodies to which they can sing along. He also loves baseball and is a co-owner of two minor league baseball teams, one in Florida and one in Wisconsin.

5  In 2004, Jimmy reinvented himself when he released his *License to Chill* album. It topped the pop charts. While his other songs had included some crossover hits from country to folk to pop, this album clearly was a pop album. After three decades of working at his craft, he had finally reached his goal to be a successful mainstream pop artist.

**38. For what purpose did the author write the passage?**

A  to present information about Parrotheads

B  to discuss the life of Jimmy Buffett

C  to encourage the reader to listen to Jimmy Buffett music

D  to critically discuss the merits of the musical and other artistic endeavors of Jimmy Buffett

**39. In the third paragraph, the underlined word is explained to the reader using which strategy?**

A  placement in context

B  mnemonic device

C  phrase following the word to define it

D  usage of a contrasting word that is the opposite of the word to explain its meaning

**40. The first sentence of the fourth paragraph describes which literary concept?**

A  visual imagery

B  irony

C  a simile

D  a metaphor

**41. Which of the following would BEST describe Jimmy Buffett's involvement in the restaurant business?**

A  He has lent his name and endorsement to three restaurant chains, but has little involvement in them.

B  He sold the name of his famous songs to restaurateurs for the purpose of familiarity to customers.

C  He is the partial owner, and an involved operator, in restaurants with names related to his music.

D  He allows his music to be played in any restaurant as long as he is paid royalties.

Read the following fictional account and answer questions 42 through 45.

# Choosing Your Friends Carefully

The boys in the corner were slamming down their dominoes as if to say "In your face!" as they found just the right domino to stop their opponent. Jill had only recently become Mike's friend. Jill was so painfully shy that she had only two friends. She could barely speak to Mike when he moved next door, but despite this, he would always say "hello" when he saw her. She finally worked up the courage to return his friendliness. When he offered his invitation to meet his friends, she was thrilled.

However, now in the playground full of clowning, rowdy boys, she felt out of place and uneasy. As they took a seat at a picnic table, Mike smiled at her and she felt slightly relieved.

Suddenly, a group formed around two boys on the playground. They were arguing over who owned a particular skateboard. They were grabbing and pulling at the board, when one boy managed to wrestle the board away from the other. Holding the skateboard, he began running away from the other boy, with the crowd following the altercation. He was almost out of the playground when a teacher they all knew appeared. Immediately, all the boys who had been following the fight began to run in different directions.

"Let's get out of here," Mike said, grabbing Jill and running.

"But we didn't do anything wrong," said Jill, struggling to keep up.

"It doesn't matter, because I don't want my friends to think that we ratted on them to the teacher."

Jill felt so uneasy and a little panicked. She thought back to her evenings at home where she played with her cat who loved the attention she showered on him. She wished right now that she were back home where it was quiet and no one was running from teachers.

The teacher yelled at their retreating backs, but they kept going. When they had finally turned the corner and were out of sight, they stopped running.

"Let's go meet some of my friends in another park," Mike said.

"I don't know if I can do that. My mom might be upset if I get home after dark," Jill said.

"Oh, come on. Don't be a chicken! If you don't go, I'll stop being friends with you. I'm not even sure why I bothered trying to become friends with you anyway."

Jill was crushed. She knew the other kids thought Mike was cool, and she wanted to be cool as well.

"I'll go," she said quickly.

They walked to a basketball court where a group of boys were playing a pickup game. It was starting to get dark. Jill knew her mother would be looking for her and would probably be upset when she got home. On the court, there was a particularly loud boy, talking about what a great basketball player he was.

"Who's that?" Jill asked. "He doesn't seem like a very nice person."

"Oh, that's just Jed. He's <u>holding court</u>. He's always bragging about something."

All of a sudden, a group of kids came onto the basketball court holding a box of candy bars and yelling triumphantly about how they had just taken them from the corner store. They began passing them out to everyone on the court. Mike grabbed two and passed one to Jill. At that point, Jill had made up her mind.

"Mike, I'm not hungry, but I am tired, so I'm going home. I'll see you tomorrow. Thanks for putting up with me, but I'm just not this kind of person. If you want to hang out at my house, that's fine, but I don't belong here."

With that, Jill turned and walked away, confident for the first time in her life.

42. **Which is TRUE about the setting(s) of the passage?**

A   There are three settings.

B   There is only one setting.

C   There are two settings, each equally as important as the other.

D   The setting cannot be determined from the passage.

43. **When Mike explains that Jed is *holding court*, this is an example of which literary concept?**

A   simile

B   irony

C   metaphor

D   alliteration

44. **What was the purpose of Jill's memories of her cat and being at home?**

A   to show she really liked to play with her cat

B   to show that she was just like Mike

C   to explain that she was just a regular person

D   to show a setting in which she felt comfortable

45. **What is the organization of the passage?**

A   mostly chronological, with a few flashbacks

B   some foreshadowing, but mostly chronological

C   inclusion of both flashbacks and foreshadowing, but no chronological order at all

D   straight facts presented to support a thesis statement

The section you are about to start is the Writing portion of the CAHSEE. This part of the test is composed of multiple-choice questions followed by a writing task.

The following is a rough draft of an essay discussing how people are changing. It may contain errors in grammar, punctuation, sentence structure, and capitalization. Some of the questions may refer to underlined or numbered sentences or phrases within the text. Read the essay and answer questions 46 through 50.

# Our Changing Population

(1) As we enter the 21st century, we are noticing changes in the human population. (2) People are now taller and heavier than ever before. (3) While being tall has never been a problem (except for the rare instance of acromegaly, in which a person grows abnormally tall, more than eight feet, and has accompanying medical problems), obesity certainly is. (4) There is greater diversity in cognitive abilities, and the creativity of the human spirit is expressing itself in a great variety of endeavors. (5) In addition, people are now living longer and longer. (6) There was a time, not so long ago, when a person living to be 100 was a rarity. (7) Now, every town has a centenarian. (8) One thing we note, though, is that centenarians are still almost always women.

(9) The New York Board of Health has voted to ban restaurants in the New York area from using frying oils that contain artificial trans fat, which has been known to cause obesity. (10) It also clogs arteries; therefore, it causes heart disease and heart attacks. (11) A few years before, they banned smoking in restaurants. (12) The restaurant industry is up in arms about it. (13) Said one man on television, "Are they trying to run us out of business? One of these days they'll ban drinking in bars!" (14) Actually, that already happened. (15) In 1920, the 18th Amendment outlawed the manufacture, transportation, and sale of alcoholic beverages. (16) Although people often believe that Prohibition meant that it was illegal to drink or possess alcohol, it wasn't. (17) One simply couldn't make or sell it. (18) This amendment stayed in place until 1933 when it was repealed <u>via</u> the 21st Amendment. (19) Interestingly, the 19th Amendment, which gave women the right to vote, was passed between the 18th and the 21st during the time of Prohibition.

46. As used in the passage, the word *centenarian* means—

A   a person who oversees a large group of soldiers.

B   a Roman warrior.

C   a person who is exactly 100 years old.

D   a person who is at least 100 years old.

47. What is the biggest problem with the organization of the passage?

A   It contains too many big words that people don't understand.

B   It is a short story but contains too many factual elements.

C   It lacks focus, so it simply has one idea that leads to another.

D   It is chronological in nature, so it is somewhat boring.

48. According to the passage, one can conclude that—

A   all women live longer than most men.

B   men live longer than women.

C   most people who live to be 100 are women.

D   there is no difference between longevity of men and women.

49. In sentence 3, what would be the best way to improve the sentence?

A   Being obese is a problem. Being tall can be a problem, too, if one gets acromegaly and grows to be taller than eight feet.

B   While being tall has never been a problem (except in rare extreme instances), obesity certainly is.

C   While being too tall, caused by the condition known as acromegaly, is a problem, for most, it isn't; obesity, on the other hand, certainly can be a problem.

D   Leave as is.

50. In sentence 18, the word *via* could BEST be replaced with which of the following while changing the meaning the least?

A   through

B   credit

C   bill

D   amend

The following is a rough draft of an essay. It may contain errors in grammar, punctuation, sentence structure, and capitalization. Some of the questions may refer to underlined or numbered sentences or phrases within the text. Read the essay and answer questions 51 through 55.

## Mercer Island

(1) Mercer Island, located just east of Seattle, Washington, is an island of the wealthy. (2) It is connected to its mainland cousin, Bellevue, also a wealthy suburb of Seattle, by a multilane concrete bridge. (3) Even the bridge seems luxurious. (4) That, of course, was by design. (5) Unlike other islands, where the inhabitants are happy when progress is brought to the island by connection of it with the mainland, Mercer liked its <u>ability to shut out others</u>. (6) Thus, the residents were willing to agree to the construction of the state-highway commissioned bridge only after enough greenspace and landscaping had been added to meet with their approval. (7) As one resident stated, "We welcome people to the island as long as they play by our rules."

(8) Mercer Island has the best schools and the best parks and the best of everything, it seems, for its residents. (9) Some islands around the world never have any of these things. (10) Its children graduate from its good schools and go on to prestigious colleges throughout the United States. (11) But, like some things, there is a dark side. (12) It also has one of the highest adolescent obesity rates in the nation. (13) Some students, it appears, may not feel they can live up to the expectations placed on them by the mere fact that they are "from Mercer Island."

**51.** If you were to give this essay one of the following titles, which would fit BEST?

A   Mercer Island: Healthy, Wealthy, and Wise

B   Even Success Can Have Its Dark Side

C   Sophistication and Wealth Go Hand in Hand

D   Being Wealthy Affords Privilege Without Problems

**52.** Which of the following is the accurate relationship among ideas in the essay?

A   Seattle is not a part of the two independent towns of Bellevue and Mercer Island.

B   Mercer Island is located within the city limits of Seattle but Bellevue is not.

C   Mercer Island and Bellevue are located in the metropolitan area of Seattle.

D   Bellevue is a suburb of Mercer Island.

**53.** Which is the MOST effective substitution for the underlined part of sentence 5?

A   exclusion

B   acceptance

C   exception

D   exclusivity

**54.** Which of the following sentences does NOT fit the paragraph well and should be deleted?

A   Sentence 8

B   Sentence 9

C   Sentence 10

D   Sentence 11

**55.** The organization of this passage can be best described as—

A   a myopic description of a geographic locale.

B   a comparison of an island with its mainland opposite.

C   a thesis statement with supporting details.

D   a geographic and sociological description of a place.

The following is a rough draft of an essay. It may contain errors in grammar, punctuation, sentence structure, and capitalization. Some of the questions may refer to underlined or numbered sentences or phrases within the text. Read the essay and answer questions 56 through 60.

## High-Context and Low-Context Societies

(1) A helpful distinction between low-context and high-context cultures is made by anthropologist Edward Hall. (2) The United States, Canada, Europe, Israel, and Australia are examples of low-context cultures. (3) Individuals from these parts of the world prefer a direct, literal style of interaction. (4) People are expected to say more or less exactly what they mean. (5) Self-expression skills such as clarity, fluency, and brevity are valued by low-context cultures. (6) Speakers often seek to convince and persuade their listeners.

(7) Parts of Asia, the Middle East and Africa are examples of high-context cultures. (8) The preferred style of interaction is an indirect one in which meaning is carried less by the literal meaning of the words and more by contextual clues such as the place, time, and situation and the relationships between the speakers. (9) High-context cultures value harmony, subtlety, sensitivity, and tact more than clarity. (10) Speakers often seek to connect with their listeners.

(11) Differences between low- and high-context cultures cause conflicts of meaning, pacing, volume, gesture, space, and touch. (12) To the Japanese, a profuse apology is an expression of goodwill, part of a pattern of mutual self-depreciation that sets the tone for a discussion between equals. (13) To Americans, an apology is an admission of guilt that puts the speaker in a one-down position. (14) It's easy for Japanese to think that Americans are tactless oafs and for Americans to think that Japanese are passive and insecure.

56. **What is one of the biggest problems with this passage?**

A   It is unfocused and difficult to follow.

B   There are too many passive sentences.

C   It is biased against high-context societies.

D   The chronological nature of the passage is confusing.

57. **How would the addition of this sentence affect the passage?**

> I personally believe that the low-context societies are more efficient, and therefore, their model should be adopted by the rest of the world.

A   It would be a factual statement that would add credibility to the passage.

B   It would be a statement of opinion that would deviate from the factual nature of the passage.

C   It is an opinion that matches the opinions already stated in the passage.

D   It is an opinion, but it strengthens the argument of the passage.

58. **What is the role of the final paragraph of the passage?**

A   It explains that there is not a difference between high-context and low-context cultures.

B   It exemplifies that the Americans are a high-context population.

C   It shows that high-context cultures are less cordial than low-context cultures.

D   It acts as an example to strengthen the argument that there is a difference between high-context and low-context cultures.

59. **Which of the following titles would be a more creative, yet accurate, replacement for the passage?**

A   High- vs. Low-Context Societies

B   Edward Hall and His Theory

C   An Apology: Polite or Uncomfortable?

D   High or Low: Japan or America

60. **Which of the following would be the BEST way to combine sentences 3 and 4 into a single sentence?**

A   However, individuals from these parts of the world prefer a direct, literal style of interaction if people are expected to say more or less exactly what they mean.

B   If individuals from these parts of the world prefer a direct, literal style of interaction, then people are expected to say more or less exactly what they mean.

C   When people from these parts of the world are expected to say more or less exactly what they mean, they are preferring a direct, literal style of interaction.

D   Individuals from these parts of the world prefer a direct, literal style of interaction in which people are expected to say more or less exactly what they mean.

For questions 61 through 66, choose the answer that is the most effective substitute for each underlined part of the sentence. If no substitution is necessary, choose "Leave as is."

61. The rest of the room looked drab next to the <u>curtains, they had been not only cleaned</u> but also color-restored.

    A   curtains; they had been not only cleaned

    B   curtains: they were cleaned

    C   curtains where they had been cleaned

    D   Leave as is.

62. Some people <u>living in Phoenix</u> believe that progress should be halted because the population is straining the sparse water supplies.

    A   that are living in Phoenix

    B   who do indeed live in Phoenix

    C   who are residing in Phoenix

    D   Leave as is.

63. The father, as well as her sisters and brothers, <u>have greatly appreciated</u> the fame brought to the family by the youngest child.

    A   greatly appreciate

    B   are greatly appreciating

    C   has greatly appreciated

    D   Leave as is.

64. Turning to see if the woman walking into the store was my aunt, <u>my bike almost hit</u> a tree.

    A   I almost rode my bike into

    B   my bike was almost hit by

    C   my bike almost made me hit

    D   Leave as is.

65. Most fourth-grade students <u>have the ability to multiply</u> two-digit numbers.

    A   are capable in multiplying

    B   can multiply

    C   may be capable of multiplying

    D   Leave as is.

66. Once the furniture was moved in, the moving company representatives requested <u>they're money in a cashier's check</u>.

    A   there money in a cashier's check

    B   they're money in a cashier's check

    C   their money in a cashier's check

    D   Leave as is.

For questions 67 through 72, choose the word or phrase that best completes the sentence.

67. By the end of the first quarter of the game, it appeared that the girls' basketball team _____ so far behind that they could not possibly pull out a victory.

   A   fell
   B   had fallen
   C   had fell
   D   have fallen

68. _____ the beliefs of many, reading for hours a day does not cause poor eyesight.

   A   Contrary for
   B   Contrary of
   C   In contrast to
   D   Contrary to

69. In Mexico, the government and the farmers decided to have the clouds seeded to see if that _____ the drought.

   A   would affect
   B   would effect
   C   affected
   D   effected

70. Despite the fact that previous mountain climbers had failed to reach the summit, all of the members of the current climbing team _____ the journey.

   A   are excited to begin
   B   were excited about beginning
   C   is excited about starting
   D   were excited to end

71. The rumors were _____ show is not being cancelled.

   A   incorrect, the
   B   incorrect, but
   C   incorrect; the
   D   correct: that the

72. The use of seat belts has greatly reduced the _____ of traffic deaths in the United States, so most states have now made their use mandatory.

   A   incidence
   B   number
   C   account
   D   denotation

# REMINDER

✓ Write a response to the writing prompt shown.

✓ You may title your passage if you like, but it is not required.

✓ You may not use a dictionary. If you do not know how to spell a word, sound out the word and do the best you can.

✓ Dictionaries are NOT allowed. If cannot spell a word, try sounding the word out. Then write the word in the best way you can.

✓ Make sure you write clearly! Any erasures or strike-outs should be as neat as possible.

## 73. Writing Task

Increasing numbers of employers are instituting mandatory drug testing for employees. Many employees feel that such tests are an invasion of privacy.

What are your views on this issue? Support your position with specific reasons and examples from your own experience, observations, or reading.

# Writing Checklist

This writing list will help you make your writing better. Make sure you check the following:

☐ Read the description of the prompt carefully.

☐ Organize your essay with a strong introduction, body, and conclusion.

☐ Support your ideas with specific, detailed examples.

☐ Use words that your audience can understand and that fit the purpose of the writing task.

☐ Use different types of sentences to make your writing interesting.

☐ Check for errors in grammar, spelling, punctuation, capitalization, and sentence formation.

# Answers and Explanations

**1. B**

This is a specific detail question that is directly answered in the final sentence of the passage. "White Christmas" was considered the most patriotic song because it became an anthem for people everywhere who were away from home on Christmas. Choices A and C are incorrect because the passage doesn't describe how they affected Americans. Choice D is the name of a movie, not a song.

**2. D**

The author of the passage indicates that the composer stated that his song was the best song ever written. Over time, that song did indeed become one of the best-selling, longest-lasting recordings of all time. Therefore, we can conclude that the author of the passage felt the composer's attitude about his music was well deserved.

**3. C**

This main idea question asks for the identification of the best title. While the first two, choices A and B, may be accurate, the actual passage is strictly about the composer and the particular song, "White Christmas." Choices A and B are less focused, and choice D is too broad.

**4. B**

The question is asking for you to identify the answer that the passage does NOT address. Most of the passage mentions his songwriting (choice D).

While there is only limited information about his childhood (choice A) and his father's life (choice C), there is no mention of his mother's life (choice B) in the passage at all.

### 5. A

This question is asking for a synonym or synonym phrase for the word *rudimentary*, which means a basic principle or element. The only answer that is synonymous with this definition is choice A because he learned only the *very basic* skills of writing music.

### 6. A

Choice A, *will reminisce*, means to discuss things from the past, or *. . .from days gone by.* This is the action the author is describing in that line in the poem.

### 7. C

This inference question asks us to read between the lines. Because the narrator of the poem is Joe, and he is asking Bill to sit down and reminisce with him, we can assume that they have not remained in close contact, but that Joe is asking his old friend Bill to sit down and talk about old times. So based on this assumption, choices A and B can be eliminated. Obviously, choice D is not accurate because he would not want to sit with him if they disliked each other. Therefore, only choice C can be inferred.

### 8. A

Joe, as the narrator, mentions to Bill *You've taught your name to half the globe*, but describes himself as having less acclaim than an old mare, so this eliminates choices B, C, and D. Thus, A is the best answer to this relationship among ideas question.

### 9. D

The poem is about getting together with a friend from one's childhood to reminisce. While Joe mentions he has not had the good luck that Bill appears to have had, choice A is not correct because the main theme of the poem is about old friends finding common ground after many years of doing different things in life. There is nothing in the poem that suggests choices B or C could be the correct answer.

## 10. B

This is a question asking for a matching example that exemplifies *teaching across the curriculum* described in the passage. Because the idea is that materials should be included in *various subjects* when a concept is being taught, choice A is not correct because it simply uses language arts concepts. Choice C is simply describing the strategy of cooperative learning. While choice D involves students in doing more than one subject, it does not describe the concept of learning a set of concepts using various subjects. On the other hand, choice B involves students using math while learning their history material, therefore, it is the correct answer.

## 11. D

This is a vocabulary in context question. *Bypass* means "to go past," while *buy* means "to purchase." Therefore, choices A and B are not correct. Choice C includes *spoils*, meaning "to rot or become unusable." It does not match *bypass*, meaning "to go past." Choice D matches the two synonyms *buy* and *purchase*.

## 12. B

We can eliminate choice A right away, because the passage describes how positive transfer should be incorporated into school curricula. Choices C and D are ideas that cannot be inferred from the passage at all. The author indicates in paragraph 3 that adults, in real life, use positive transfer all the time. Therefore, we can read between the lines that he believes that, if children are not actively taught to use positive transfer, it will hinder their functioning skills in adulthood. Therefore, choice B is correct.

## 13. D

This passage is about science, but its level of writing is at a level above the elementary level, so choice A is eliminated. Choice B does not make sense, as the passage is too long to be in a survey and is not asking any questions. Choice C doesn't make any sense either, as this subject has nothing to do with a guidebook. The passage does give hints that it is a proposal (choice D) with such phrases as *needs to be investigated, we will expose,* and *we will examine.*

**14. B**

Choice A is incorrect because although nanoparticles are described, it does not explain what the study is about. Choice C is incorrect because although it mentions how this is relevant to the Great Lakes region, the study is about the impact on aquatic organisms, not about the impact on freshwater systems. Choice D is incorrect because although it states that this project will influence future environmental policy, it doesn't mention who should be worried. In the final two sentences, it is made clear that the study will look to see what effects nanoparticles will have on *Daphnia*, choice B.

**15. B**

*Daphnia* are small, aquatic fleas, not aquatic environments (choice A). Choice C doesn't make any sense, as *Daphnia* are not part of a microscope. *Daphnia* are small, planktonic crustaceans, not environmental pollutants, so it is clear that choice D is incorrect. That leaves choice B as the only answer.

**16. C**

Choices A, B, and D are not mentioned at all in the passage. The passage first discusses the fact that nanoparticles are increasing, and that their effect (hence, safety or lack of safety) has not been studied, choice C.

**17. C**

Choice A is incorrect because although the passage states that children enjoy this genre, it doesn't state who it is and isn't for. Choice B is incorrect because although good historical fiction must be both true and made-up at the same time, just because it is made-up doesn't mean it is lies. Choice D is incorrect because the passage explains how history can be taught in story form. However, the final paragraph indicates the best title, which is choice C.

**18. C**

In the fourth paragraph, the three viewpoints are listed. Therefore, this is a specific detail question. Underline the three viewpoints in the passage, and you will see that choice C is not listed among them.

**19. D**

This is an author's attitude question. Throughout the passage, she indicates that both the story aspect as well as the accuracy of the history are important in the genre. Choices A and B cannot be correct because they each emphasize only one of those aspects. Choice C may be true, but it is not addressed by the author in the passage. Choice D, on the other hand, is clearly stated in the final paragraph of the essay.

**20. B**

This is an organization question. There is nothing controversial about the topic, so choice A is not accurate. Choice C is not correct because, while two aspects of the genre are discussed, there is really only one topic. Also, neither of the two aspects (accurate history or a good story) is deemed to be more important than the other. Choice D is not accurate because no question is asked. However, choice B accurately describes the organization of the passage.

**21. B**

Choice A is not the correct answer, although the story starts out describing the girl's father. Choice C is incorrect because Tammy is mentioned only briefly in paragraph 3. Choice D is incorrect because there is no ice skater character whose name is not given. In the third paragraph, the girl's name is given. It is Brianna.

**22. C**

Choice A is incorrect, because the phrases show just the opposite—how hard the girl works when she is on the ice. Choice B is incorrect and depicts the opposite as well; the phrases show her expertise when describing all her difficult skating techniques. Choice D is incorrect because the topic sentence in that paragraph talks about her journal, which has nothing to do with her skating techniques. The underlined phrases are there to encourage the reader to be able to see the details being described and are there to add visual imagery, choice C.

### 23. A

Throughout the passage, the young ice-skater has a feeling of regret about the choices she has made to pursue her sport. There is no change of heart, so choice B is not correct. Choices C and D indicate that the character is being pragmatic or practical (both synonyms meaning "to do the necessary things"). While that may be true, the passage does not convey that her feelings at the time were about that. Instead, she was feeling regretful, choice A.

### 24. D

Choice A is incorrect because although the skater might not want to follow her father's advice, she does anyway, which is not her being unwilling. Choice B is incorrect because she is not a rebellious teenager at all—she does everything her father tells her. As for choice C, there is no indication that she is incapable of making appropriate choices; all the choices she makes are beneficial for her skating career. The only thing left is the narrator discussing her family and the fact that her father won't let her do things, so from this, we can infer that the ice-skater is a young girl living with her family. Therefore, choice D is correct.

### 25. C

Choices A and D are not the correct answers because adenosine is mentioned only briefly in the last paragraph. Choice B is incorrect because the passage states in the last paragraph that caffeine consumption, in the long run, can cause negative health effects on the body's ability to function and the brain's ability to process information. This passage contains three paragraphs. The first two deal with caffeine; the last deals with cortisol. Therefore, the whole passage deals with these two things and how they affect the body, choice C.

### 26. C

In the second sentence of the third paragraph, it clearly states that cortisol and caffeine block the relaxing effects of adenosine. Therefore, the relationship between the ideas is expressed correctly in choice C.

### 27. B

This question asks what the author of the passage would think. Both choices A and B discuss the idea of giving children caffeine. The author clearly states that caffeine, added to stress, is hard on the body. Therefore, of the two, the author would agree with choice B. Choices C and D deal with positive information for adults who consume caffeine, but throughout the passage, the author is against combining stress with caffeine for them as well.

### 28. A

Choices B and C are incorrect because no opinions are formed about any of the information in the passage. Choice D is incorrect because the entire passage is filled with facts. Choice A is correct because this is a factual passage, and the author presents only facts. Facts are items that can be verified by an outside source.

### 29. B

This passage is about ethnocentrism, and does speak of gender, but it is not about comparing ethnocentrism with gender bias, as in choice A. Both choices C and D discuss the idea of females being ethnocentric, when the passage is about the opposite of that. Thus, only choice B can be accurate, and we know this because it is described in the second paragraph.

### 30. D

This question asks what conclusion the reader can come to based on the passage. Choice A presents the opposite of what the passage says. Choice B indicates that females give more attention to females, which is inaccurate, while choice C indicates that both genders give females more attention. Only choice D is accurate, as the passage states that both genders give more attention to males.

### 31. C

An assumption question asks for something that happened before the passage was written. While both choices A and B might be accurate, they cannot be substantiated in the paragraph. In order to explain the concept, the sociologist must have read the Sadkers' research, so choice C is the correct answer. Choice D may or may not be true. The passage does not speak to it.

### 32. D

This question is asking for an exception to the rule. Choices A, B, and C all exemplify the concept of ethnocentrism by showing people doing things in an ethnocentric way. Only choice D strays from that. Therefore, it is the exception to the rule and the correct answer.

### 33. A

The passage is best described by choice A; the story starts on a sad note, but at the end you begin see a more hopeful turn of events. Choice B is obviously incorrect because the story does not start out glad. Choice C is incorrect because the ending hints at an improvement in the girl's mood. Choice D is incorrect because the girl is not happy and lively, but sad.

### 34. C

Although the underlined phrase includes the words *broke out*, it is not talking about broken windows, so choice A is incorrect. Choices B and D are incorrect because they have nothing to do with the underlined phrase. It is instead talking about the fact that windows make a break in the wall as in choice C.

### 35. B

Choice B is the correct answer because the story shows how hard the aunts tried to help Rose overcome her grief. Choice A is incorrect because the aunts cared very much about Rose, and they tried several ways to help her. Choice C is incorrect because there is no indication that the girl did not like her aunts. Choice D is incorrect because the story hints that Rose found a way to console herself.

### 36. C

Throughout the passage, the setting is obviously indoors. Therefore, only choice C can be correct.

### 37. C

There is no theme or moral presented at the beginning, so choices A and B are not accurate. While there is a dialogue in the passage, it is not the focus of the whole passage, so choice D is incorrect. Therefore, the only answer that makes sense is choice C, *chronological*. This means that the passage is written following the passage of time in order.

**38. B**

Choice A is not correct because there is only one mention of the Parrotheads (in paragraph 3). The passage is presented as factual information about Jimmy Buffett's life. There is no attempt to either encourage people to listen to his music as suggested in choice C or to critique the music as suggested in choice D.

**39. C**

Because *busking* is not a commonly used word, the writer uses a phrase following the word to define it ("playing in public for tips or donations from passersby"). Some words can be figured out from context as suggested in choice A, but that would not be possible in this passage. Mnemonic devices (choice B) take the first letter of each word to form a new word or phrase so one can remember it. That is not used in this passage. Neither is the use of an antonym to indicate meaning (choice D).

**40. B**

This is an example of irony. While Jimmy sings of a quiet, laid-back life, his own life is one of working hard and being productive. Irony involves the opposite of something that is being said, or in this case, his music about a do-nothing lifestyle is the opposite of what it takes for his music to be presented to the people through his concerts, CDs, and other ventures.

**41. C**

We see that Jimmy is an involved member of the restaurant industry through the phrase *actively participates* in paragraph 4. The opposite of this is represented by choice A. Choice B is incorrect, for he did not sell the name of his songs. Instead, he used them to create the restaurants with partners, which reflects choice C, the correct answer. Choice D is not accurate at all. As long as a restaurant owner has purchased the CD, he can play it in his restaurant.

**42. C**

The passages settings take place on a playground and a basketball court, so this is the correct answer. Even though Jill's home is mentioned, it is not really part of the story's action.

**43. C**

A metaphor uses a phrase with a different literal meaning to describe something in the passage. In this case, a boy is giving his opinion in a very persuasive way, and the writer of the passage uses the words *holding court* to describe it. Choice A is incorrect because a simile is a figure of speech that compares two unlike things and uses the words *like* or *as*. Choice B is incorrect because irony is an incongruity between the actual result of a sequence of events and the normal or expected result. Alliteration is the repetition of usually initial consonant sounds in two or more neighboring words or syllables, so choice D is incorrect.

**44. D**

Although choice A could be true, it is not the purpose of why Jill had the memory of her cat and her quiet home. Choices B and C do not make sense. Choice D is correct because Jill is in an unfamiliar setting, so to feel more comfortable, she thinks back to memories that make her feel safe.

**45. A**

Both choices B and C are incorrect because foreshadowing is to show or indicate beforehand, or to prefigure. This never happened in the passage. Choice D is incorrect because this passage is a work of fiction, and there is no thesis statement and no facts. This passage moves chronologically (meaning one thing happening after another in straight-line order). However, as the main character attempts to make connections to her own life by remembering her childhood games, she uses flashbacks, choice A.

**46. D**

When we look at the passage, the word *centenarian* is used to mean a person who is at least 100 years old. Choices A and B are referring to the word *centurion*, not centenarian. Choice C is incorrect, because it would imply that a person who was 101 or more was no longer a centenarian.

**47. C**

The passage definitely lacks focus. Choice A is not accurate because most of the words are straightforward, general-usage words. The organization of this passage has nothing to do with being a short story, so choice B is not correct. It is not chronological in nature, as mentioned in choice D, nor are chronological writings necessarily boring. Thus, choice C is the correct answer.

**48. C**

This logic question asks one for a conclusion. Choice A is not correct because it states that *all* women live longer than most men. One should be cautious of an answer containing *all*. Choice B states the opposite of what the passage states, so this can be eliminated. Choice D is inaccurate because the first paragraph is about the differences in how long men and women live. Choice C is expressed in sentence 8.

**49. B**

Choices A and C are both incorrect because they state that being tall is a problem, which is the opposite of what the sentence states. In the passage, this sentence is problematic because the parenthetical information is distracting, so right away, we know choice D is incorrect. But choice B deals with this correctly by giving the same information without being distracting.

**50. A**

This question can simply be answered by substituting the new word in the sentence and seeing which makes sense. Choice A is the only one that makes sense.

**51. B**

Choice A won't work because although the passage is about Mercer Island, this title does not address the concept of obesity. Choice B is the best title because it includes both the success side of Mercer Island as well as the dark side (obesity). Choices C and D are not correct because neither includes the negative aspect of the passage.

**52. C**

This is a relationship among ideas question. We see that Mercer Island and Bellevue are in the metropolitan area of Seattle through the words in the first paragraph describing Mercer Island as *connected to its mainland cousin, Bellevue, also a wealthy suburb of Seattle.* From this sentence alone, you can deduce that choices A, B, and D are all incorrect.

**53. D**

By substituting each answer choice in the sentence *Mercer liked its <u>ability to shut out others</u>*, we can easily see that the concept they liked was *exclusivity*, choice D, meaning "shutting out others." Choice A will not work because it is the wrong form of the word to fit in the sentence. Choice B means agreeing to something, and choice C means to make a special rule. Neither substitutes well in the sentence.

**54. B**

Sentence 9 is the only sentence that deviates from the subject of the passage, which is Mercer Island and life lived there.

**55. D**

Only choice D is accurate because this passage is simply about the geographic description and the sociological aspects of one place (Mercer Island). Choice A is not accurate because the word *myopic* means "to look at only one aspect." That is not the case with this passage. While Bellevue, a mainland suburb, is mentioned, it is not the opposite of Mercer Island. They are both wealthy suburbs, so choice B cannot be correct. Choice C is not accurate because there is no thesis statement.

**56. B**

The passage has multiple passive sentences. The author should have written more active sentences to make the writing stronger, so choice B is the correct answer. Choice A is incorrect because the paragraphs are focused and fairly easy to follow. Choice C is incorrect because the paragraph does not have a bias toward either high- or low-context societies. Choice D is incorrect because the passage follows a logical chronology.

**57. B**

The sentence listed in the question is one of opinion, so choice A can't be correct. Only facts are presented in the original passage, so choices C and D are not accurate. That leaves choice B. It is accurate because the added sentence would be an opinion that would deviate from the facts written in the passage.

**58. D**

Choice A is not accurate because it states that there is NOT a difference. The passage clearly states there is. Choice B is not accurate because the Americans are low-context. Choice C is also inaccurate because the passage states the opposite. Thus, choice D is accurate. It does present an example to show the differences in the last paragraph.

**59. C**

While choice A could be plausible, it is not creative. Choice B is incorrect because the passage is not about Edward Hall. He is merely mentioned as one person who has looked at this concept. Choice D is not accurate because it does not contain the word *context*. Instead, it simply uses *high* or *low*. Thus, choice C is the answer. It is both creative and on topic. It would draw the reader in.

**60. D**

Choice A will not work because the transition *However* indicates that the words before concerned a differing point. Choice B begins with *If*, which makes it question the validity the point. Choice C uses not only awkward wording, but also *When* to suggest that it is not a constant. Thus, choice D, with its simple usage of the transition *in which*, is the best way to combine the two sentences.

**61. A**

A semicolon is needed, so choice A is the answer. As the sentence is originally written, it is a run-on sentence, so choice D is incorrect. Choices B and C are not accurate because *but* following the underlined part needs a *not only* to balance it, as in choice A.

**62. D**

This passage is correct as it is written. The simple, yet accurately used, *living in Phoenix* works best. Choice A is not correct because *that* cannot refer to people; instead, *who* is needed. Choices B and C are both too wordy.

**63. C**

Although it may seem that the subject is plural, it actually is the singular *father*. Thus, it needs a singular verb, *has*.

**64. A**

This is a case of a misplaced modifier. As it is written, and in choices B and C, it sounds as if the bike is performing all the action, not the person riding it. Because of this, choice D is incorrect as well. Choice A corrects this misplaced modifier with the usage of the subject *I*.

**65. B**

This is a circumstance of using the most straightforward wording, so choice D is incorrect. Also, the word *can*, meaning "is able to," is needed instead of *may*, meaning "allowed to," so choice C is incorrect. Choice B is correct. Choice A makes the sentence awkward and is too wordy.

**66. C**

Choices B and D are incorrect because *they're* means "they are," which doesn't make sense in this sentence. Choice A is incorrect because *there* is an adverb meaning "at that place" or "to that place," which doesn't make sense in this sentence either. The appropriate *their*, meaning "to show possession," is used in choice C.

**67. B**

The past tense *had fallen* is needed in this sentence to make it grammatically correct.

**68. D**

*Contrary* means "a fact or condition incompatible with another," while *contrast* means "to compare or appraise in respect to differences." There is nothing in the sentence being contrasted, so choice C is incorrect. The idiom is *contrary to*, not *for* or *of*, so choices A and B are incorrect, which leaves choice D as the right answer.

**69. A**

The word *affect*, meaning "to influence," is needed here. Thus, choices B and D cannot be correct because they use the word *effect*, which means "to cause to come into being; to bring about." Choice C is not correct because it is past tense, which does fit the context of the sentence.

**70. B**

Choices A and C cannot be correct because of the verbs *are* and *is*. The sentence talks about previous mountain climbers, and *is* and *are* are present terms that do not make sense in this sentence. The word *despite* depicts a contradiction between actions, so ending the journey, choice D, would not serve as a contradiction as beginning the journey would, so choice B is correct.

**71. C**

Choice A is ruled out because, with only a comma, the sentence is a run-on sentence. Choice B creates a nonsensical sentence. Choice D includes a colon, which could have been accurate. However, by using the word *that* to begin the second part, it is grammatically incorrect. Therefore, only choice C is correct.

**72. B**

When something can be counted, one uses the word *number* (choice B). *Incidence* (choice A), meaning an occurrence of an action, sounds like it could be a choice, but one cannot reduce an incidence, like one can reduce a number. While *count* could have been accurate, *account* (choice C) means something entirely different. *Denotation* simply means a sign or meaning . It has nothing to do with measurement.

## 73. WRITING TASK

## A sample answer that received a 4:

Mandatory drug testing is a requirement for employment for some companies even though some employees object to them as an invasion of their privacy. I believe that mandatory drug testing is a right an employer can insist upon, that it improves the safety of the workplace, and that it contributes to a better society overall.

Firstly, I believe that the employer has the right to set the rules, or what is sometimes called the conditions of employment. Therefore, if I am going to work for an employer, I have to follow his rules. If he wants me to wear a uniform, or to start to work at a particular time each day, I have to follow that in order to get paid. Drug testing would simply be one more rule I would need to follow.

Secondly, having a drug-free environment in which the employees can work is important. If I work for a company, it is important to me to know that my coworkers won't put me at risk by being careless. Drugs can cause a person to be careless. I believe that having the rule would make my workplace safer.

Finally, I believe that a company should be responsible to society. By assuring that its employees do not use drugs, as a condition of their employment, the company is having a positive influence on the community in which it exists. Its employees are setting a good example for the youth, and the employees themselves are benefiting by staying off drugs in order to maintain their jobs.

Overall, I believe mandatory drug testing is a good rule for all employers to consider. It will make their employees better workers, their environment safer, and the society at large better. I fully endorse this rule.

## A sample answer that received a 3:

Some companies today, in increasing numbers, are requiring drug tests for their employees. I completely object to this rule because not only is it an invasion of privacy, but it is an invasion of my personal rights to my body, and it is discriminatory.

The first reason I object to drug testing is that it is an invasion of my privacy. The employer that I work for does not get to control the things I do when I am not at work. As long as I am able to do the work, she should not have any right to the things I do privately.

The second reason I object to drug testing is that it is an invasion of my personal rights to my body. I should be allowed to choose if I have to give bodily fluids or hair for testing. My individual rights to have control of my body would be invaded if I was required to take a drug test.

The third reason I object to drug testing is that it is discriminatory. Alcohol is a drug, but people who abuse it would not be eliminated from the job, but persons who tested positive for drugs would be. Also, probably more drug testing would be done on younger people because they tend to be the people who are more involved in drug usage.

In conclusion, I believe that employers who require mandatory drug testing are invading their employees privacy, their rights to their bodies, and are discriminatory. Besides, trust should be the first rule of the workplace.

## A sample answer that received a 2:

Some companies require drug testing in order to be hired. I believe that this is a good rule even though some people don't like it. The reasons I believe it is both a good rule, and a bad rule, are outlined in the following paragraphs.

On the first hand, I have always been taught about the second golden rule. It is stated as: *He who has the gold rules.* So, if the employer says it, I have to do it. End of story.

On the second hand, I live in America. I have a right to not have my privacy invaded. If I don't want to take a drug test, I shouldn't have to.

Finally, I believe that if I objected to taking a drug test in order to be employed by that particular company I would have to simple understand that I'm not going to have that job. Besides, drugs kill people.

## A sample answer that received a 1:

Employers who require their employees to take drug tests are not right. A person's job is simply his job. His personal life is his own. So, I believe that mandatory drug testing is not good.

I also think that employers should be more flexible with their employees. No one is perfect so they should give their workers a break. I've had a boss who was very demanding. Eventually, I quit because she was making too many demands (like scrubbing the floor before locking up). Employers need to lighten up.